CAPTAIN AMERICA
Sam Wilson

HERCULES

SPIDER-MAN
Peter Parker

THOR
Jane Foster

VISION

WASP
Nadia Pym

THE AVENGERS

[Kang War One]

WRITER Mark Waid
ARTIST Mike del Mundo
COLOR ARTISTS Mike del Mundo with Marco D'Alfonso
LETTERER VC's Cory Petit
COVER ART Alex Ross

ASSISTANT EDITOR Alanna Smith
EDITOR Tom Brevoort

[AVENGERS CREATED BY STAN LEE & JACK KIRBY]

COLLECTION EDITOR JENNIFER GRÜNWALD
ASSISTANT EDITOR CAITLIN O'CONNELL
ASSOCIATE MANAGING EDITOR KATERI WOODY
EDITOR, SPECIAL PROJECTS MARK D. BEAZLEY
VP PRODUCTION & SPECIAL PROJECTS JEFF YOUNGQUIST
SVP PRINT, SALES & MARKETING DAVID GABRIEL
BOOK DESIGNER JAY BOWEN

EDITOR IN CHIEF AXEL ALONSO
CHIEF CREATIVE OFFICER JOE QUESADA
PRESIDENT DAN BUCKLEY
EXECUTIVE PRODUCER ALAN FINE

AVENGERS: UNLEASHED VOL. 1 — KANG WAR ONE. Contains material originally published in magazine form as AVENGERS #1-6. First printing 2017. ISBN# 978-1-302-90611-5. Published by MARVEL WORLDWIDE, INC., a subsidiary of MARVEL ENTERTAINMENT, LLC. OFFICE OF PUBLICATION: 135 West 50th Street, New York, NY 10020. **Printed in the U.S.A.** DAN BUCKLEY, President, Marvel Entertainment; JOE QUESADA, Chief Creative Officer; TOM BREVOORT, SVP of Publishing; DAVID BOGART, SVP of Business Affairs & Operations, Publishing & Partnership; C.B. CEBULSKI, VP of Brand Management & Development, Asia; DAVID GABRIEL, SVP of Sales & Marketing, Publishing; JEFF YOUNGQUIST, VP of Production & Special Projects; DAN CARR, Executive Director of Publishing Technology; ALEX MORALES, Director of Publishing Operations; SUSAN CRESPI, Production Manager; STAN LEE, Chairman Emeritus. For information regarding advertising in Marvel Comics or on Marvel.com, please contact Vit DeBellis, Integrated Sales Manager, at vdebellis@marvel.com. For Marvel subscription inquiries, please call 888 511 5400. **Manufactured between 4/28/2017 and 5/29/2017 by QUAD/GRAPHICS WASECA, WASECA, MN, USA.**

10 9 8 7 6 5 4 3 2 1

[1]

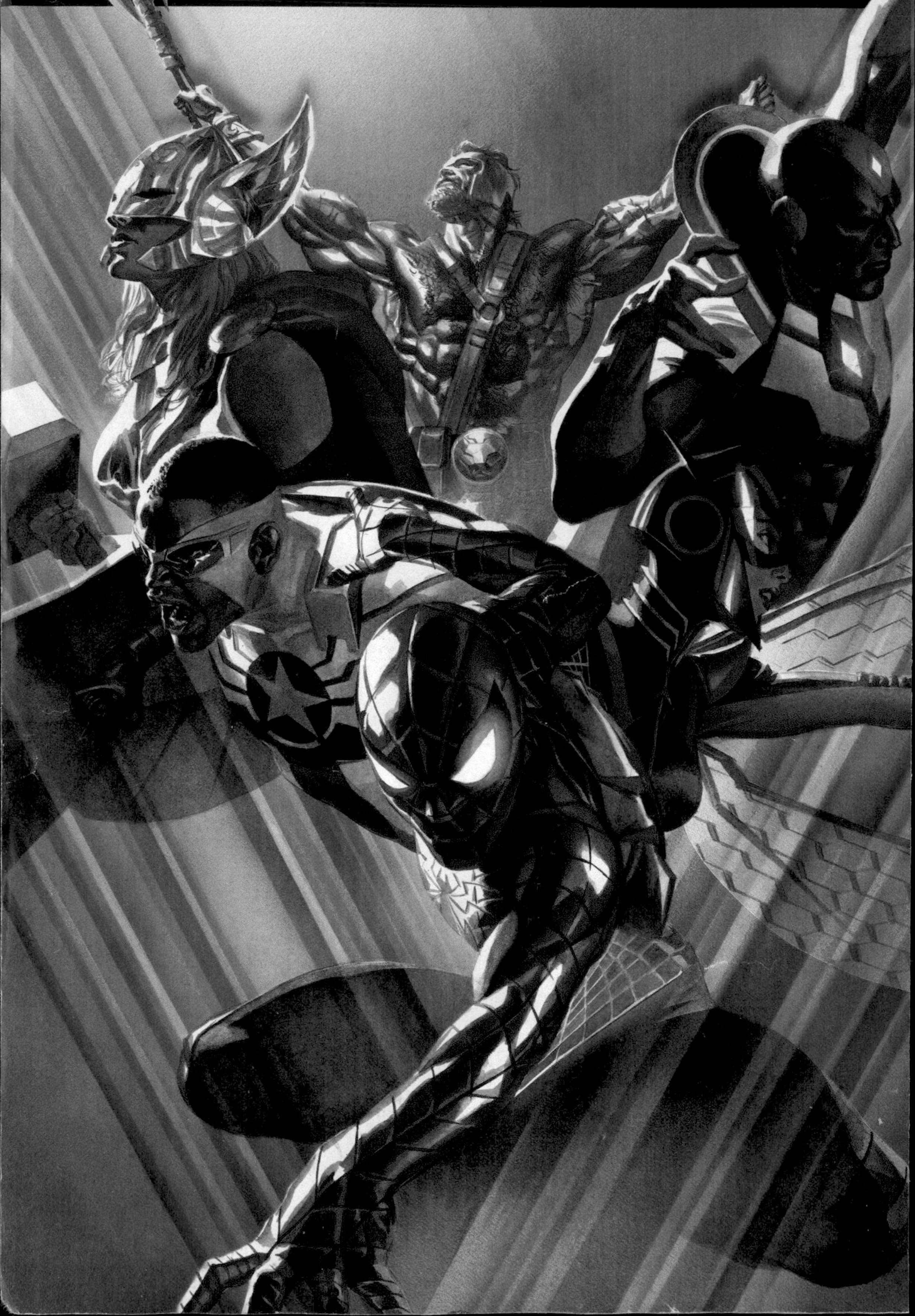

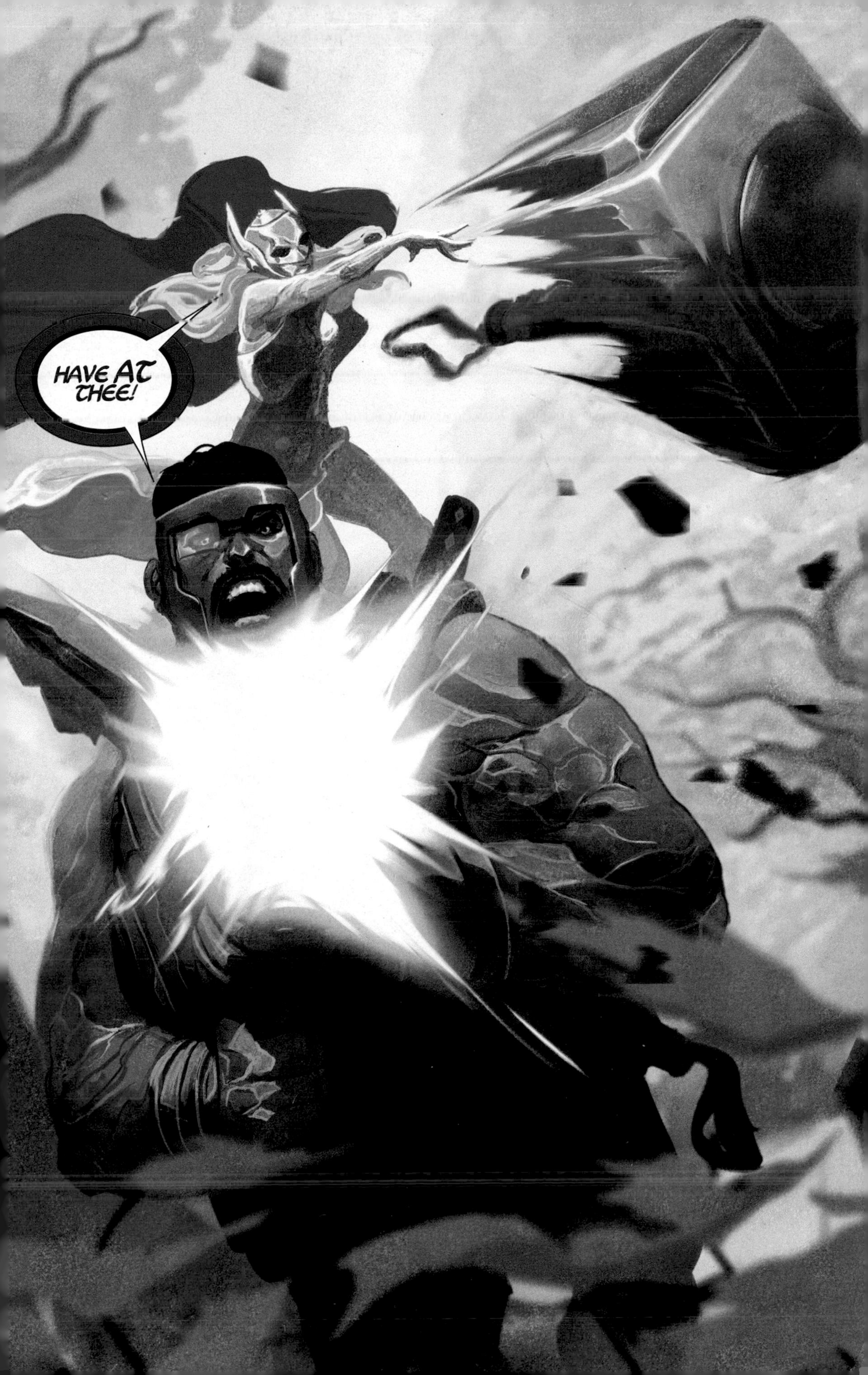
HAVE AT THEE!

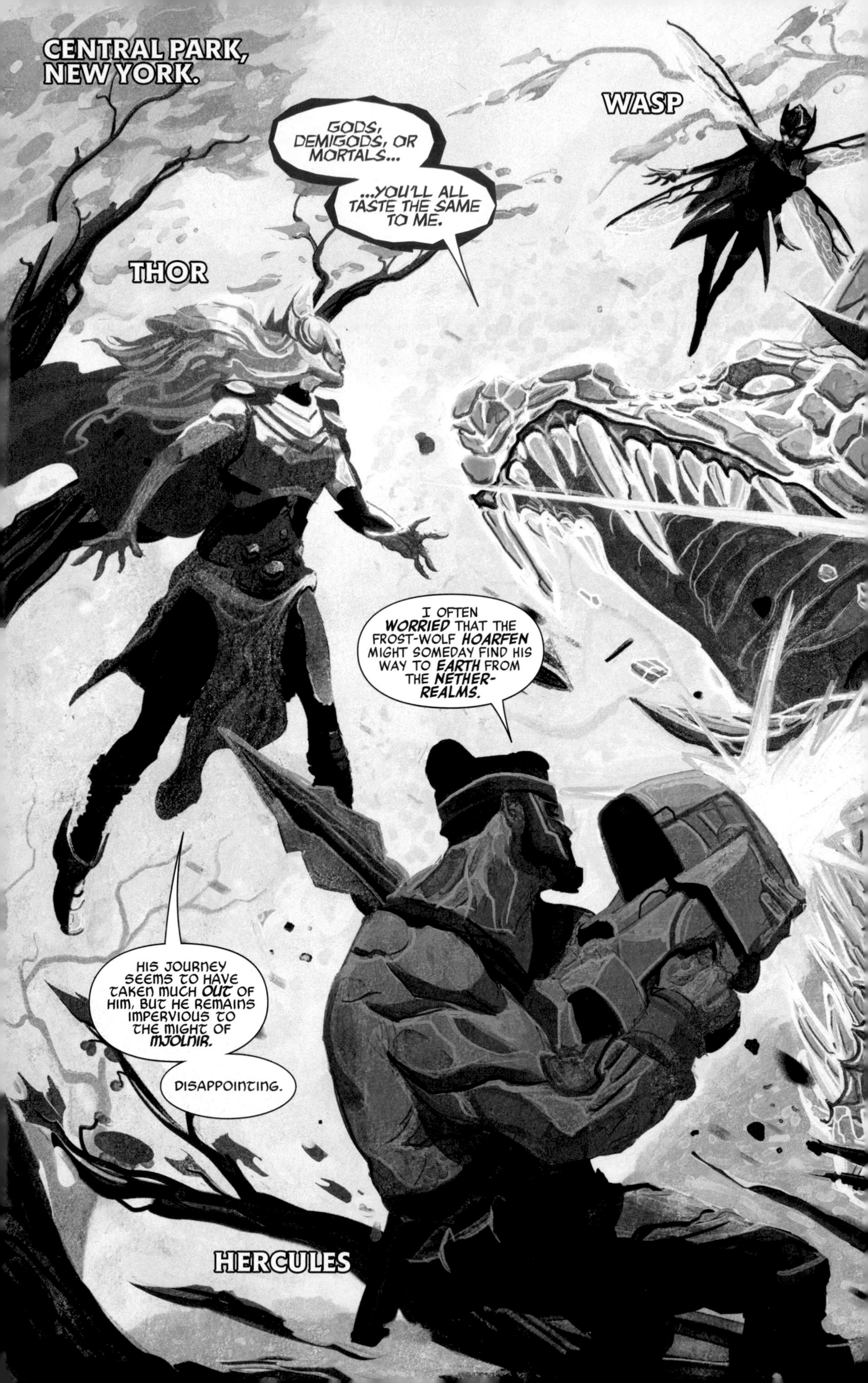
CENTRAL PARK, NEW YORK.
WASP
GODS, DEMIGODS, OR MORTALS...
...YOU'LL ALL TASTE THE SAME TO ME.
THOR
I OFTEN WORRIED THAT THE FROST-WOLF HOARFEN MIGHT SOMEDAY FIND HIS WAY TO EARTH FROM THE NETHER-REALMS.
HIS JOURNEY SEEMS TO HAVE TAKEN MUCH OUT OF HIM, BUT HE REMAINS IMPERVIOUS TO THE MIGHT OF MJOLNIR.
DISAPPOINTING.
HERCULES

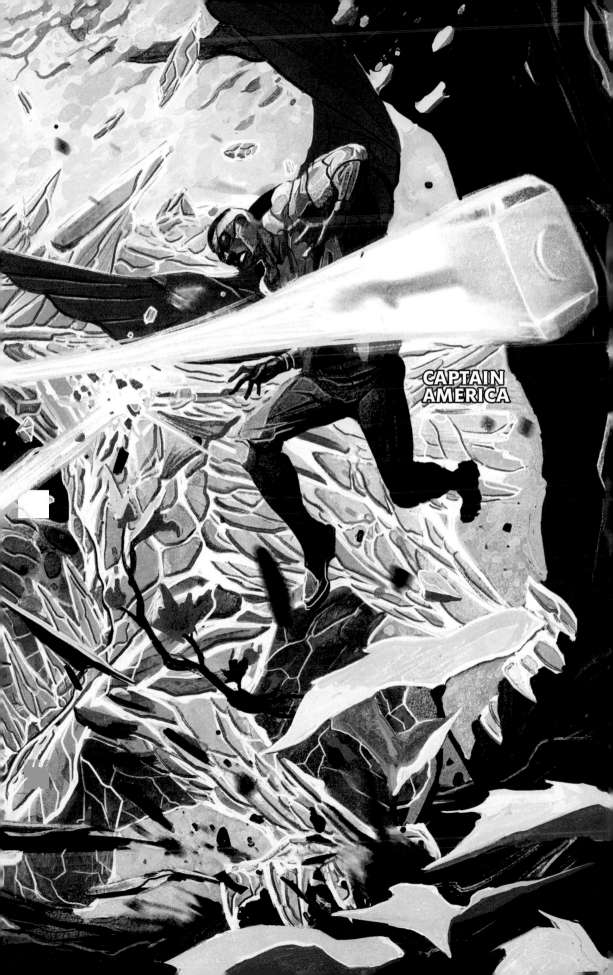

CAPTAIN
AMERICA

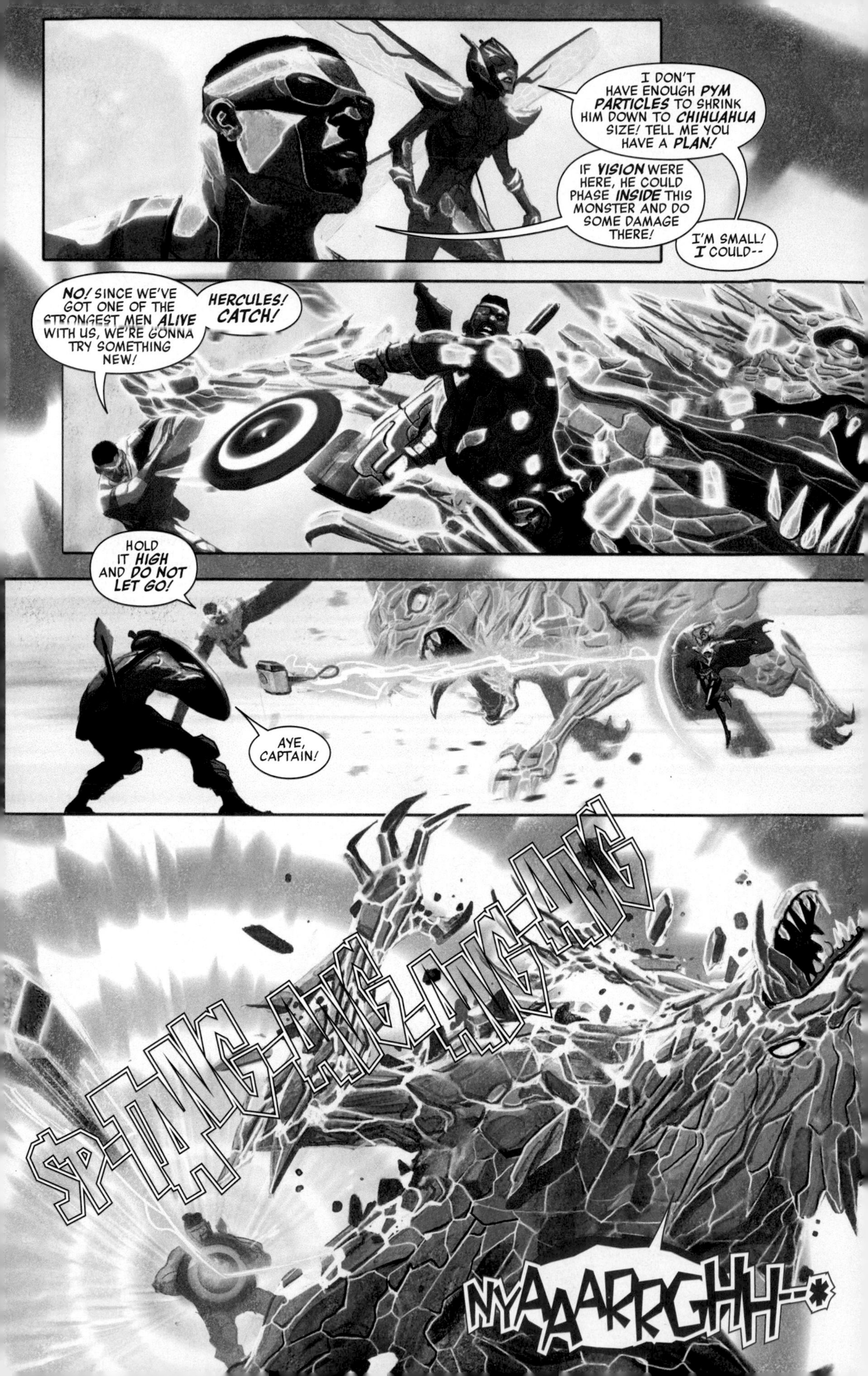
I DON'T HAVE ENOUGH PYM PARTICLES TO SHRINK HIM DOWN TO CHIHUAHUA SIZE! TELL ME YOU HAVE A PLAN!
IF VISION WERE HERE, HE COULD PHASE INSIDE THIS MONSTER AND DO SOME DAMAGE THERE!
I'M SMALL! I COULD--
NO! SINCE WE'VE GOT ONE OF THE STRONGEST MEN ALIVE WITH US, WE'RE GONNA TRY SOMETHING NEW!
HERCULES! CATCH!
HOLD IT HIGH AND DO NOT LET GO!
AYE, CAPTAIN!
SP-TANG-ANG-ANG-ANG
NYAAARRGHH--*

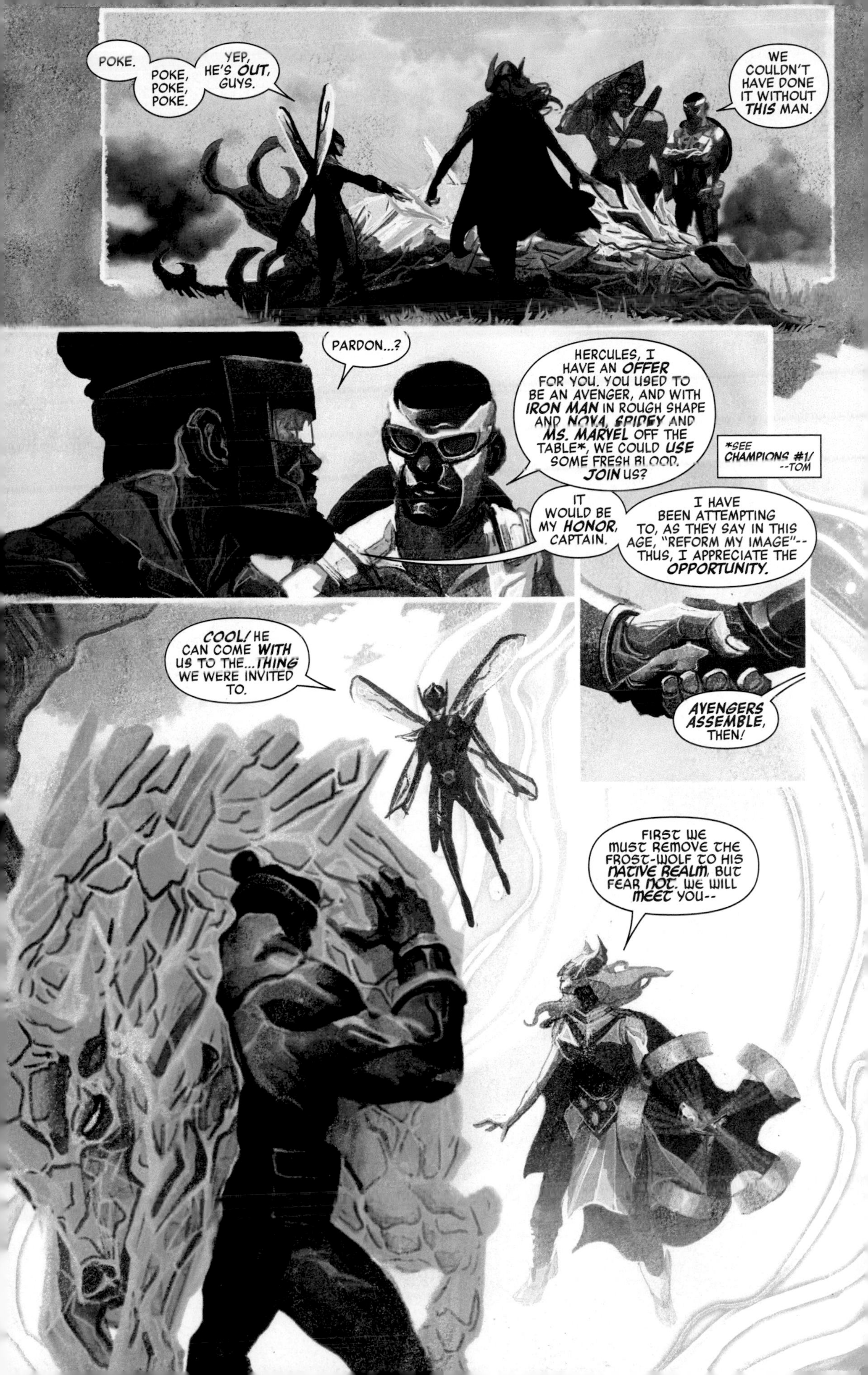
POKE.
POKE, POKE, POKE.
YEP, HE'S OUT, GUYS.
WE COULDN'T HAVE DONE IT WITHOUT THIS MAN.
PARDON...?
HERCULES, I HAVE AN OFFER FOR YOU. YOU USED TO BE AN AVENGER, AND WITH IRON MAN IN ROUGH SHAPE AND NOVA, SPIDEY AND MS. MARVEL OFF THE TABLE*, WE COULD USE SOME FRESH BLOOD. JOIN US?
*SEE CHAMPIONS #1! --TOM
IT WOULD BE MY HONOR, CAPTAIN.
I HAVE BEEN ATTEMPTING TO, AS THEY SAY IN THIS AGE, "REFORM MY IMAGE"-- THUS, I APPRECIATE THE OPPORTUNITY.
AVENGERS ASSEMBLE, THEN!
COOL! HE CAN COME WITH US TO THE...THING WE WERE INVITED TO.
FIRST WE MUST REMOVE THE FROST-WOLF TO HIS NATIVE REALM, BUT FEAR NOT. WE WILL MEET YOU--

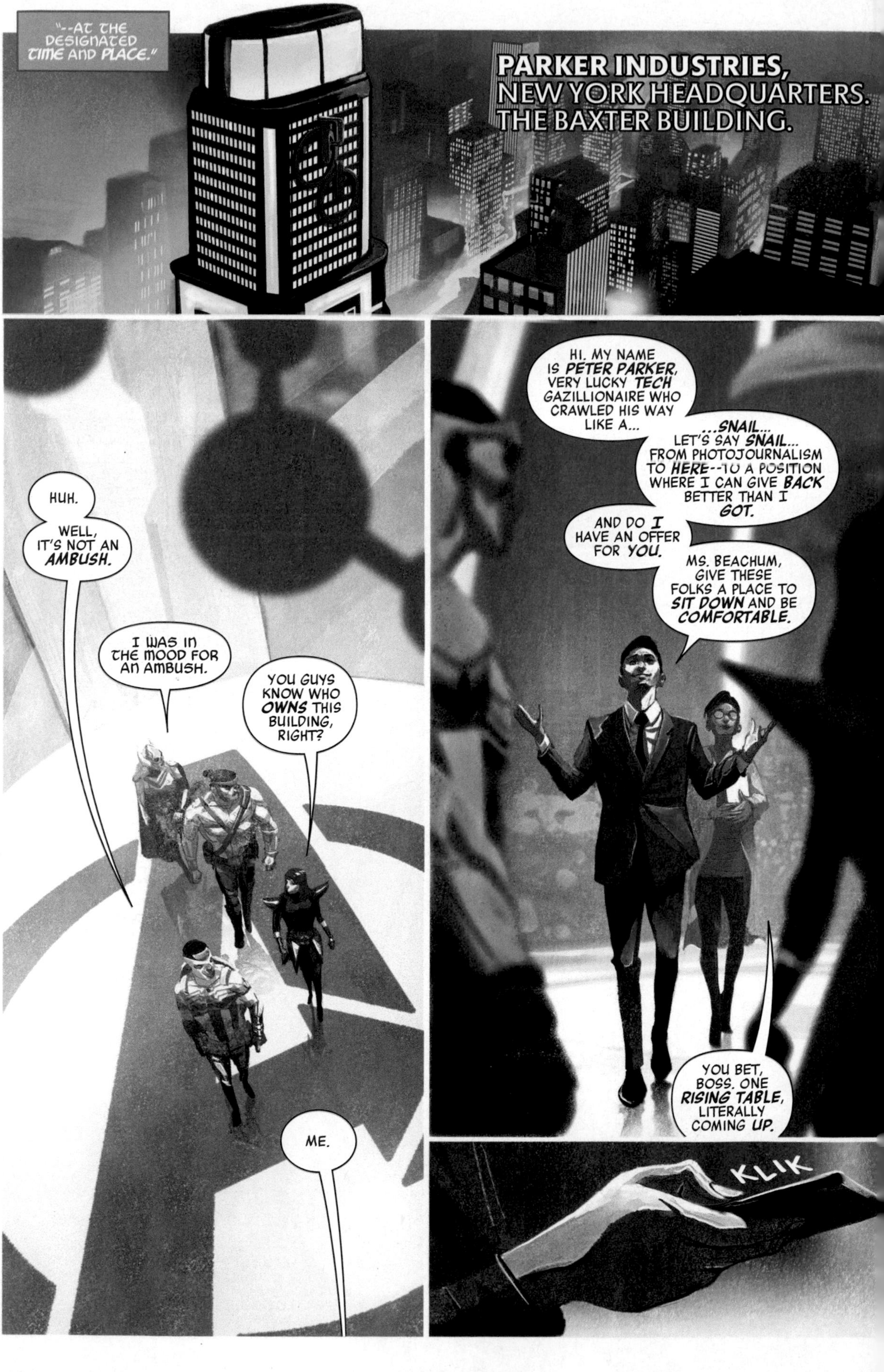
"--AT THE DESIGNATED TIME AND PLACE."
PARKER INDUSTRIES, NEW YORK HEADQUARTERS. THE BAXTER BUILDING.
HUH.
WELL, IT'S NOT AN AMBUSH.
I WAS IN THE MOOD FOR AN AMBUSH.
YOU GUYS KNOW WHO OWNS THIS BUILDING, RIGHT?
ME.
HI. MY NAME IS PETER PARKER, VERY LUCKY TECH GAZILLIONAIRE WHO CRAWLED HIS WAY LIKE A...
...SNAIL... LET'S SAY SNAIL... FROM PHOTOJOURNALISM TO HERE--TO A POSITION WHERE I CAN GIVE BACK BETTER THAN I GOT.
AND DO I HAVE AN OFFER FOR YOU.
MS. BEACHUM, GIVE THESE FOLKS A PLACE TO SIT DOWN AND BE COMFORTABLE.
YOU BET, BOSS. ONE RISING TABLE, LITERALLY COMING UP.
KLIK

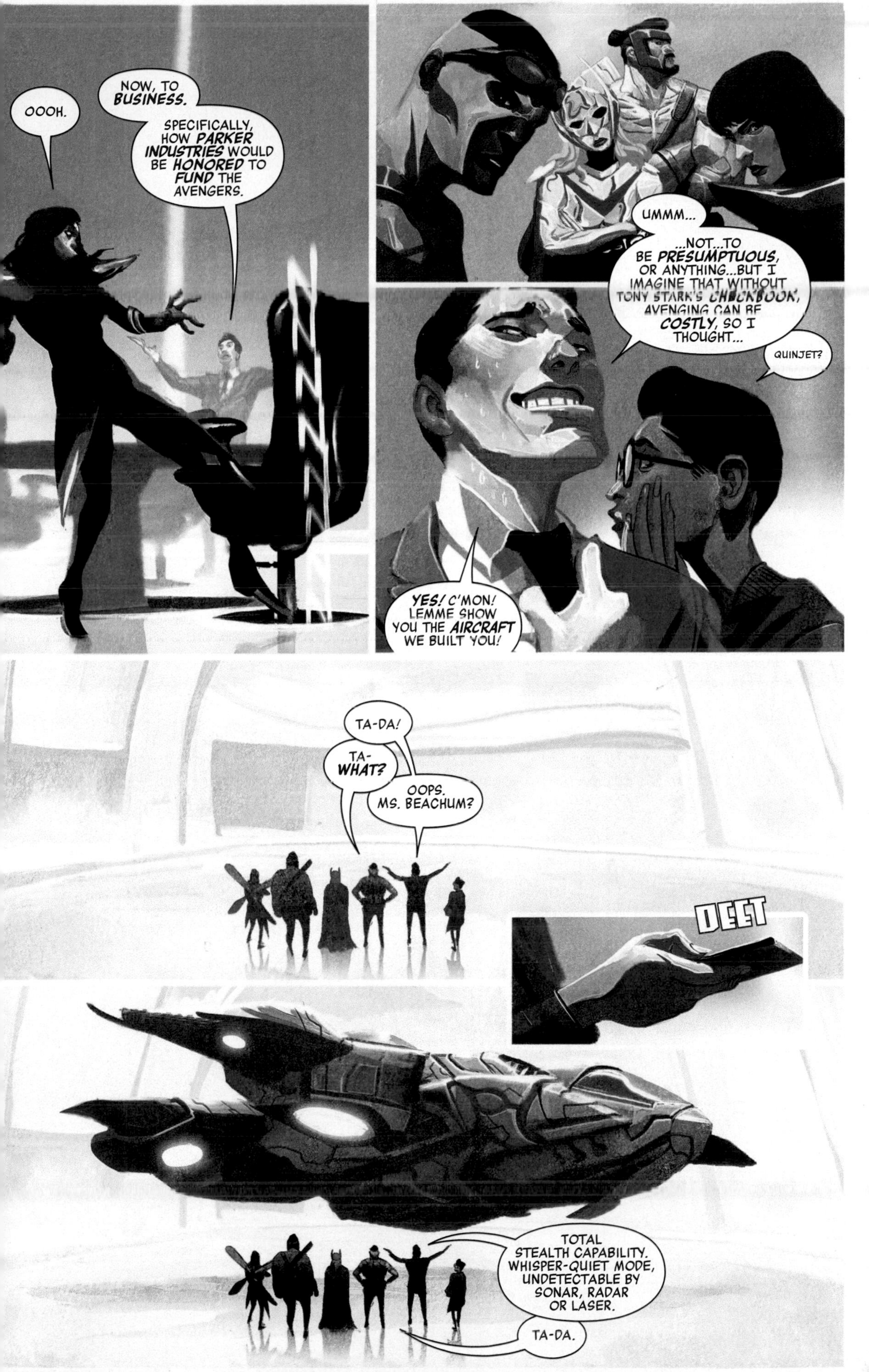
OOOH.
NOW, TO BUSINESS.
SPECIFICALLY, HOW PARKER INDUSTRIES WOULD BE HONORED TO FUND THE AVENGERS.
UMMM...
...NOT...TO BE PRESUMPTUOUS, OR ANYTHING...BUT I IMAGINE THAT WITHOUT TONY STARK'S CHECKBOOK, AVENGING CAN BE COSTLY, SO I THOUGHT...
QUINJET?
YES! C'MON! LEMME SHOW YOU THE AIRCRAFT WE BUILT YOU!
TA-DA!
TA-WHAT?
OOPS. MS. BEACHUM?
DEET
TOTAL STEALTH CAPABILITY. WHISPER-QUIET MODE, UNDETECTABLE BY SONAR, RADAR OR LASER.
TA-DA.

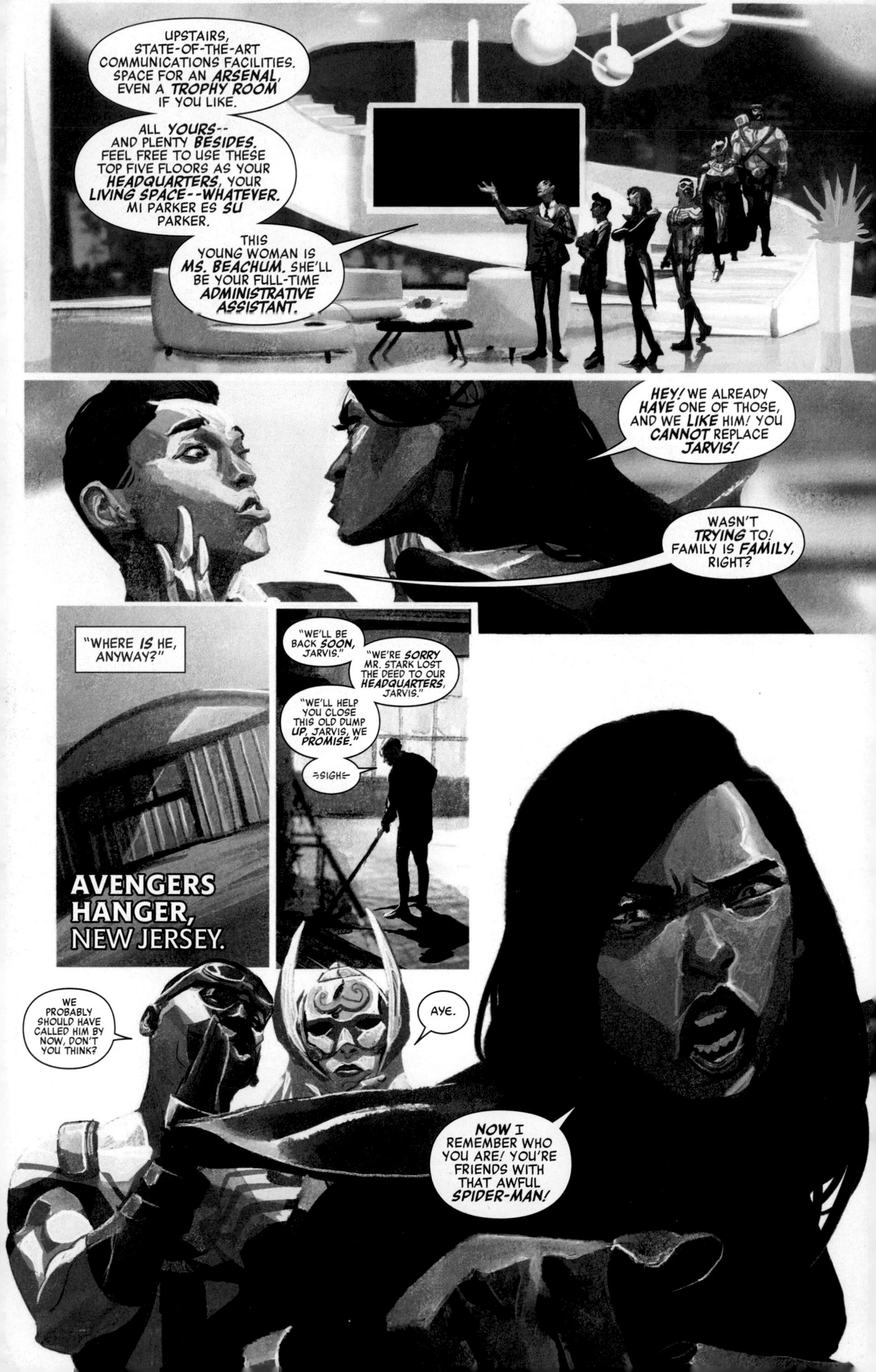
UPSTAIRS, STATE-OF-THE-ART COMMUNICATIONS FACILITIES. SPACE FOR AN ARSENAL, EVEN A TROPHY ROOM IF YOU LIKE.
ALL YOURS-- AND PLENTY BESIDES. FEEL FREE TO USE THESE TOP FIVE FLOORS AS YOUR HEADQUARTERS, YOUR LIVING SPACE--WHATEVER. MI PARKER ES SU PARKER.
THIS YOUNG WOMAN IS MS. BEACHUM. SHE'LL BE YOUR FULL-TIME ADMINISTRATIVE ASSISTANT.
HEY! WE ALREADY HAVE ONE OF THOSE, AND WE LIKE HIM! YOU CANNOT REPLACE JARVIS!
WASN'T TRYING TO! FAMILY IS FAMILY, RIGHT?
"WHERE IS HE, ANYWAY?"
AVENGERS HANGER, NEW JERSEY.
"WE'LL BE BACK SOON, JARVIS."
"WE'RE SORRY MR. STARK LOST THE DEED TO OUR HEADQUARTERS, JARVIS."
"WE'LL HELP YOU CLOSE THIS OLD DUMP UP, JARVIS, WE PROMISE."
=SIGH=
WE PROBABLY SHOULD HAVE CALLED HIM BY NOW, DON'T YOU THINK?
AYE.
NOW I REMEMBER WHO YOU ARE! YOU'RE FRIENDS WITH THAT AWFUL SPIDER-MAN!

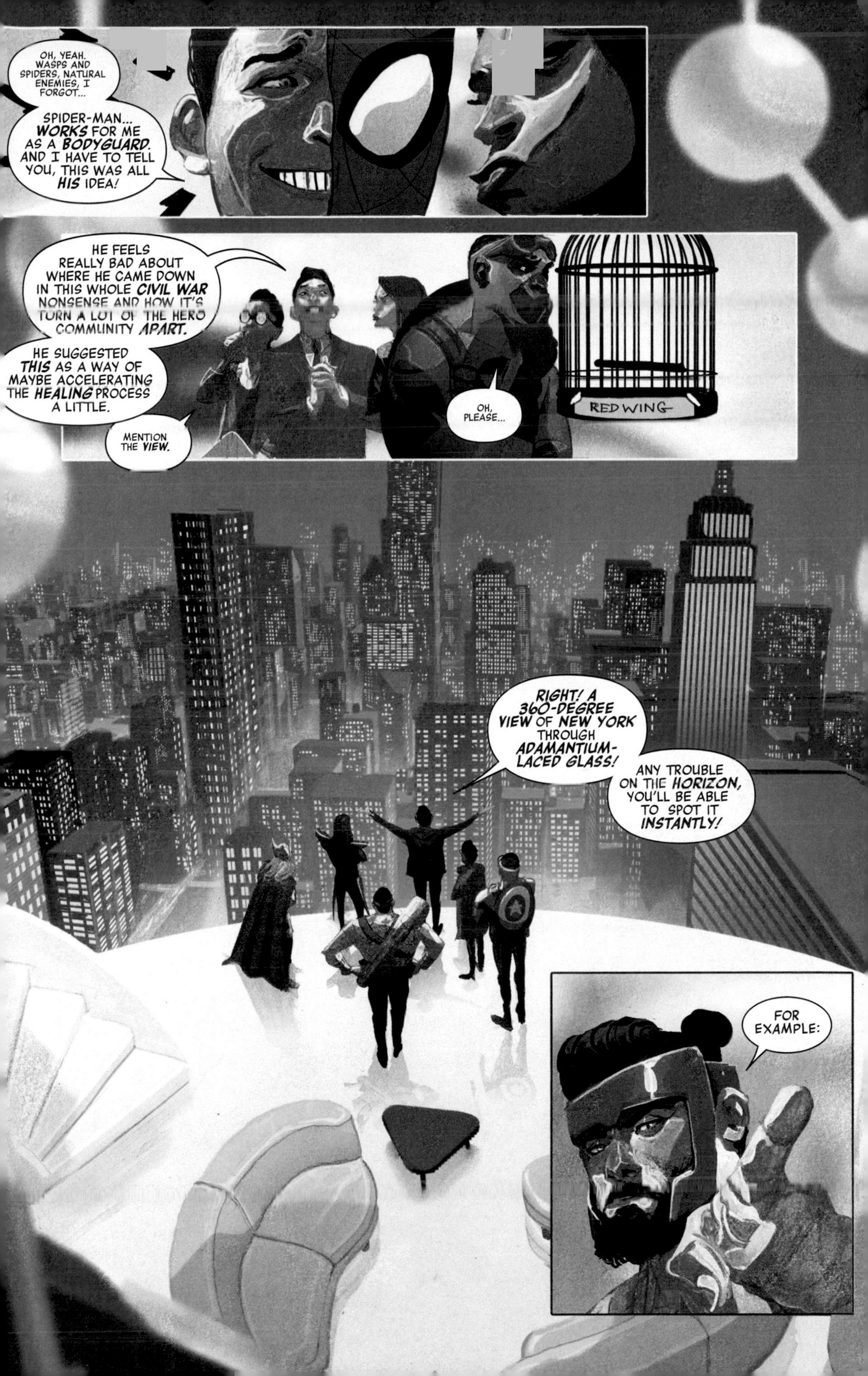
OH, YEAH. WASPS AND SPIDERS, NATURAL ENEMIES, I FORGOT...
SPIDER-MAN... WORKS FOR ME AS A BODYGUARD. AND I HAVE TO TELL YOU, THIS WAS ALL HIS IDEA!
HE FEELS REALLY BAD ABOUT WHERE HE CAME DOWN IN THIS WHOLE CIVIL WAR NONSENSE AND HOW IT'S TORN A LOT OF THE HERO COMMUNITY APART.
HE SUGGESTED THIS AS A WAY OF MAYBE ACCELERATING THE HEALING PROCESS A LITTLE.
MENTION THE VIEW.
OH, PLEASE...
REDWING
RIGHT! A 360-DEGREE VIEW OF NEW YORK THROUGH ADAMANTIUM-LACED GLASS!
ANY TROUBLE ON THE HORIZON, YOU'LL BE ABLE TO SPOT IT INSTANTLY!
FOR EXAMPLE:

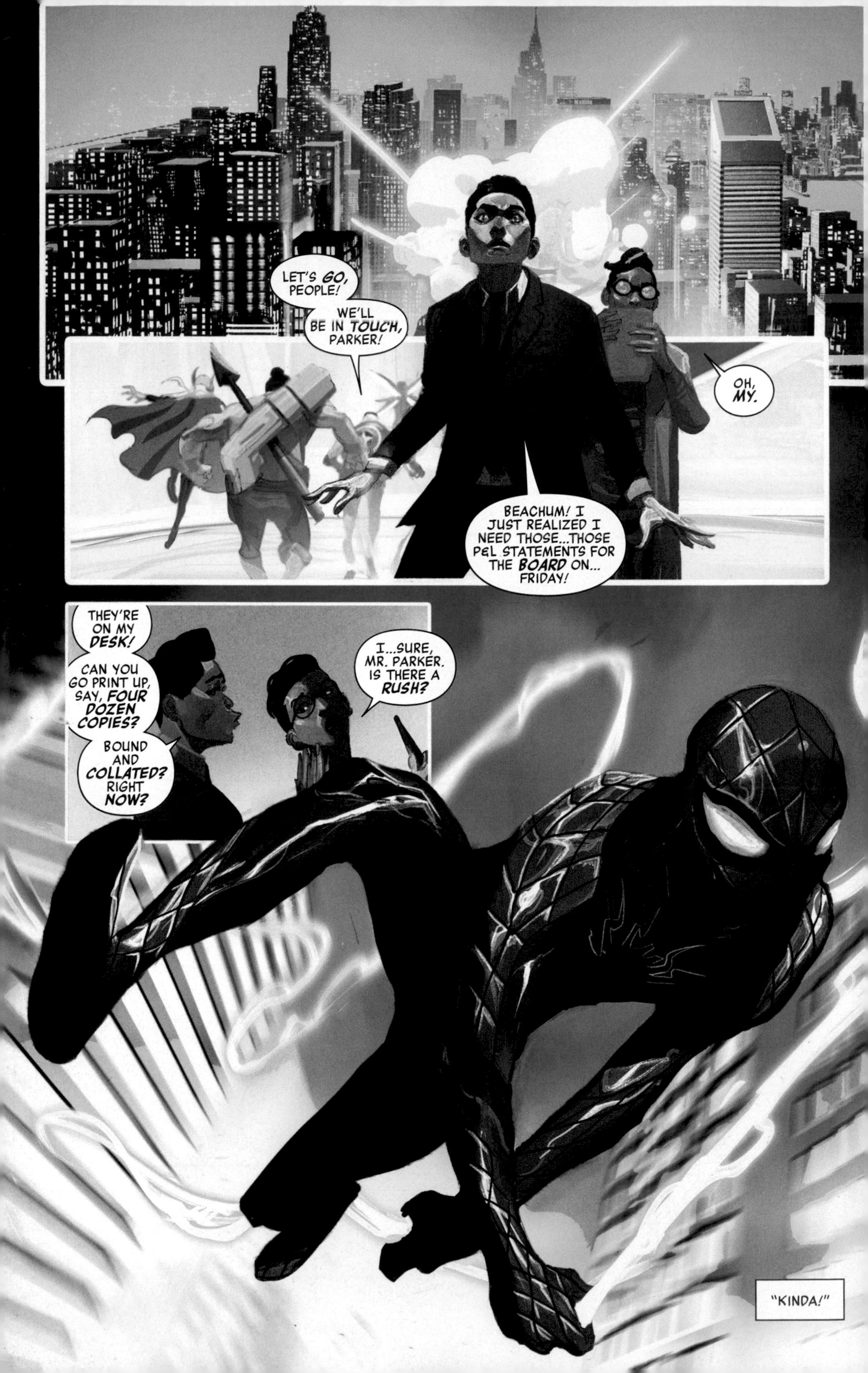
LET'S GO, PEOPLE!
WE'LL BE IN TOUCH, PARKER!
OH, MY.
BEACHUM! I JUST REALIZED I NEED THOSE...THOSE P&L STATEMENTS FOR THE BOARD ON... FRIDAY!
THEY'RE ON MY DESK!
CAN YOU GO PRINT UP, SAY, FOUR DOZEN COPIES?
BOUND AND COLLATED? RIGHT NOW?
I...SURE, MR. PARKER. IS THERE A RUSH?
"KINDA!"

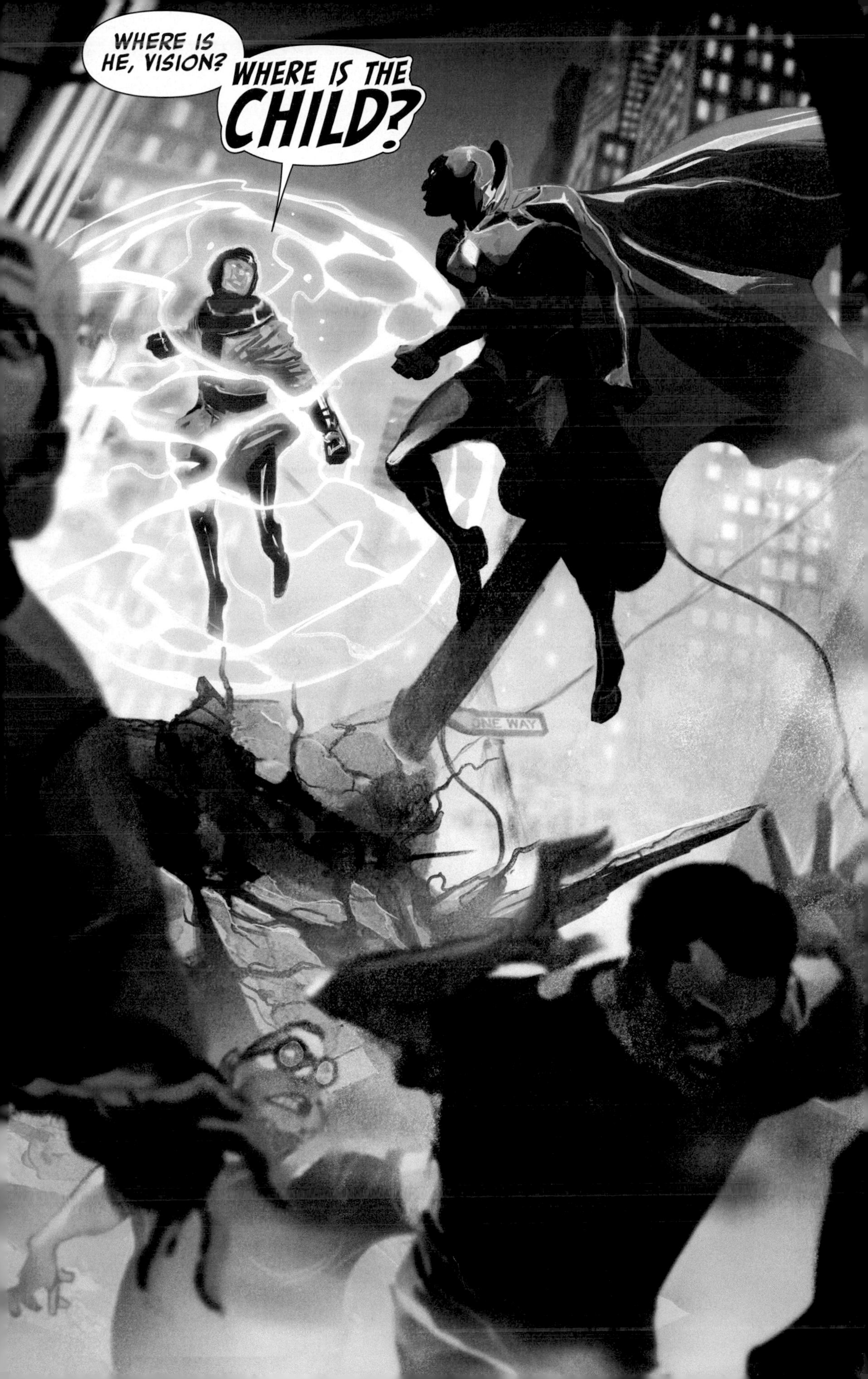
WHERE IS HE, VISION? WHERE IS THE CHILD?
ONE WAY

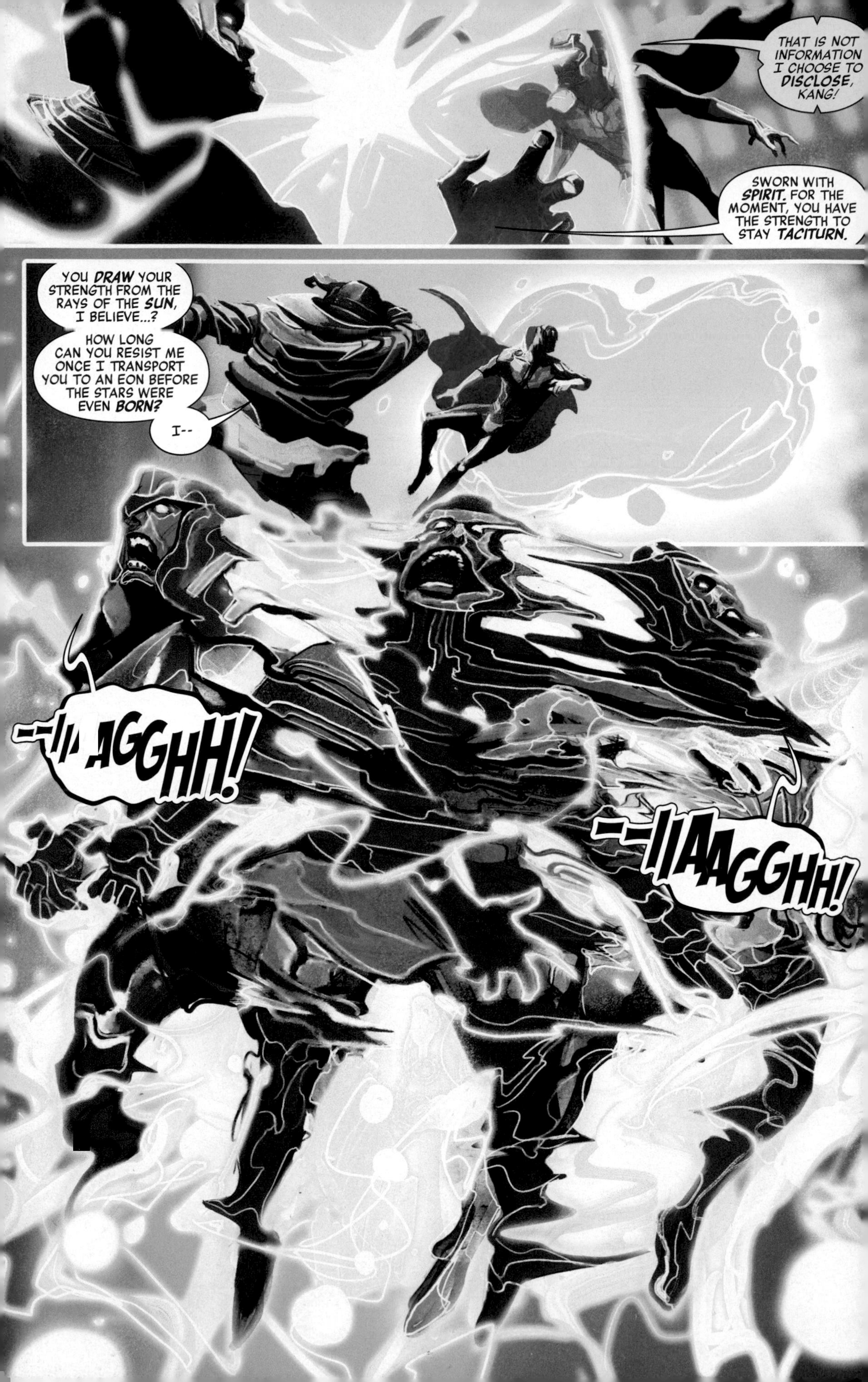
THAT IS NOT INFORMATION I CHOOSE TO DISCLOSE, KANG!
SWORN WITH SPIRIT. FOR THE MOMENT, YOU HAVE THE STRENGTH TO STAY TACITURN.
YOU DRAW YOUR STRENGTH FROM THE RAYS OF THE SUN, I BELIEVE...?
HOW LONG CAN YOU RESIST ME ONCE I TRANSPORT YOU TO AN EON BEFORE THE STARS WERE EVEN BORN?
I--
--IIAGGHH!
--IIAAGGHH!

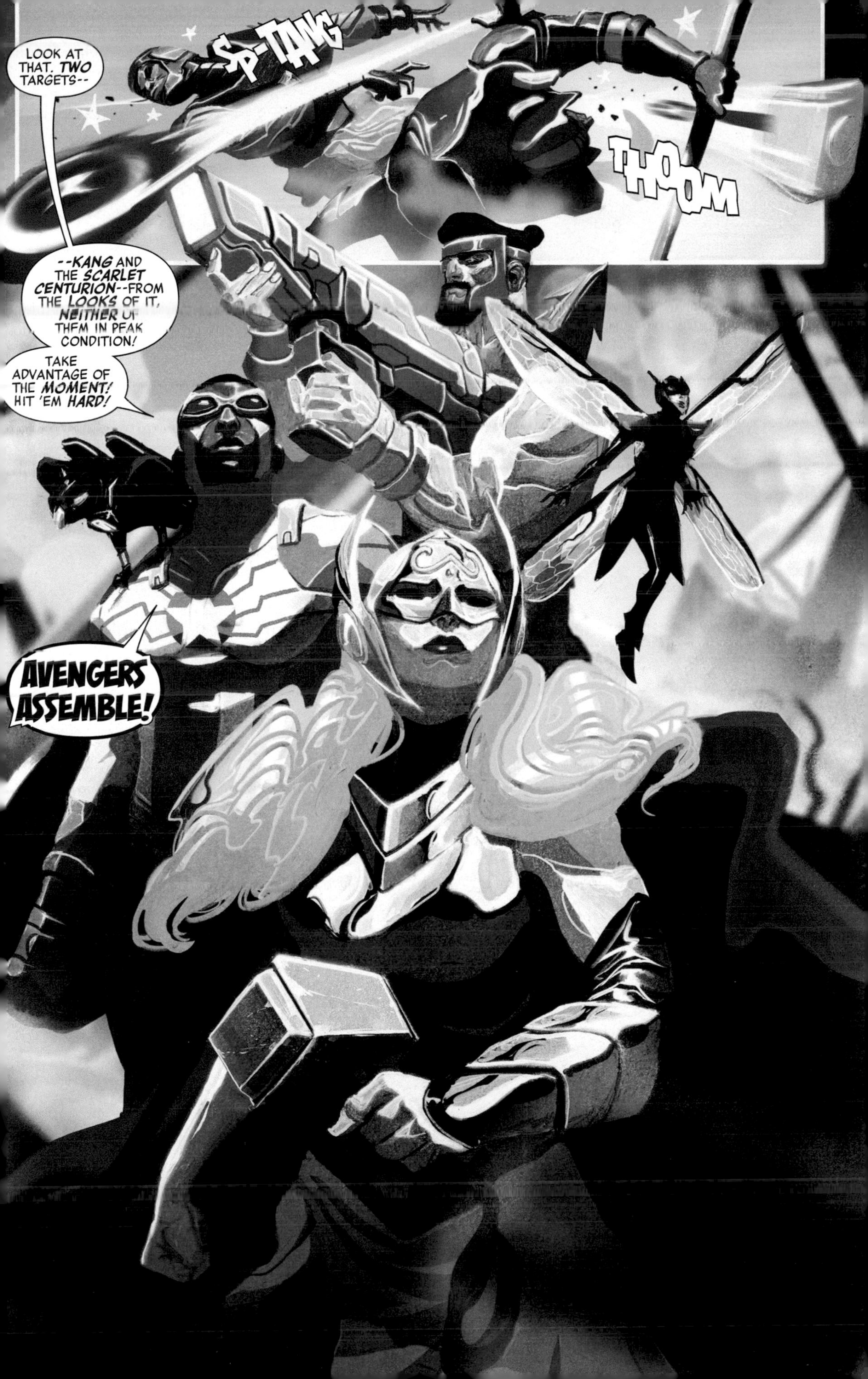

LOOK AT THAT. TWO TARGETS--
SP-TANG
THOOM
--KANG AND THE SCARLET CENTURION--FROM THE LOOKS OF IT, NEITHER OF THEM IN PEAK CONDITION!
TAKE ADVANTAGE OF THE MOMENT! HIT 'EM HARD!
AVENGERS ASSEMBLE!

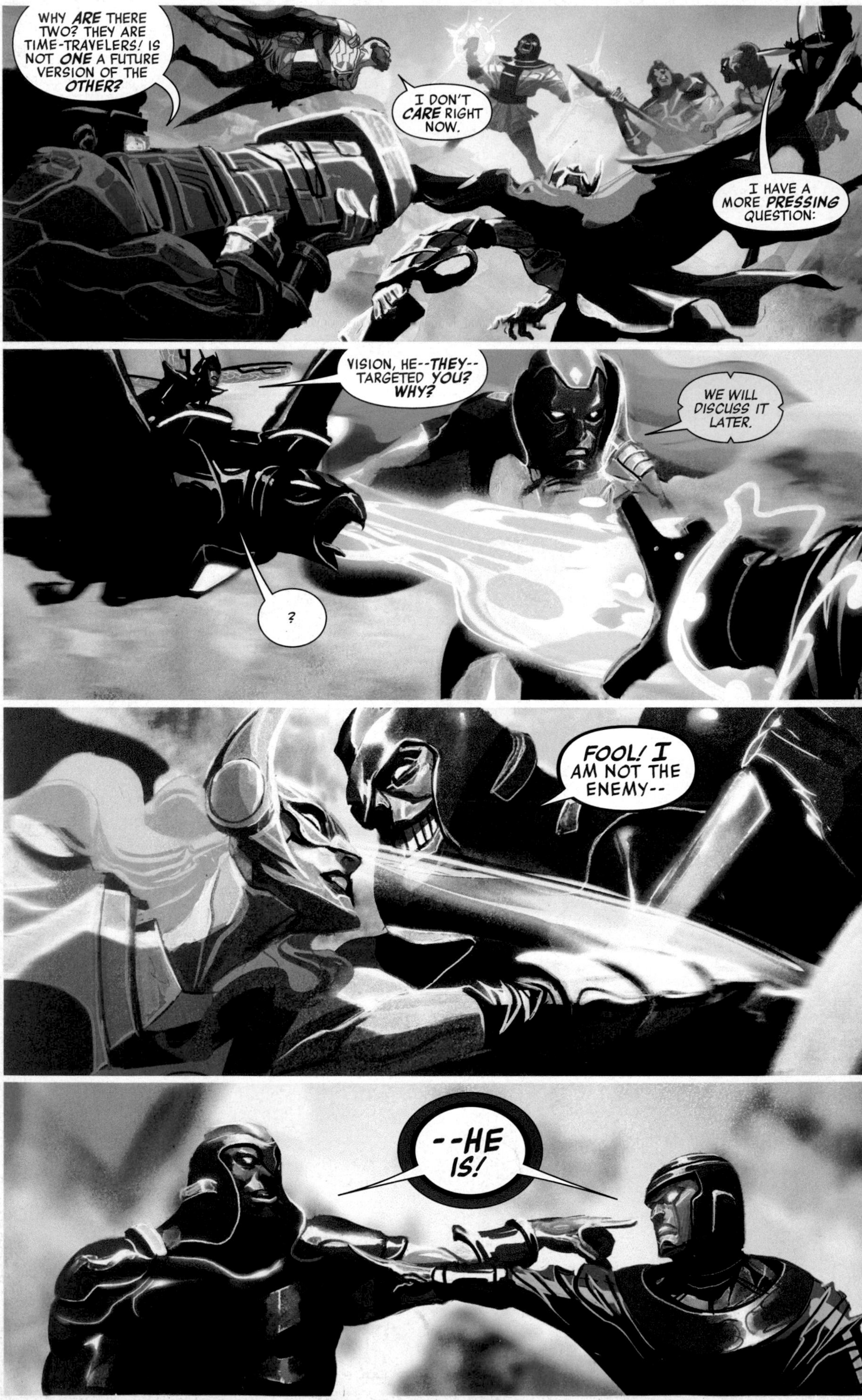
WHY ARE THERE TWO? THEY ARE TIME-TRAVELERS! IS NOT ONE A FUTURE VERSION OF THE OTHER?
I DON'T CARE RIGHT NOW.
I HAVE A MORE PRESSING QUESTION:
VISION, HE--THEY--TARGETED YOU? WHY?
WE WILL DISCUSS IT LATER.
?
FOOL! I AM NOT THE ENEMY--
--HE IS!

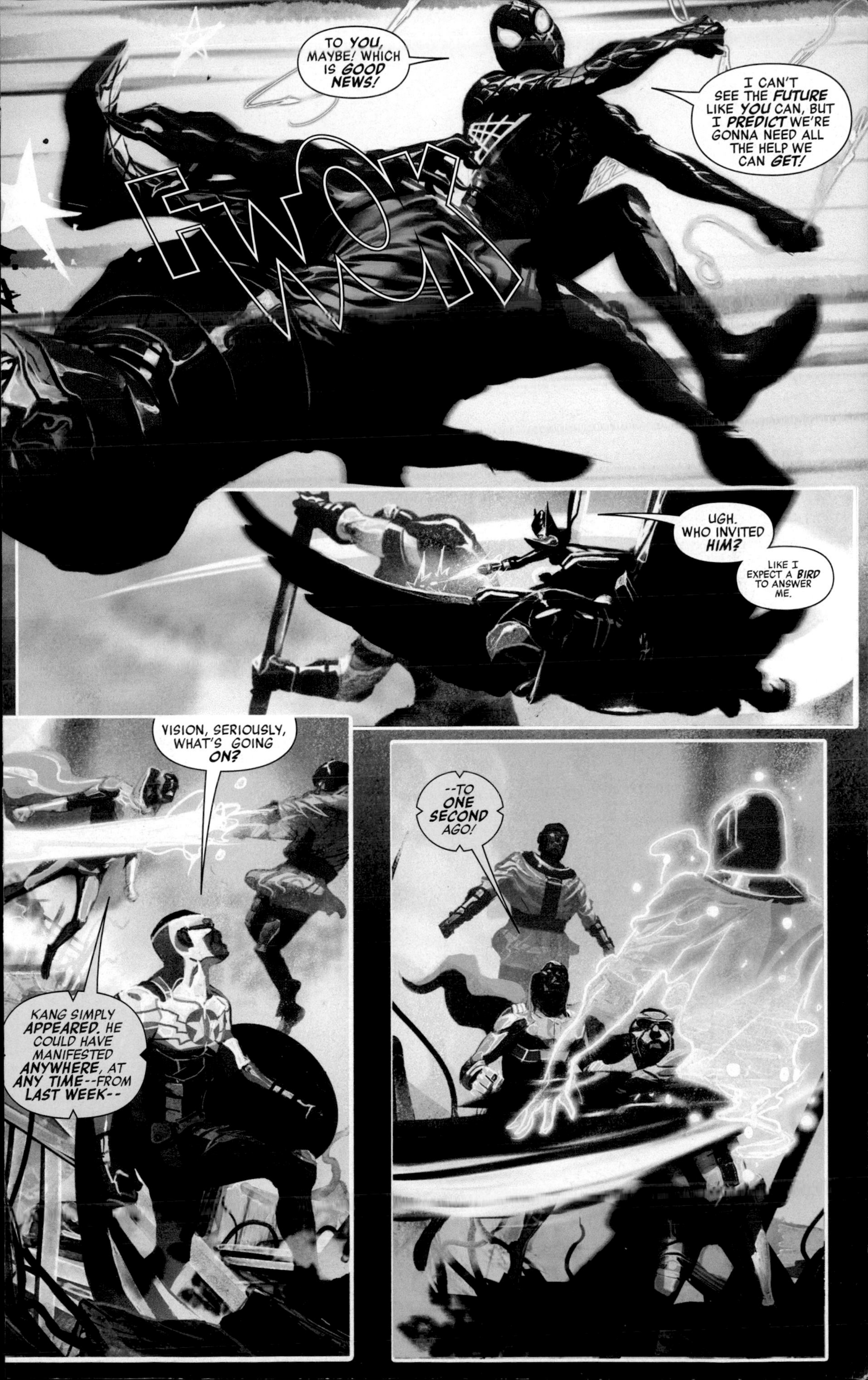
TO YOU, MAYBE! WHICH IS GOOD NEWS!
I CAN'T SEE THE FUTURE LIKE YOU CAN, BUT I PREDICT WE'RE GONNA NEED ALL THE HELP WE CAN GET!
FWOM
UGH. WHO INVITED HIM?
LIKE I EXPECT A BIRD TO ANSWER ME.
VISION, SERIOUSLY, WHAT'S GOING ON?
KANG SIMPLY APPEARED. HE COULD HAVE MANIFESTED ANYWHERE, AT ANY TIME--FROM LAST WEEK--
--TO ONE SECOND AGO!

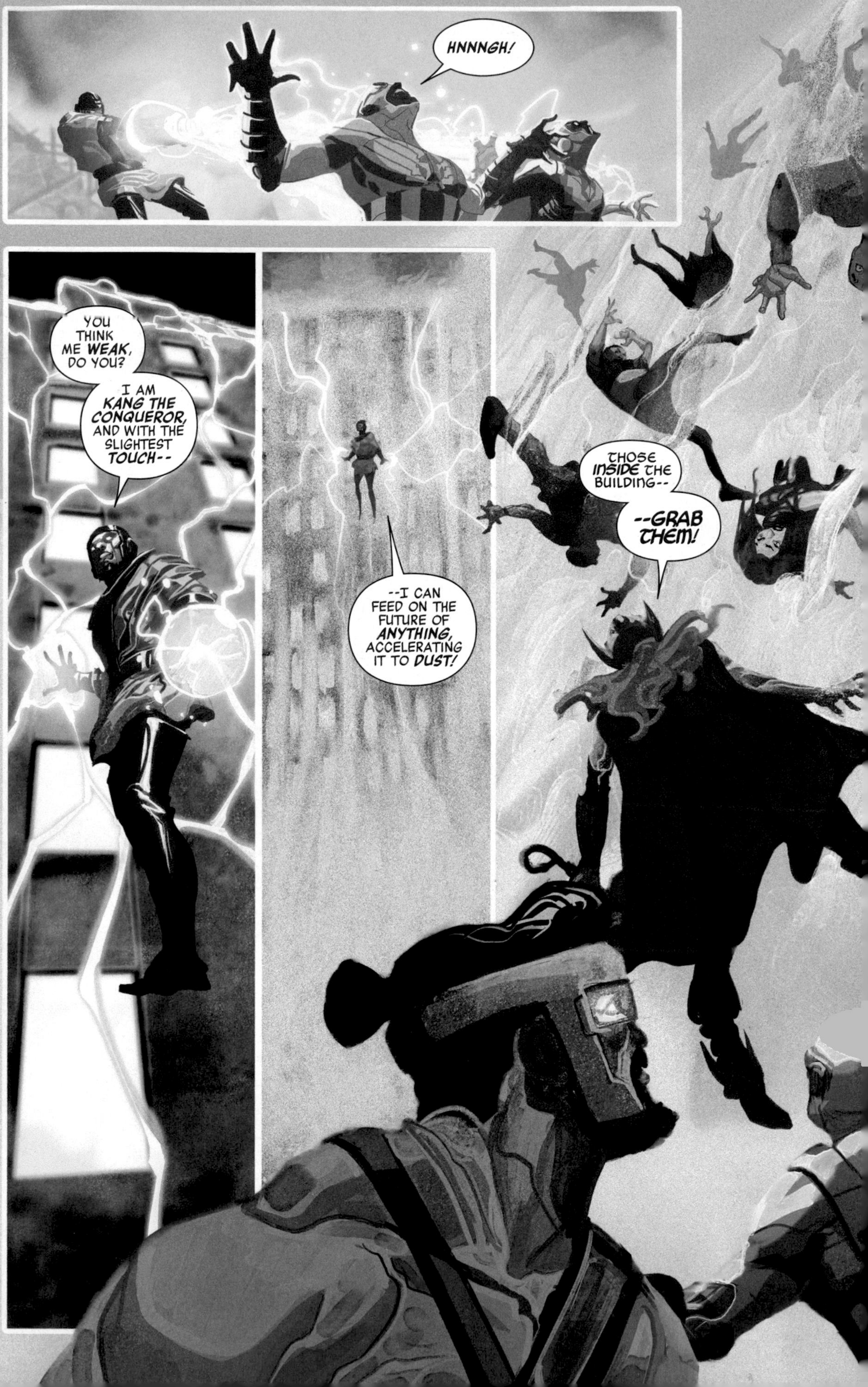
HNNNGH!
YOU THINK ME WEAK, DO YOU?
I AM KANG THE CONQUEROR, AND WITH THE SLIGHTEST TOUCH--
--I CAN FEED ON THE FUTURE OF ANYTHING, ACCELERATING IT TO DUST!
THOSE INSIDE THE BUILDING--
--GRAB THEM!

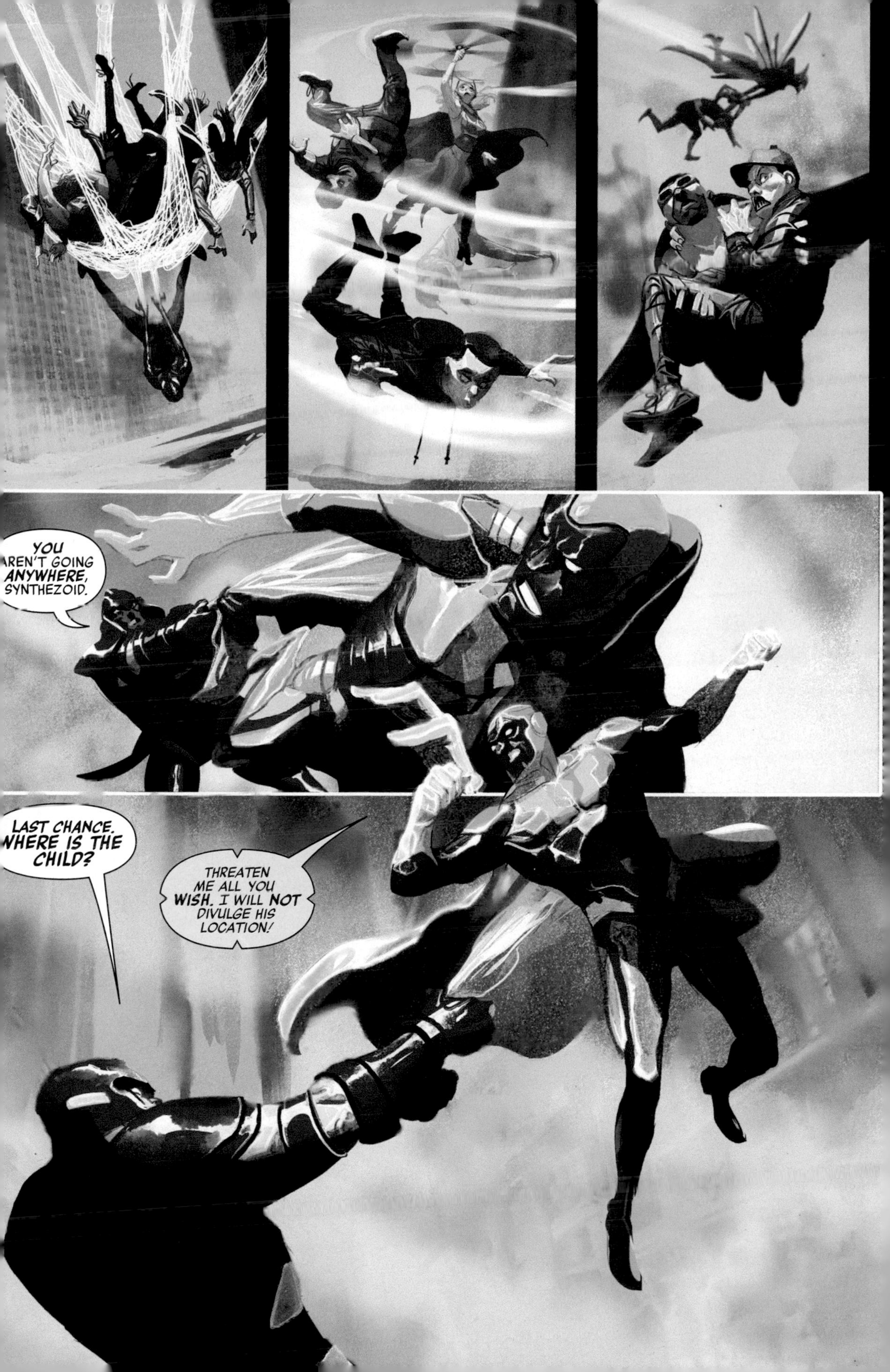
YOU AREN'T GOING ANYWHERE, SYNTHEZOID.
LAST CHANCE. WHERE IS THE CHILD?
THREATEN ME ALL YOU WISH. I WILL NOT DIVULGE HIS LOCATION!

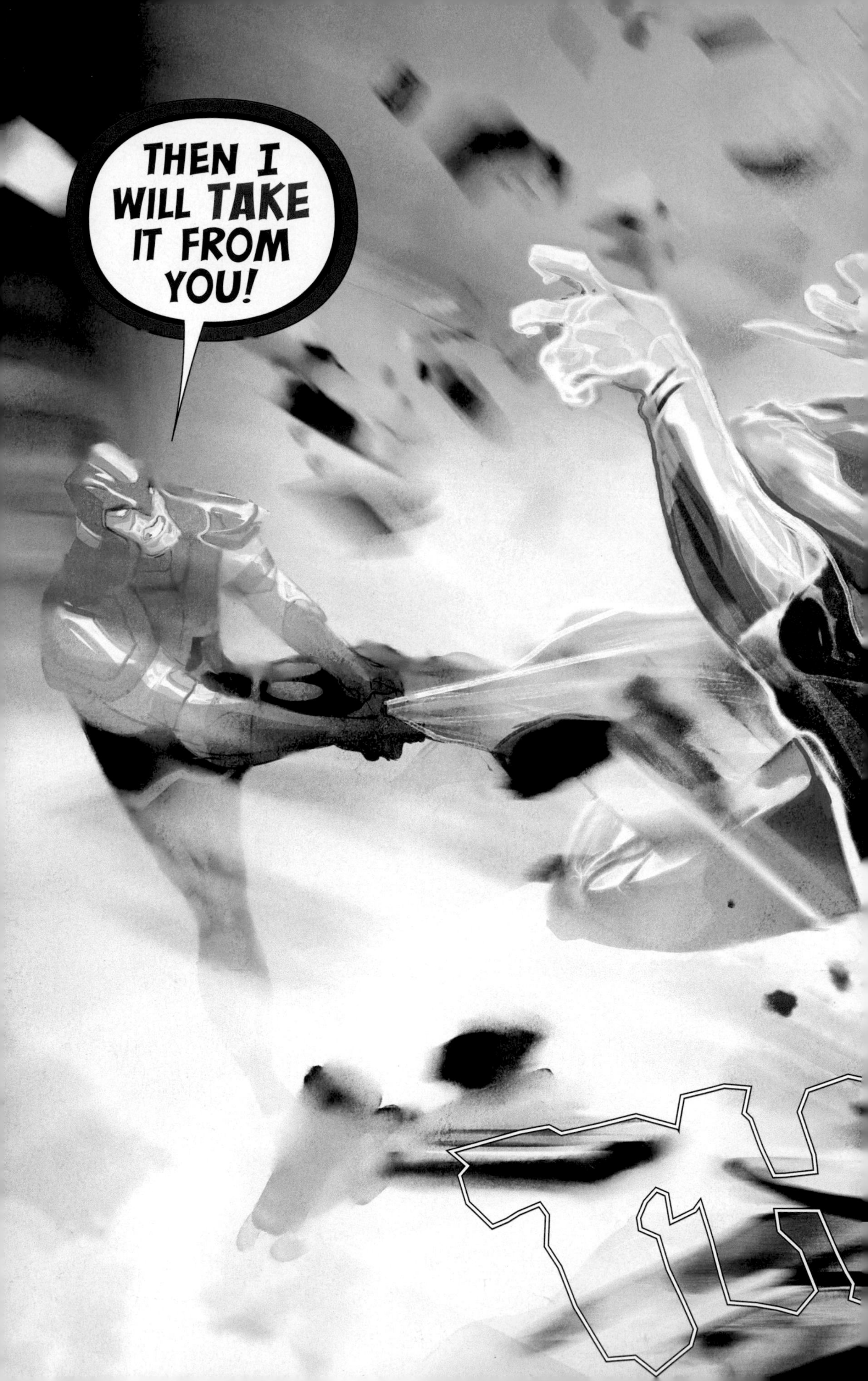
THEN I WILL TAKE IT FROM YOU!

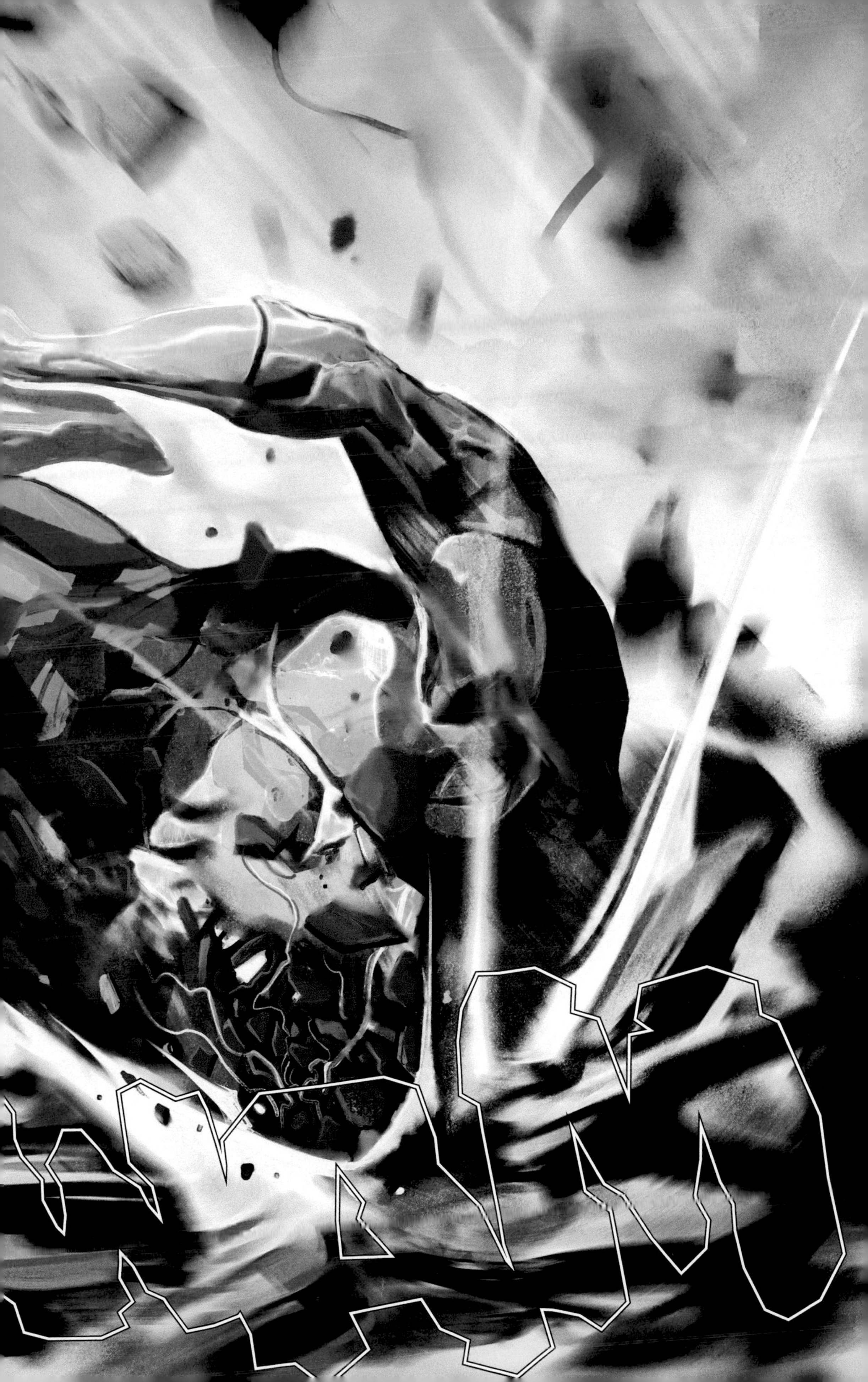

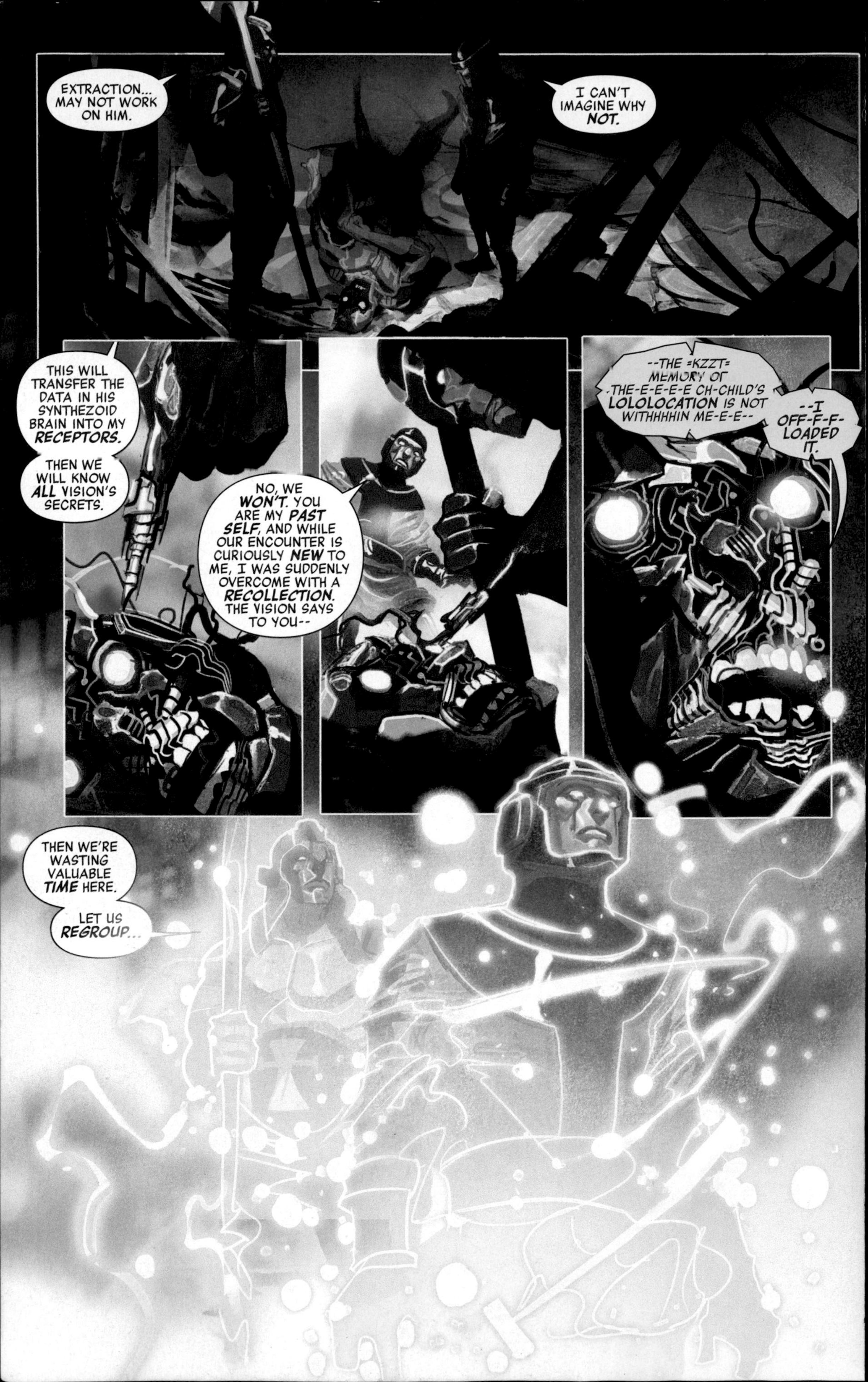
EXTRACTION... MAY NOT WORK ON HIM.
I CAN'T IMAGINE WHY NOT.
THIS WILL TRANSFER THE DATA IN HIS SYNTHEZOID BRAIN INTO MY RECEPTORS.
THEN WE WILL KNOW ALL VISION'S SECRETS.
NO, WE WON'T. YOU ARE MY PAST SELF, AND WHILE OUR ENCOUNTER IS CURIOUSLY NEW TO ME, I WAS SUDDENLY OVERCOME WITH A RECOLLECTION. THE VISION SAYS TO YOU--
--THE =KZZT= MEMORY OF THE-E-E-E CH-CHILD'S LOLOLOCATION IS NOT WITHHHHIN ME-E-E--
--I OFF-F-F-LOADED IT.
THEN WE'RE WASTING VALUABLE TIME HERE.
LET US REGROUP...

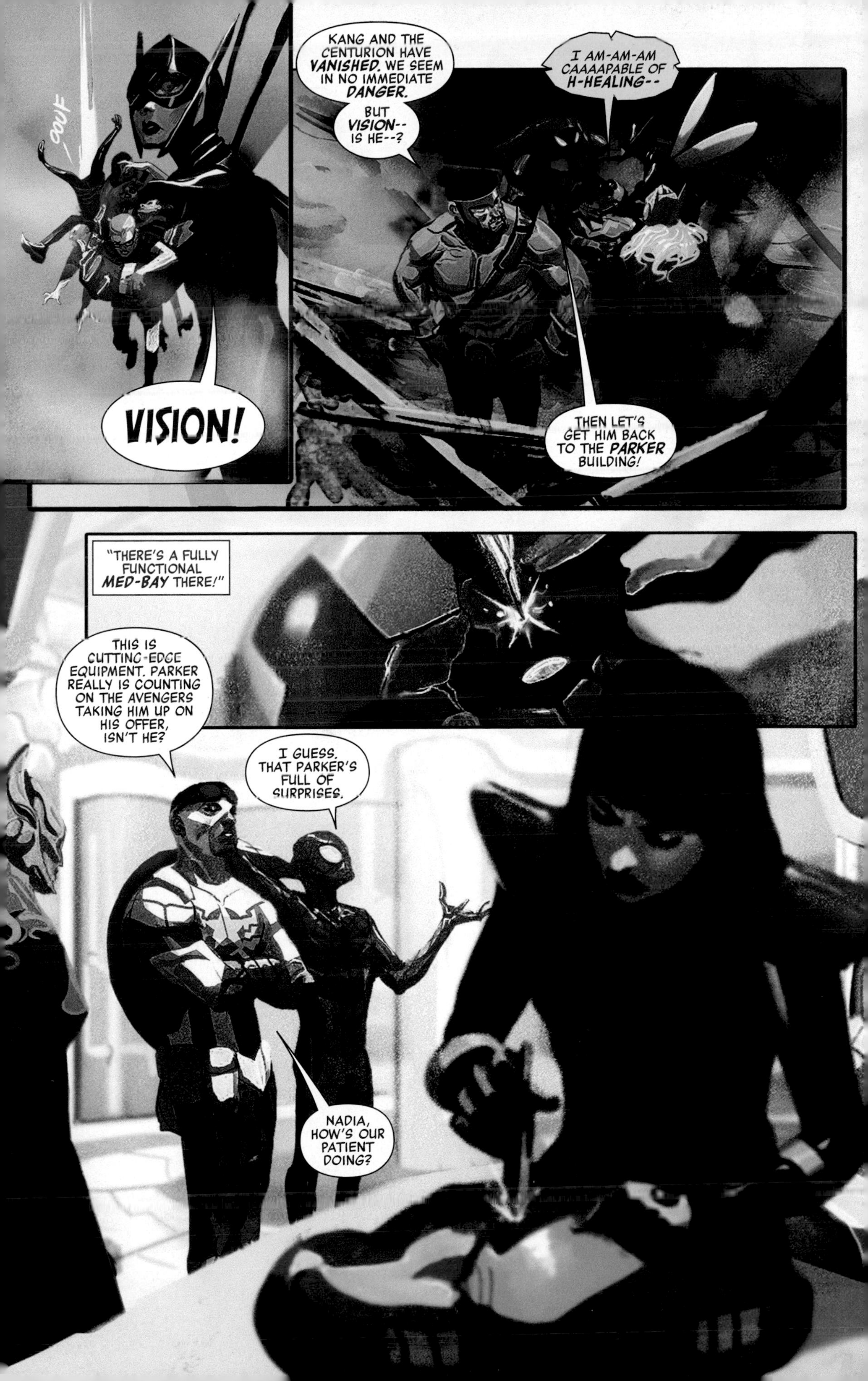
OOUF
VISION!
KANG AND THE CENTURION HAVE VANISHED. WE SEEM IN NO IMMEDIATE DANGER.
BUT VISION-- IS HE--?
I AM-AM-AM CAAAAPABLE OF H-HEALING--
THEN LET'S GET HIM BACK TO THE PARKER BUILDING!
"THERE'S A FULLY FUNCTIONAL MED-BAY THERE!"
THIS IS CUTTING-EDGE EQUIPMENT. PARKER REALLY IS COUNTING ON THE AVENGERS TAKING HIM UP ON HIS OFFER, ISN'T HE?
I GUESS. THAT PARKER'S FULL OF SURPRISES.
NADIA, HOW'S OUR PATIENT DOING?

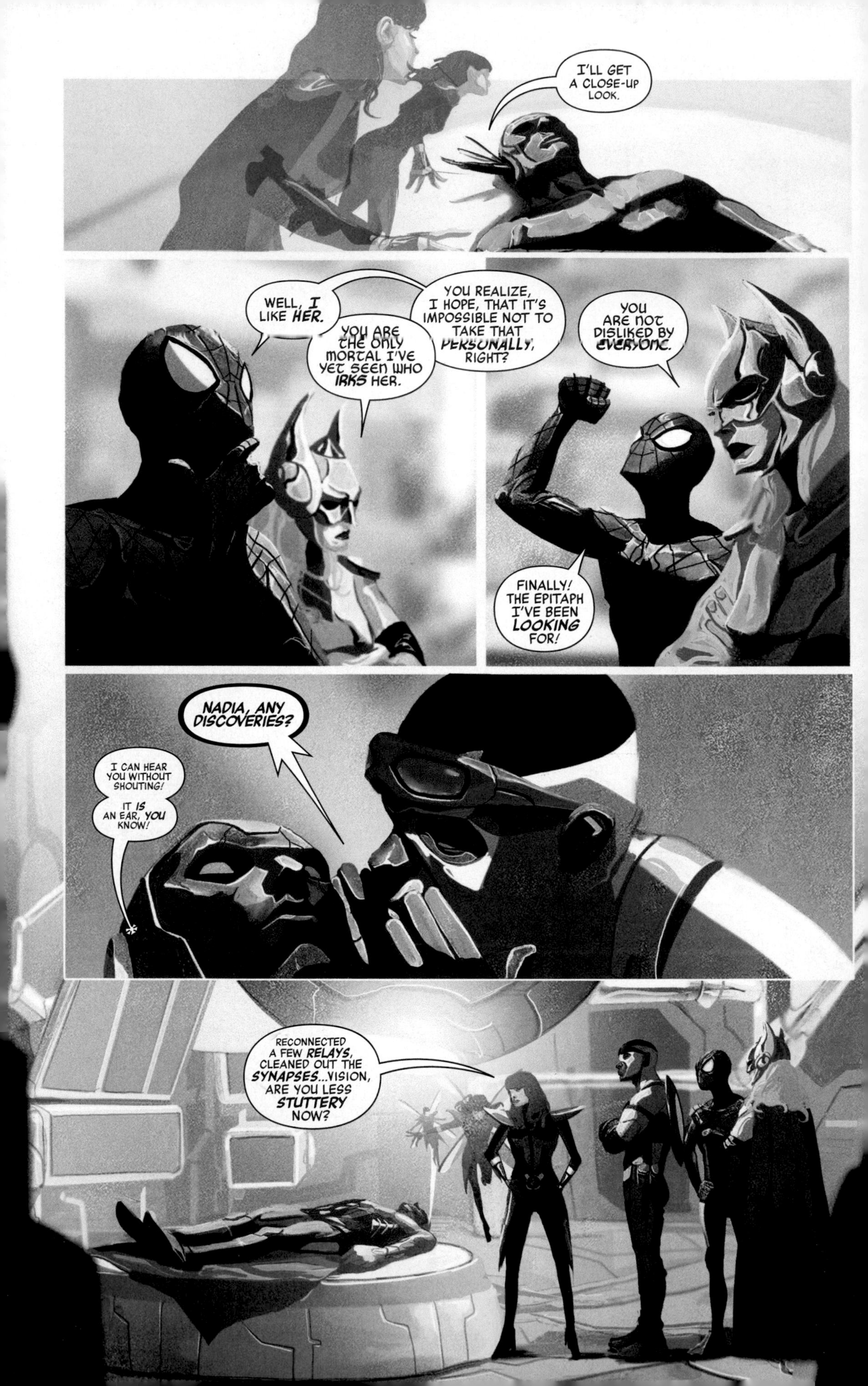
I'LL GET A CLOSE-UP LOOK.
WELL, *I* LIKE *HER.*
YOU REALIZE, I HOPE, THAT IT'S IMPOSSIBLE NOT TO TAKE THAT *PERSONALLY*, RIGHT?
YOU ARE THE ONLY MORTAL I'VE YET SEEN WHO *IRKS* HER.
YOU ARE NOT DISLIKED BY *EVERYONE.*
FINALLY! THE EPITAPH I'VE BEEN *LOOKING* FOR!
NADIA, ANY DISCOVERIES?
I CAN HEAR YOU WITHOUT SHOUTING!
IT *IS* AN EAR, *YOU* KNOW!
RECONNECTED A FEW *RELAYS*, CLEANED OUT THE *SYNAPSES*...VISION, ARE YOU LESS *STUTTERY* NOW?

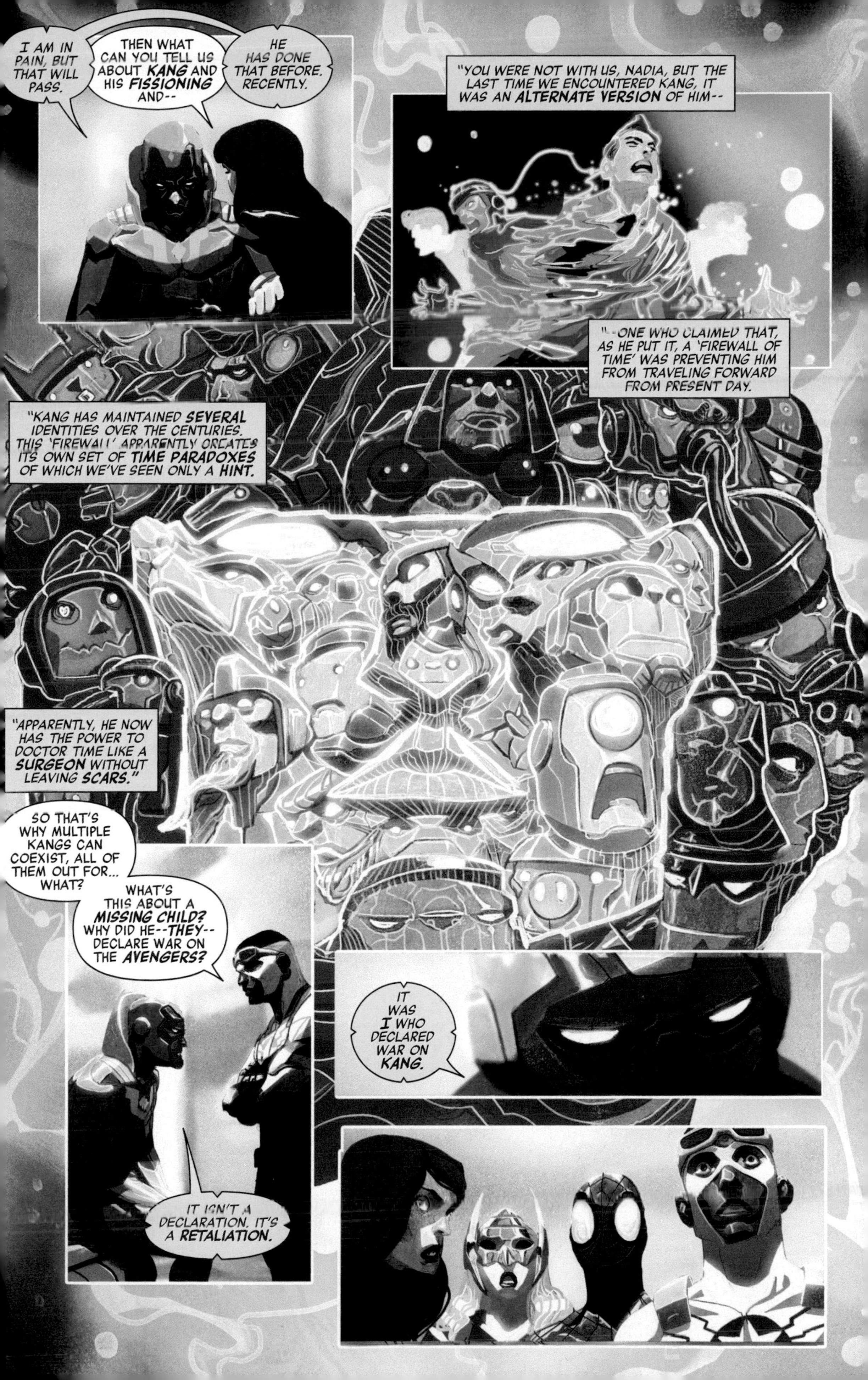

I AM IN PAIN, BUT THAT WILL PASS.
THEN WHAT CAN YOU TELL US ABOUT KANG AND HIS FISSIONING AND--
HE HAS DONE THAT BEFORE. RECENTLY.
"YOU WERE NOT WITH US, NADIA, BUT THE LAST TIME WE ENCOUNTERED KANG, IT WAS AN ALTERNATE VERSION OF HIM--
"--ONE WHO CLAIMED THAT, AS HE PUT IT, A 'FIREWALL OF TIME' WAS PREVENTING HIM FROM TRAVELING FORWARD FROM PRESENT DAY.
"KANG HAS MAINTAINED SEVERAL IDENTITIES OVER THE CENTURIES. THIS 'FIREWALL' APPARENTLY CREATES ITS OWN SET OF TIME PARADOXES OF WHICH WE'VE SEEN ONLY A HINT.
"APPARENTLY, HE NOW HAS THE POWER TO DOCTOR TIME LIKE A SURGEON WITHOUT LEAVING SCARS."
SO THAT'S WHY MULTIPLE KANGS CAN COEXIST, ALL OF THEM OUT FOR... WHAT?
WHAT'S THIS ABOUT A MISSING CHILD? WHY DID HE--THEY--DECLARE WAR ON THE AVENGERS?
IT ISN'T A DECLARATION. IT'S A RETALIATION.
IT WAS I WHO DECLARED WAR ON KANG.

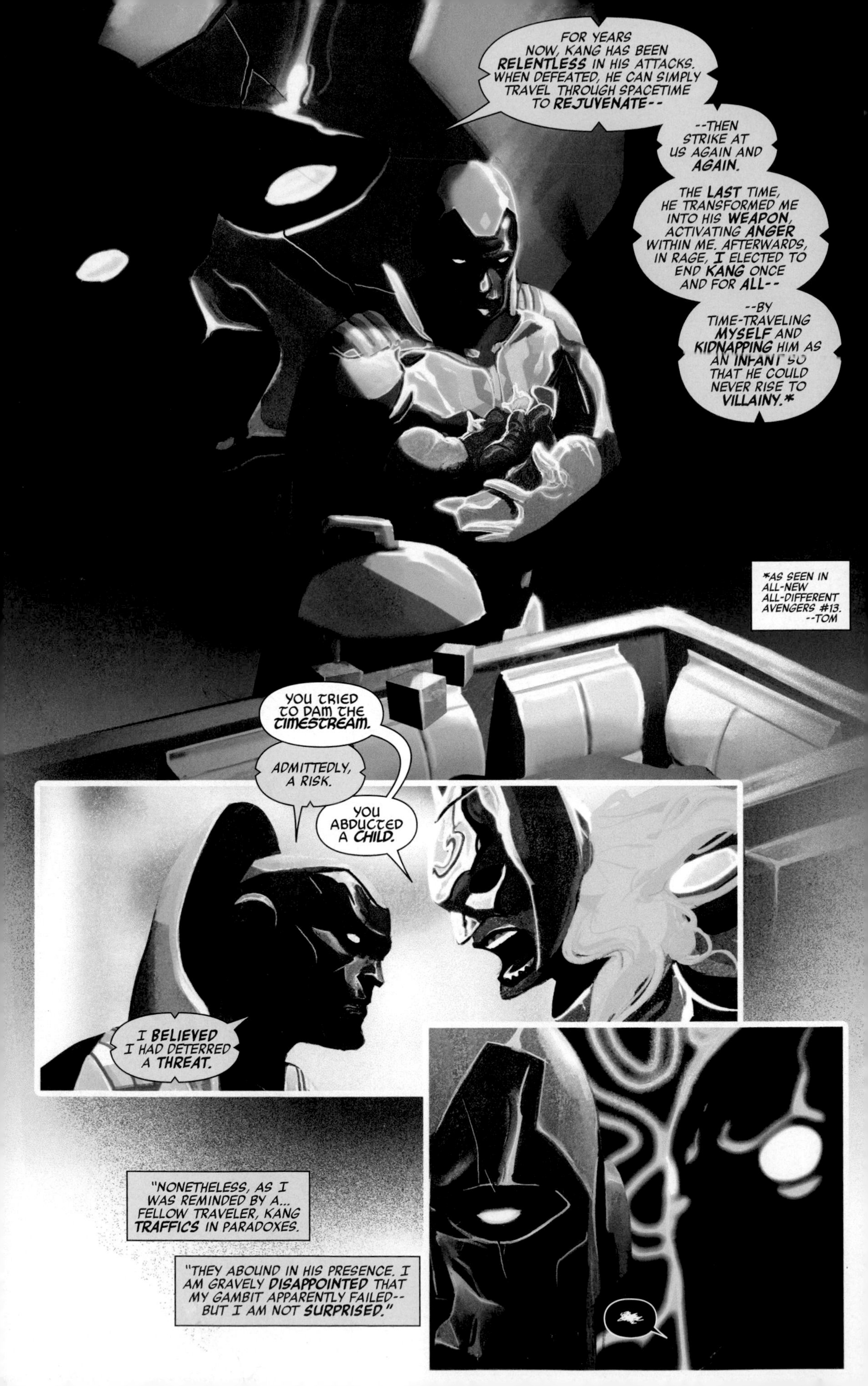
FOR YEARS NOW, KANG HAS BEEN RELENTLESS IN HIS ATTACKS. WHEN DEFEATED, HE CAN SIMPLY TRAVEL THROUGH SPACETIME TO REJUVENATE--
--THEN STRIKE AT US AGAIN AND AGAIN.
THE LAST TIME, HE TRANSFORMED ME INTO HIS WEAPON, ACTIVATING ANGER WITHIN ME. AFTERWARDS, IN RAGE, I ELECTED TO END KANG ONCE AND FOR ALL--
--BY TIME-TRAVELING MYSELF AND KIDNAPPING HIM AS AN INFANT SO THAT HE COULD NEVER RISE TO VILLAINY.*
*AS SEEN IN ALL-NEW ALL-DIFFERENT AVENGERS #13. --TOM
YOU TRIED TO DAM THE TIMESTREAM.
ADMITTEDLY, A RISK.
YOU ABDUCTED A CHILD.
I BELIEVED I HAD DETERRED A THREAT.
"NONETHELESS, AS I WAS REMINDED BY A... FELLOW TRAVELER, KANG TRAFFICS IN PARADOXES.
"THEY ABOUND IN HIS PRESENCE. I AM GRAVELY DISAPPOINTED THAT MY GAMBIT APPARENTLY FAILED--BUT I AM NOT SURPRISED."

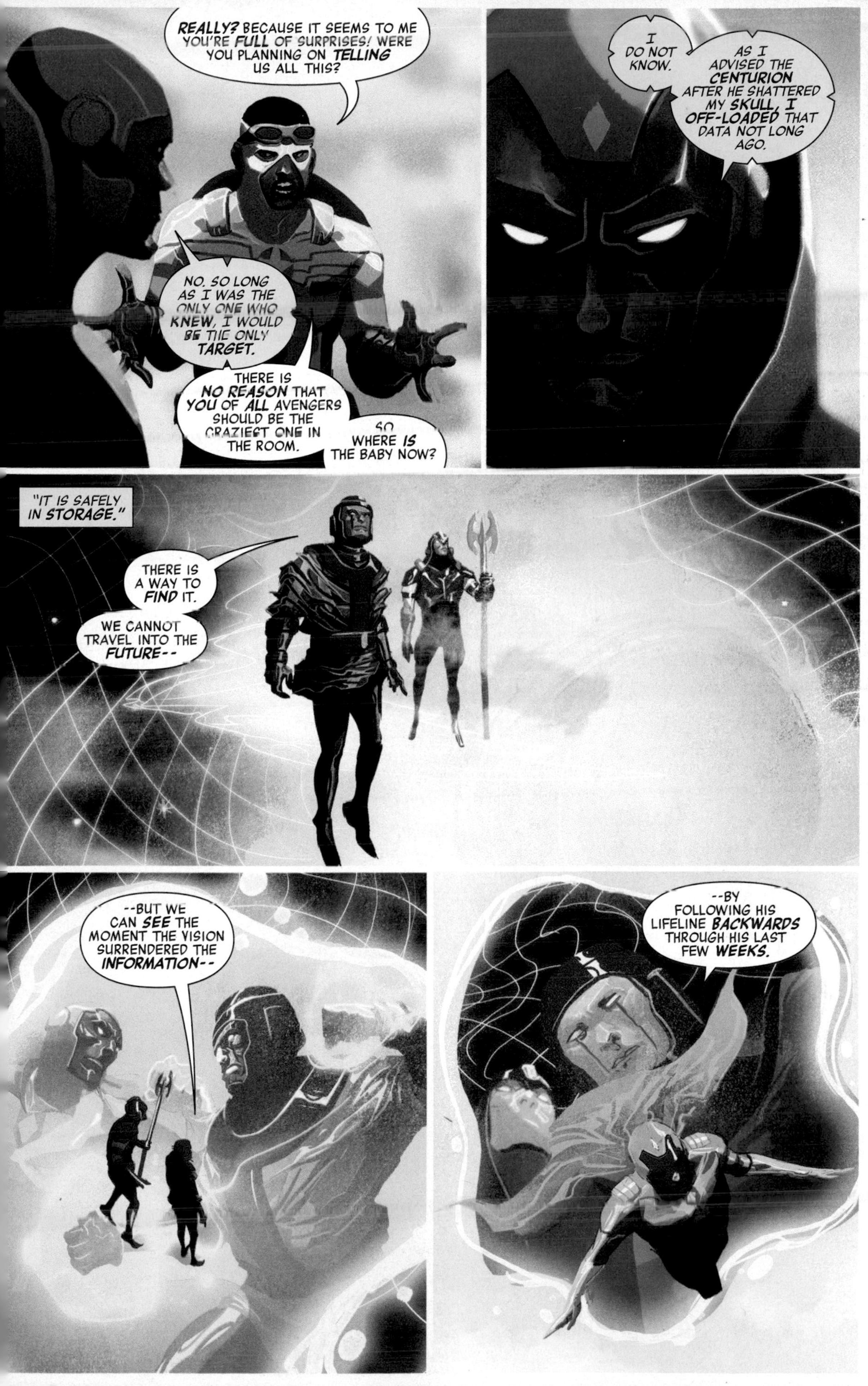
REALLY? BECAUSE IT SEEMS TO ME YOU'RE FULL OF SURPRISES! WERE YOU PLANNING ON TELLING US ALL THIS?
NO. SO LONG AS I WAS THE ONLY ONE WHO KNEW, I WOULD BE THE ONLY TARGET.
THERE IS NO REASON THAT YOU OF ALL AVENGERS SHOULD BE THE CRAZIEST ONE IN THE ROOM.
SO WHERE IS THE BABY NOW?
I DO NOT KNOW.
AS I ADVISED THE CENTURION AFTER HE SHATTERED MY SKULL, I OFF-LOADED THAT DATA NOT LONG AGO.
"IT IS SAFELY IN STORAGE."
THERE IS A WAY TO FIND IT.
WE CANNOT TRAVEL INTO THE FUTURE--
--BUT WE CAN SEE THE MOMENT THE VISION SURRENDERED THE INFORMATION--
--BY FOLLOWING HIS LIFELINE BACKWARDS THROUGH HIS LAST FEW WEEKS.

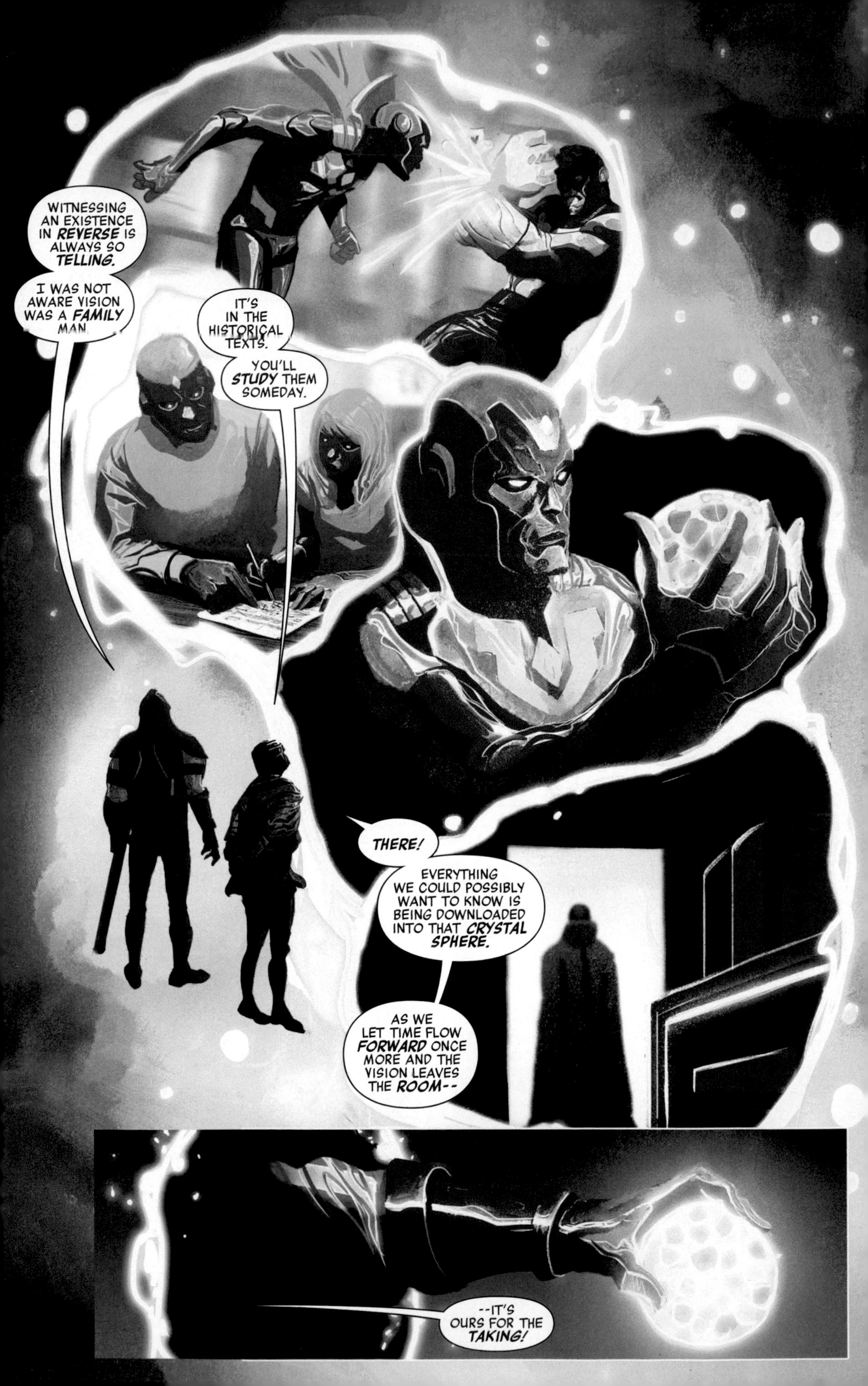
WITNESSING AN EXISTENCE IN REVERSE IS ALWAYS SO TELLING.
I WAS NOT AWARE VISION WAS A FAMILY MAN.
IT'S IN THE HISTORICAL TEXTS.
YOU'LL STUDY THEM SOMEDAY.
THERE!
EVERYTHING WE COULD POSSIBLY WANT TO KNOW IS BEING DOWNLOADED INTO THAT CRYSTAL SPHERE.
AS WE LET TIME FLOW FORWARD ONCE MORE AND THE VISION LEAVES THE ROOM--
--IT'S OURS FOR THE TAKING!

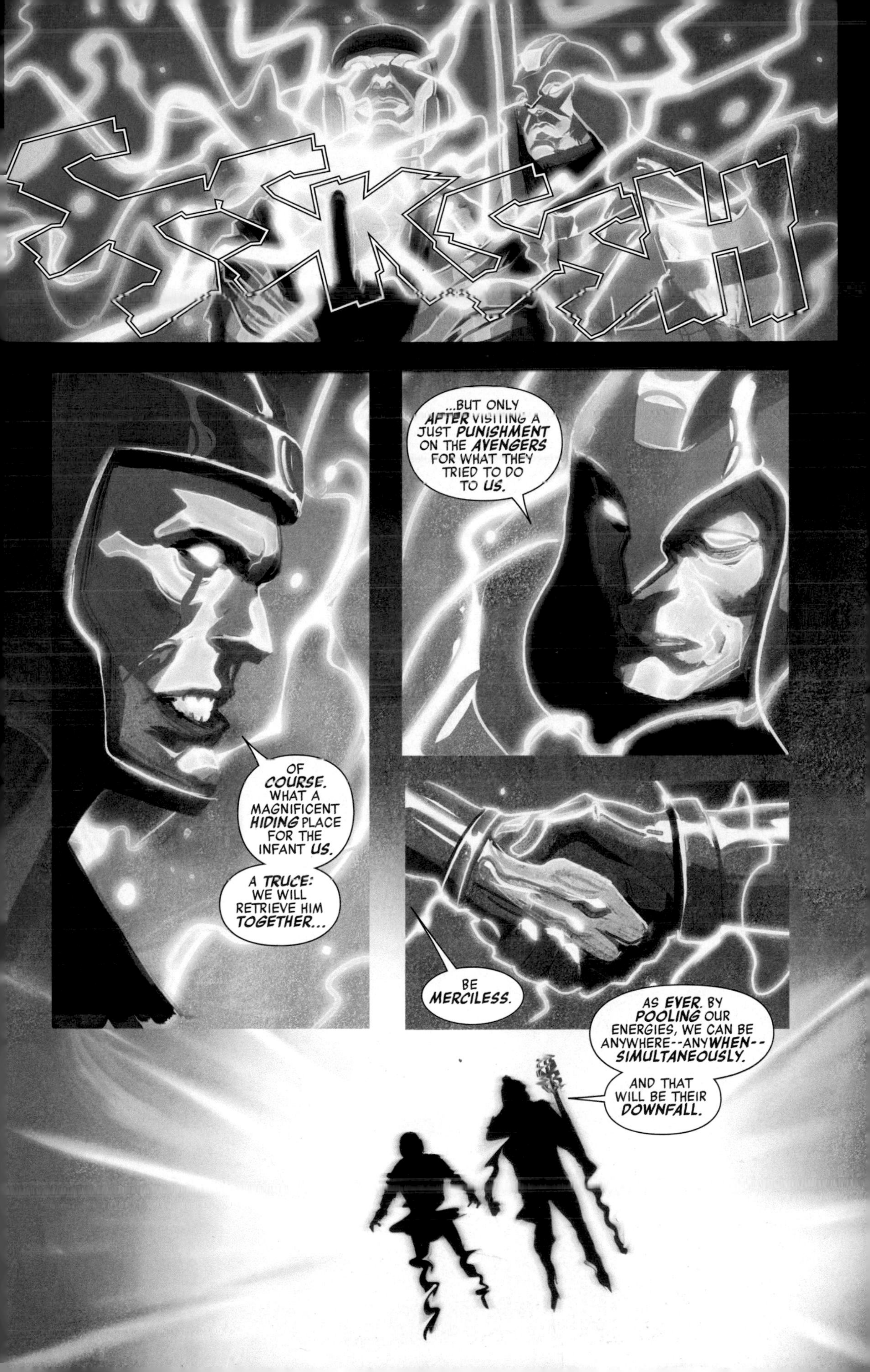
SKRSSH
...BUT ONLY AFTER VISITING A JUST PUNISHMENT ON THE AVENGERS FOR WHAT THEY TRIED TO DO TO US.
OF COURSE. WHAT A MAGNIFICENT HIDING PLACE FOR THE INFANT US.
A TRUCE: WE WILL RETRIEVE HIM TOGETHER...
BE MERCILESS.
AS EVER. BY POOLING OUR ENERGIES, WE CAN BE ANYWHERE--ANYWHEN--SIMULTANEOUSLY.
AND THAT WILL BE THEIR DOWNFALL.

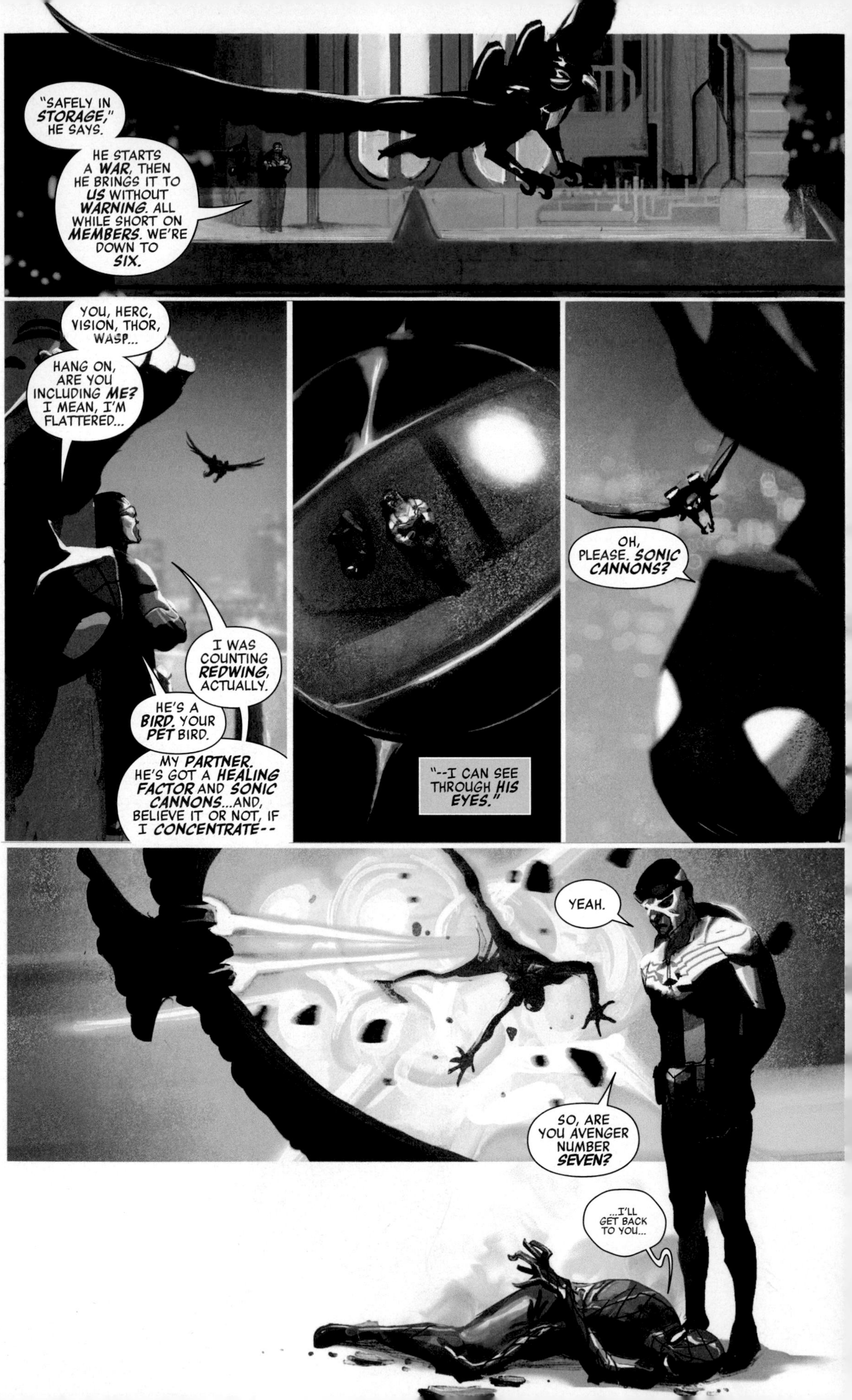

"SAFELY IN STORAGE," HE SAYS.
HE STARTS A WAR, THEN HE BRINGS IT TO US WITHOUT WARNING. ALL WHILE SHORT ON MEMBERS. WE'RE DOWN TO SIX.
YOU, HERC, VISION, THOR, WASP...
HANG ON, ARE YOU INCLUDING ME? I MEAN, I'M FLATTERED...
I WAS COUNTING REDWING, ACTUALLY.
HE'S A BIRD. YOUR PET BIRD.
MY PARTNER. HE'S GOT A HEALING FACTOR AND SONIC CANNONS...AND, BELIEVE IT OR NOT, IF I CONCENTRATE--
"--I CAN SEE THROUGH HIS EYES."
OH, PLEASE. SONIC CANNONS?
YEAH.
SO, ARE YOU AVENGER NUMBER SEVEN?
...I'LL GET BACK TO YOU...

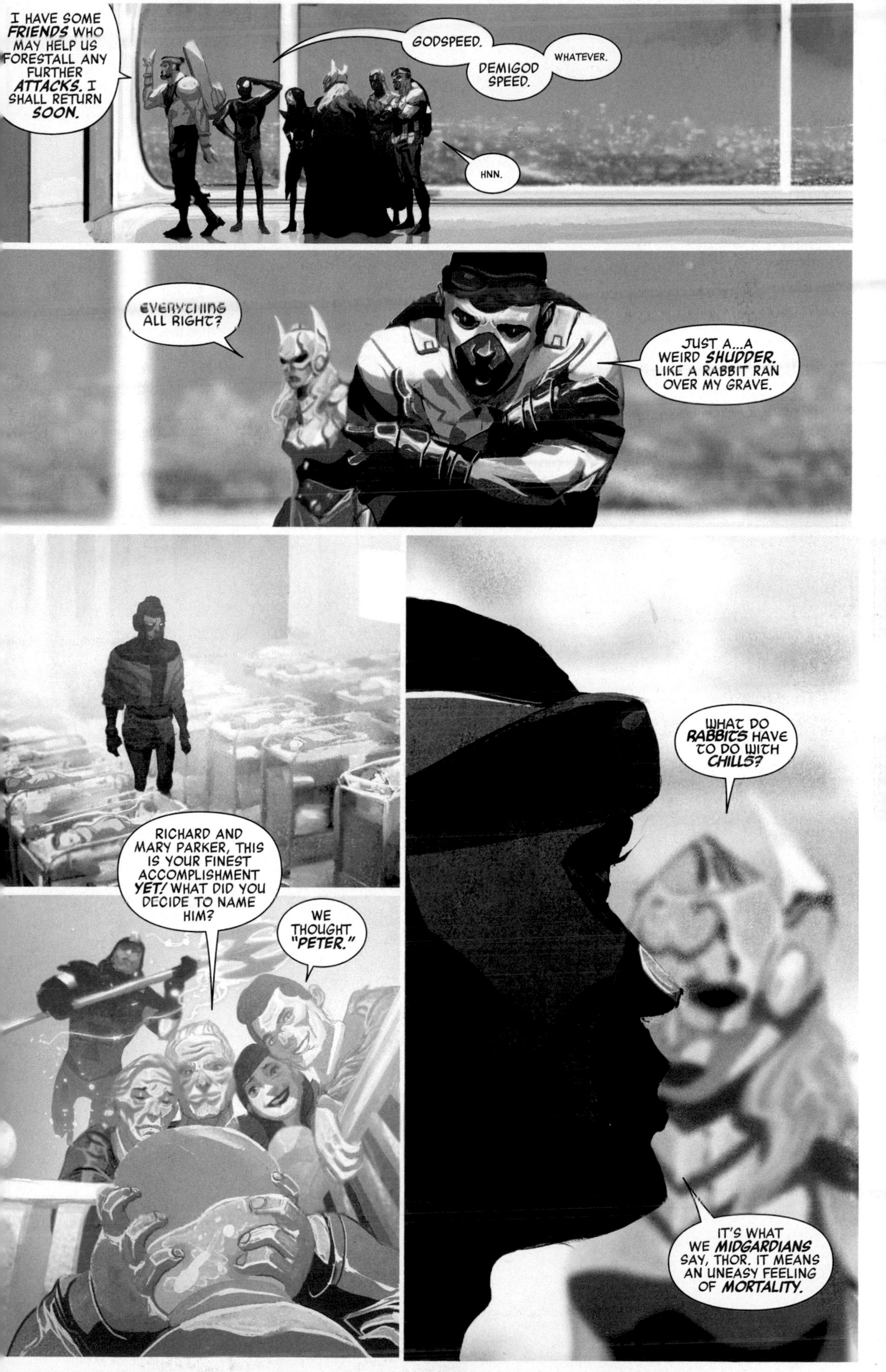

I HAVE SOME FRIENDS WHO MAY HELP US FORESTALL ANY FURTHER ATTACKS. I SHALL RETURN SOON.
GODSPEED.
DEMIGOD SPEED.
WHATEVER.
HNN.
EVERYTHING ALL RIGHT?
JUST A...A WEIRD SHUDDER. LIKE A RABBIT RAN OVER MY GRAVE.
RICHARD AND MARY PARKER, THIS IS YOUR FINEST ACCOMPLISHMENT YET! WHAT DID YOU DECIDE TO NAME HIM?
WE THOUGHT "PETER."
WHAT DO RABBITS HAVE TO DO WITH CHILLS?
IT'S WHAT WE MIDGARDIANS SAY, THOR. IT MEANS AN UNEASY FEELING OF MORTALITY.

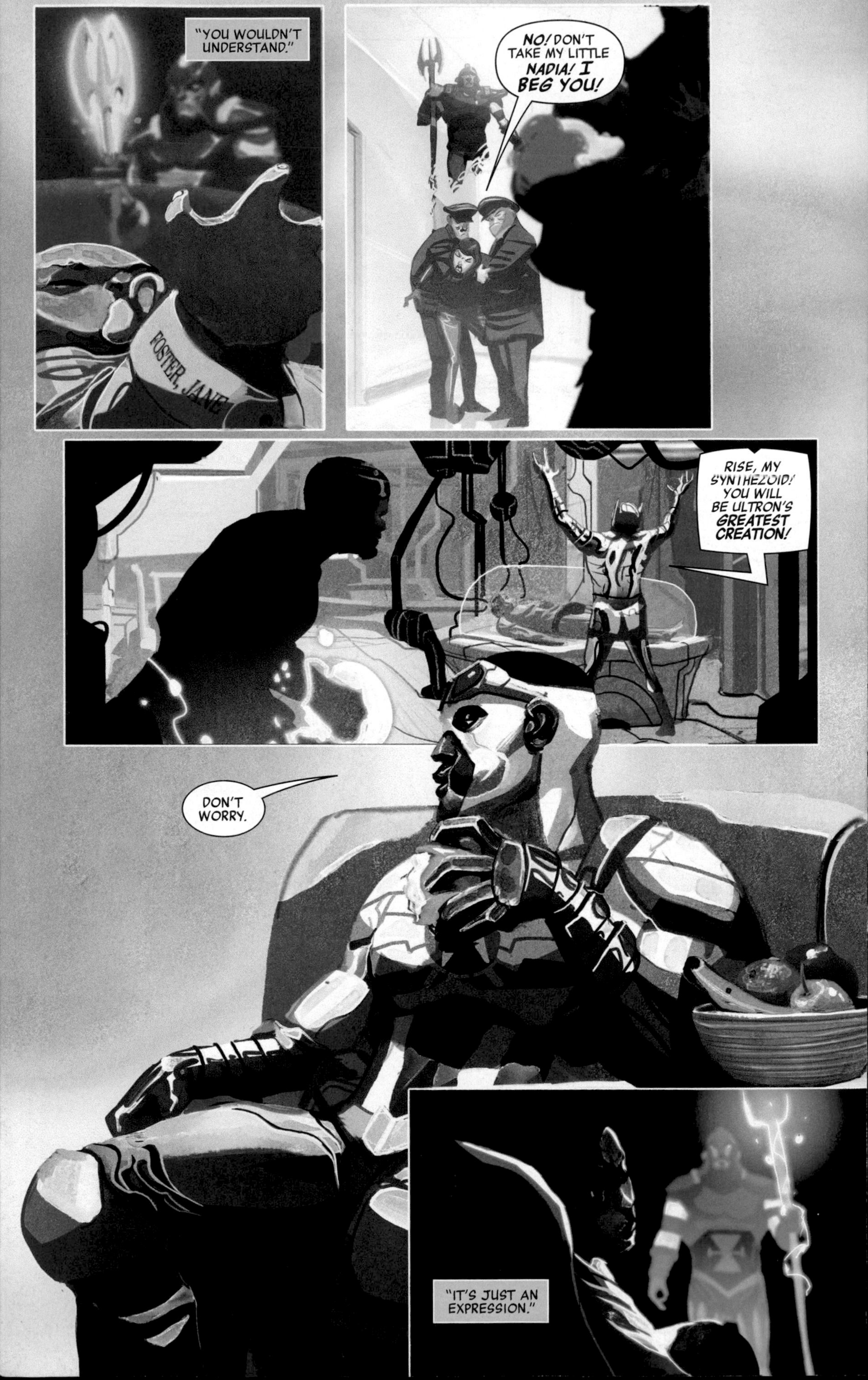
"YOU WOULDN'T UNDERSTAND."
FOSTER, JANE
NO! DON'T TAKE MY LITTLE NADIA! I BEG YOU!
RISE, MY SYNTHEZOID! YOU WILL BE ULTRON'S GREATEST CREATION!
DON'T WORRY.
"IT'S JUST AN EXPRESSION."

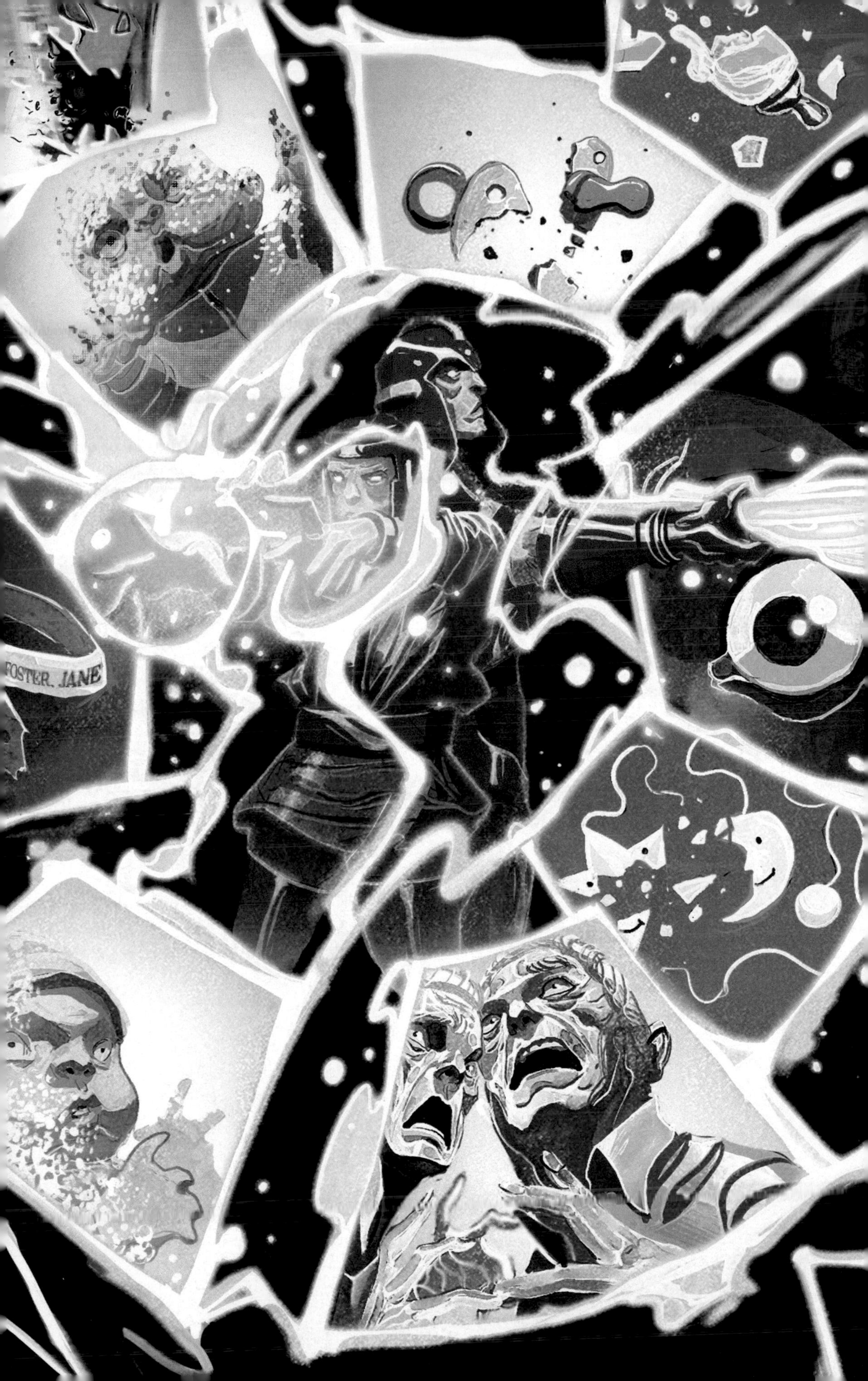
FOSTER, JANE

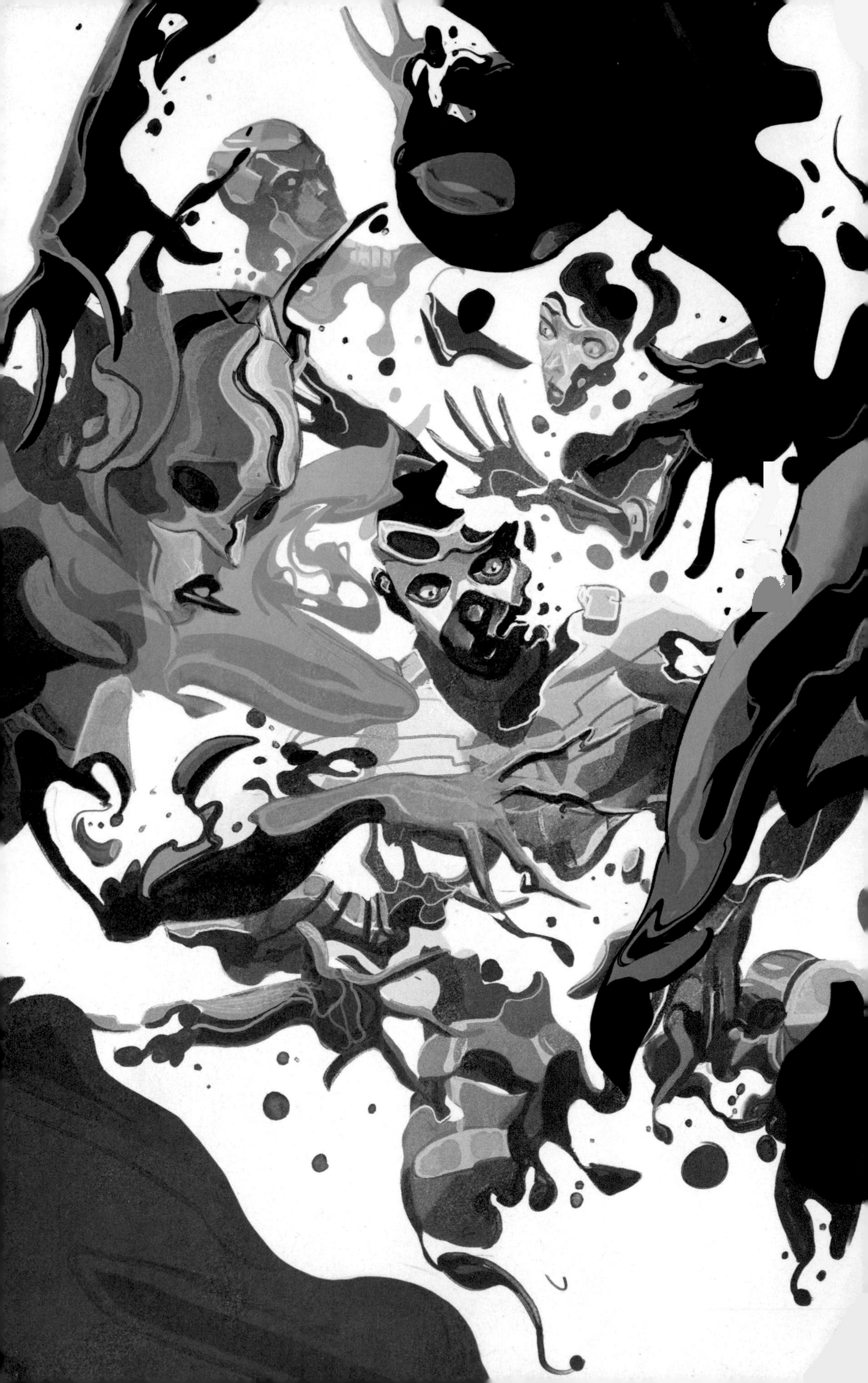

[2]

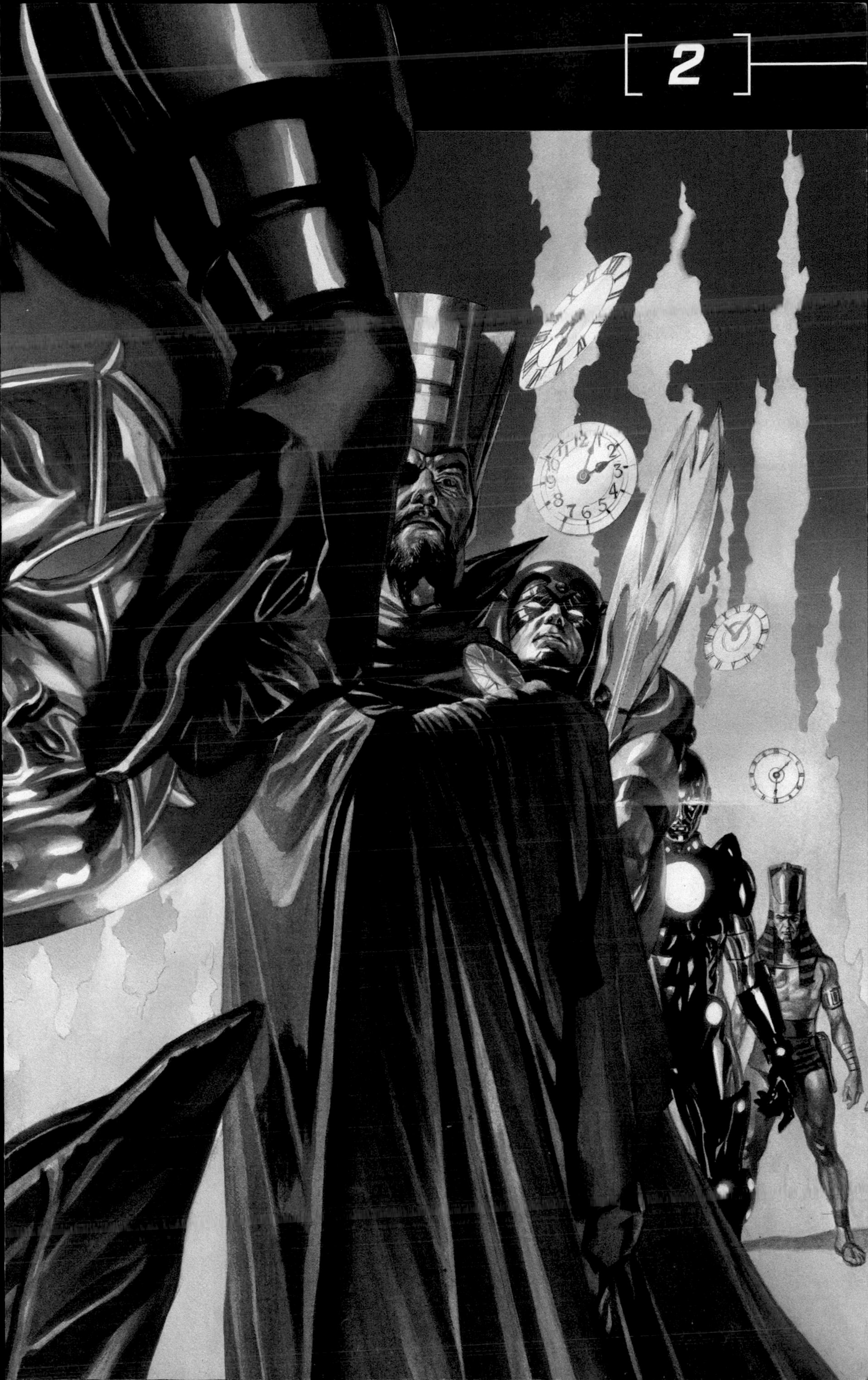

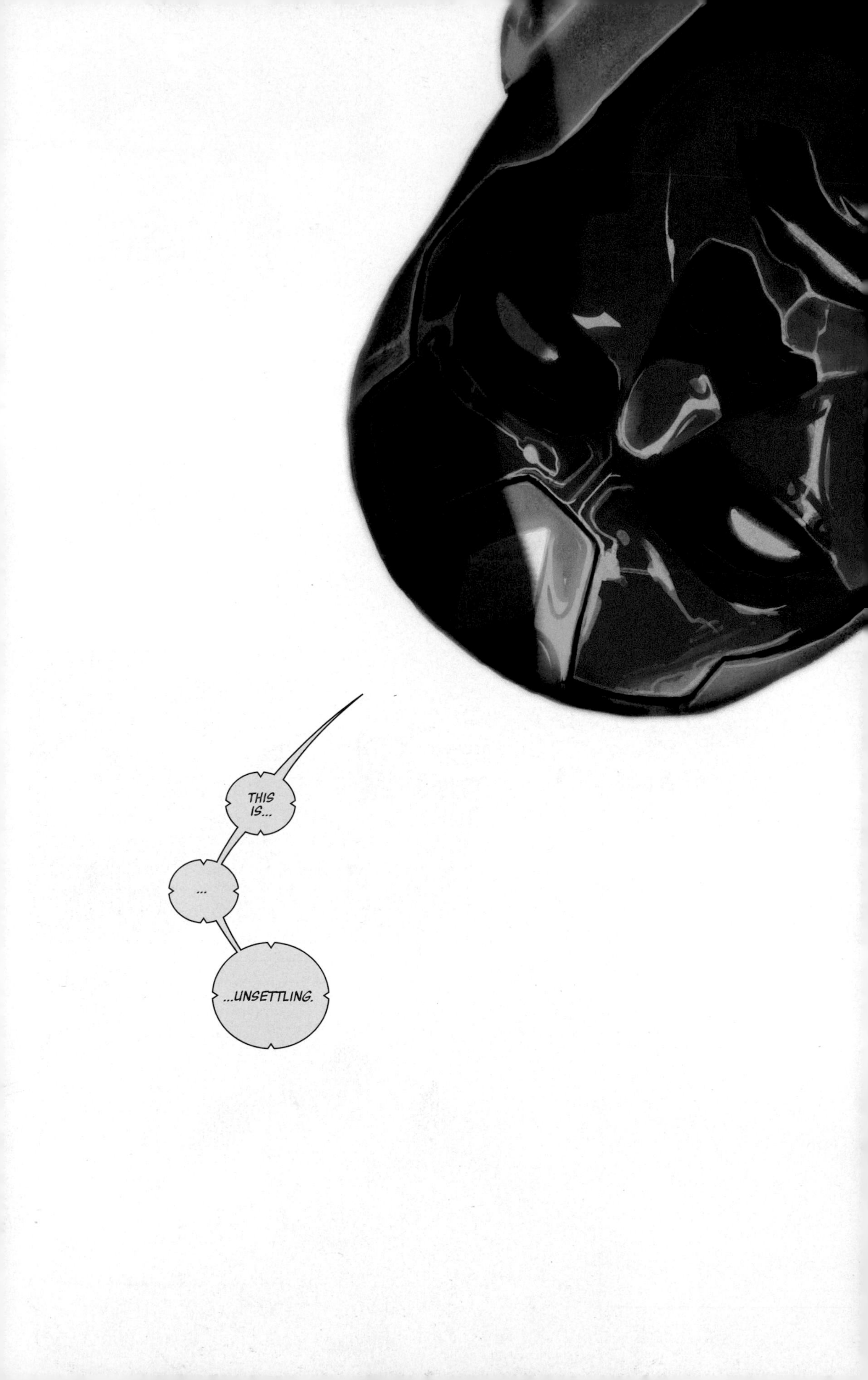
THIS IS...
...
...UNSETTLING.

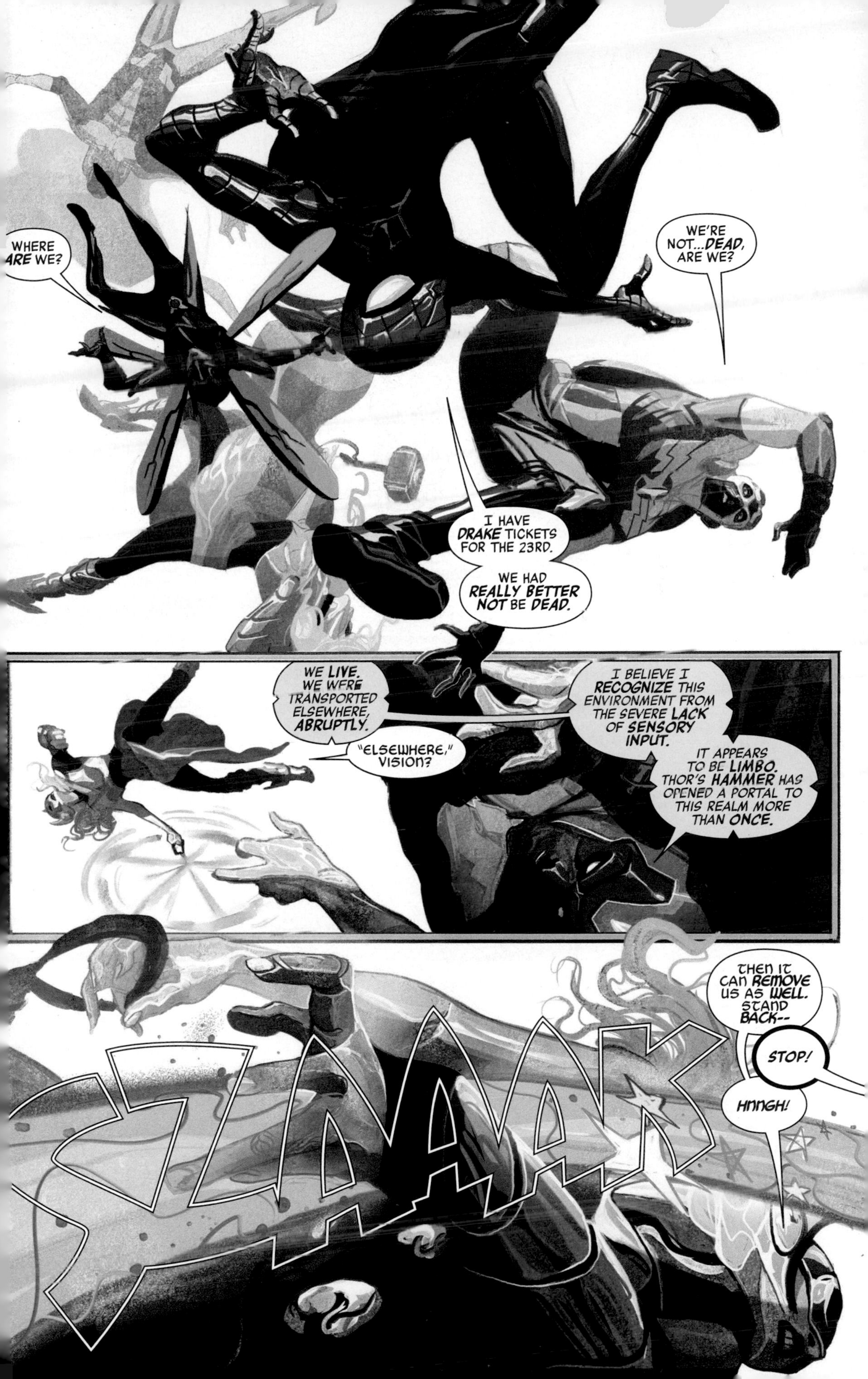
WHERE ARE WE?
WE'RE NOT...DEAD, ARE WE?
I HAVE DRAKE TICKETS FOR THE 23RD.
WE HAD REALLY BETTER NOT BE DEAD.
WE LIVE. WE WERE TRANSPORTED ELSEWHERE, ABRUPTLY.
"ELSEWHERE," VISION?
I BELIEVE I RECOGNIZE THIS ENVIRONMENT FROM THE SEVERE LACK OF SENSORY INPUT.
IT APPEARS TO BE LIMBO. THOR'S HAMMER HAS OPENED A PORTAL TO THIS REALM MORE THAN ONCE.
THEN IT CAN REMOVE US AS WELL. STAND BACK--
STOP!
HNNGH!
SZZAAAK

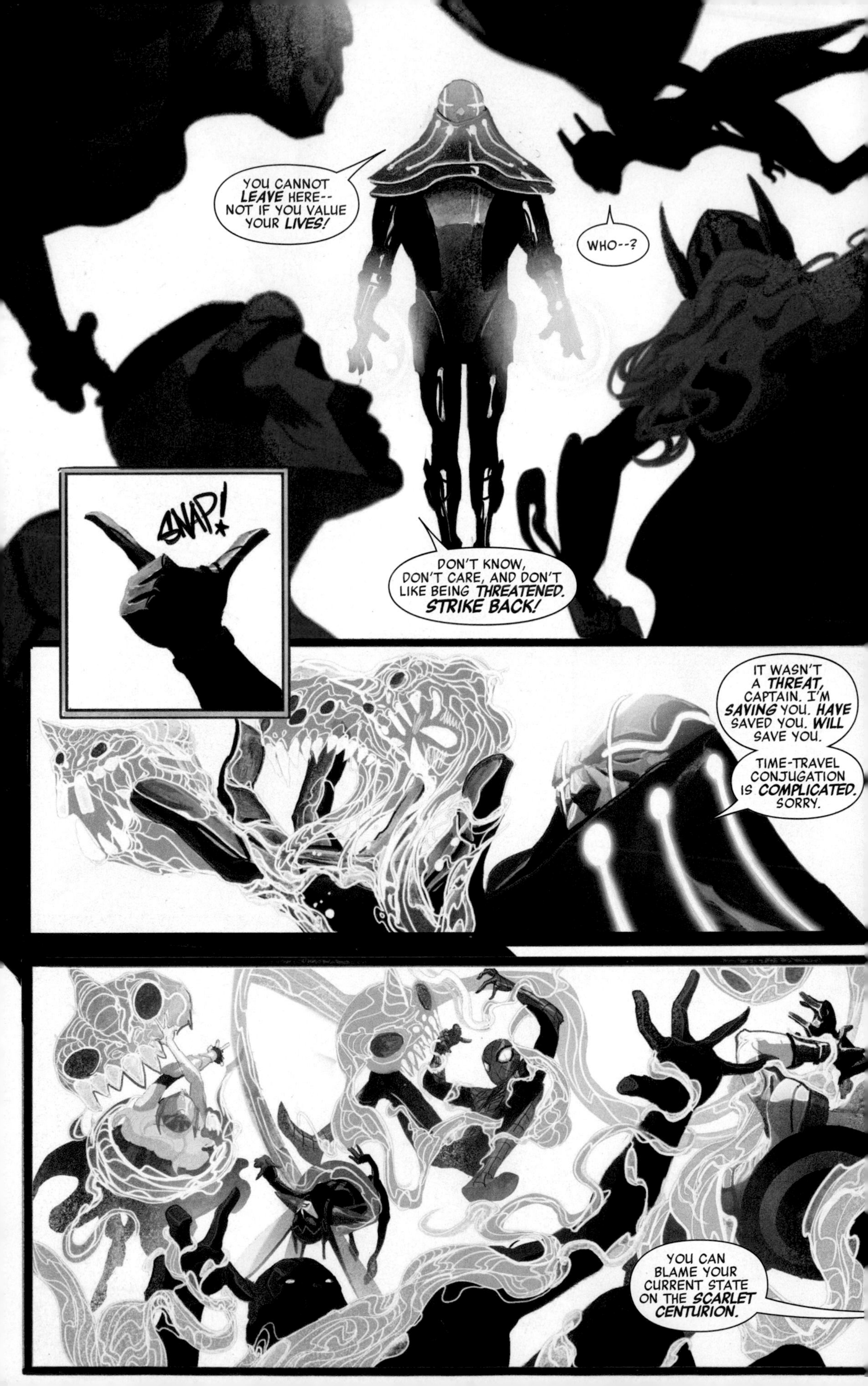
YOU CANNOT LEAVE HERE-- NOT IF YOU VALUE YOUR LIVES!
WHO--?
DON'T KNOW, DON'T CARE, AND DON'T LIKE BEING THREATENED. STRIKE BACK!
SNAP!
IT WASN'T A THREAT, CAPTAIN. I'M SAVING YOU. HAVE SAVED YOU. WILL SAVE YOU.
TIME-TRAVEL CONJUGATION IS COMPLICATED. SORRY.
YOU CAN BLAME YOUR CURRENT STATE ON THE SCARLET CENTURION.

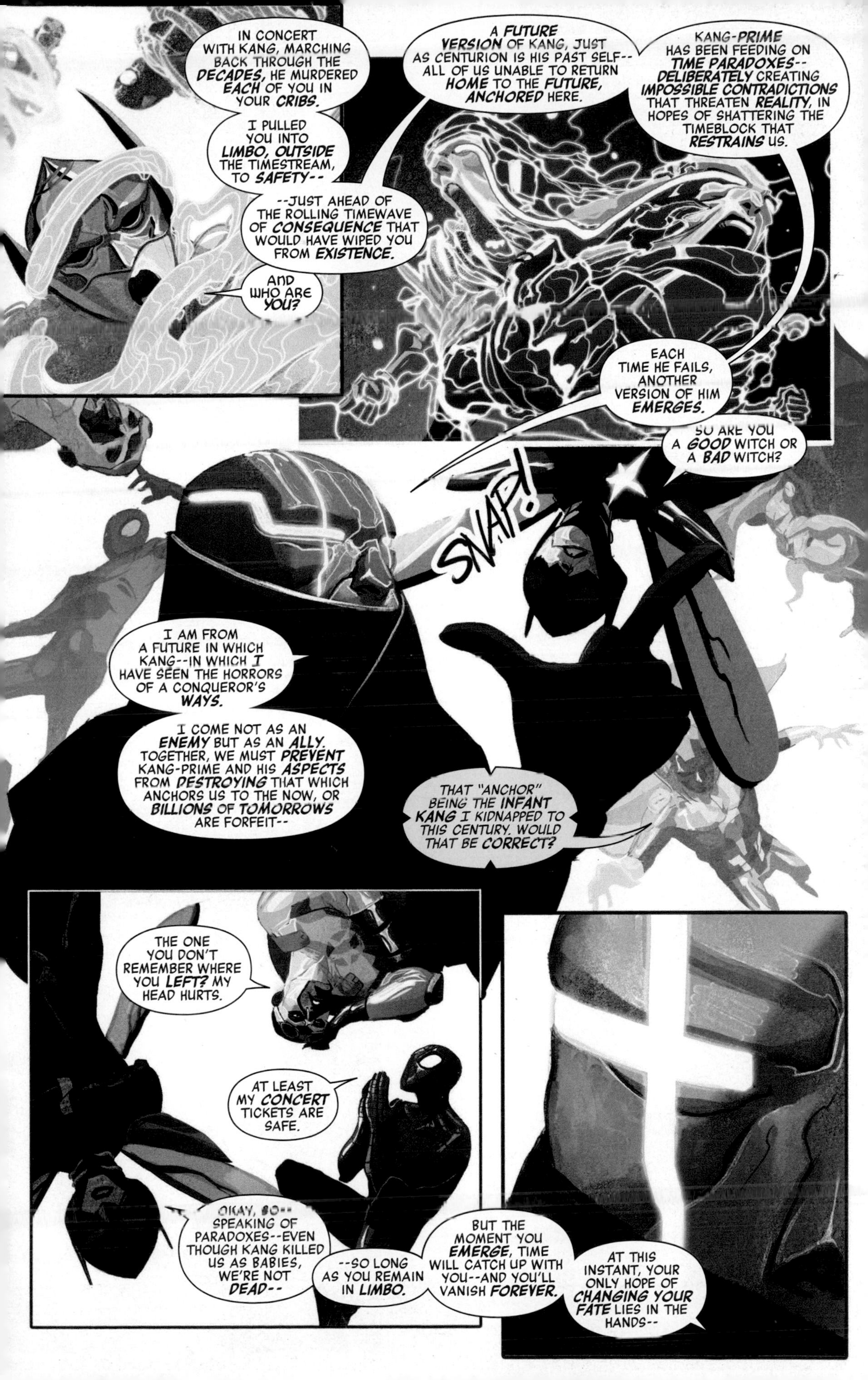
IN CONCERT WITH KANG, MARCHING BACK THROUGH THE DECADES, HE MURDERED EACH OF YOU IN YOUR CRIBS.
I PULLED YOU INTO LIMBO, OUTSIDE THE TIMESTREAM, TO SAFETY--
--JUST AHEAD OF THE ROLLING TIMEWAVE OF CONSEQUENCE THAT WOULD HAVE WIPED YOU FROM EXISTENCE.
AND WHO ARE YOU?
A FUTURE VERSION OF KANG, JUST AS CENTURION IS HIS PAST SELF--ALL OF US UNABLE TO RETURN HOME TO THE FUTURE, ANCHORED HERE.
KANG-PRIME HAS BEEN FEEDING ON TIME PARADOXES--DELIBERATELY CREATING IMPOSSIBLE CONTRADICTIONS THAT THREATEN REALITY, IN HOPES OF SHATTERING THE TIMEBLOCK THAT RESTRAINS US.
EACH TIME HE FAILS, ANOTHER VERSION OF HIM EMERGES.
SO ARE YOU A GOOD WITCH OR A BAD WITCH?
SNAP!
I AM FROM A FUTURE IN WHICH KANG--IN WHICH I HAVE SEEN THE HORRORS OF A CONQUEROR'S WAYS.
I COME NOT AS AN ENEMY BUT AS AN ALLY. TOGETHER, WE MUST PREVENT KANG-PRIME AND HIS ASPECTS FROM DESTROYING THAT WHICH ANCHORS US TO THE NOW, OR BILLIONS OF TOMORROWS ARE FORFEIT--
THAT "ANCHOR" BEING THE INFANT KANG I KIDNAPPED TO THIS CENTURY. WOULD THAT BE CORRECT?
THE ONE YOU DON'T REMEMBER WHERE YOU LEFT? MY HEAD HURTS.
AT LEAST MY CONCERT TICKETS ARE SAFE.
OKAY, SO--SPEAKING OF PARADOXES--EVEN THOUGH KANG KILLED US AS BABIES, WE'RE NOT DEAD--
--SO LONG AS YOU REMAIN IN LIMBO.
BUT THE MOMENT YOU EMERGE, TIME WILL CATCH UP WITH YOU--AND YOU'LL VANISH FOREVER.
AT THIS INSTANT, YOUR ONLY HOPE OF CHANGING YOUR FATE LIES IN THE HANDS--

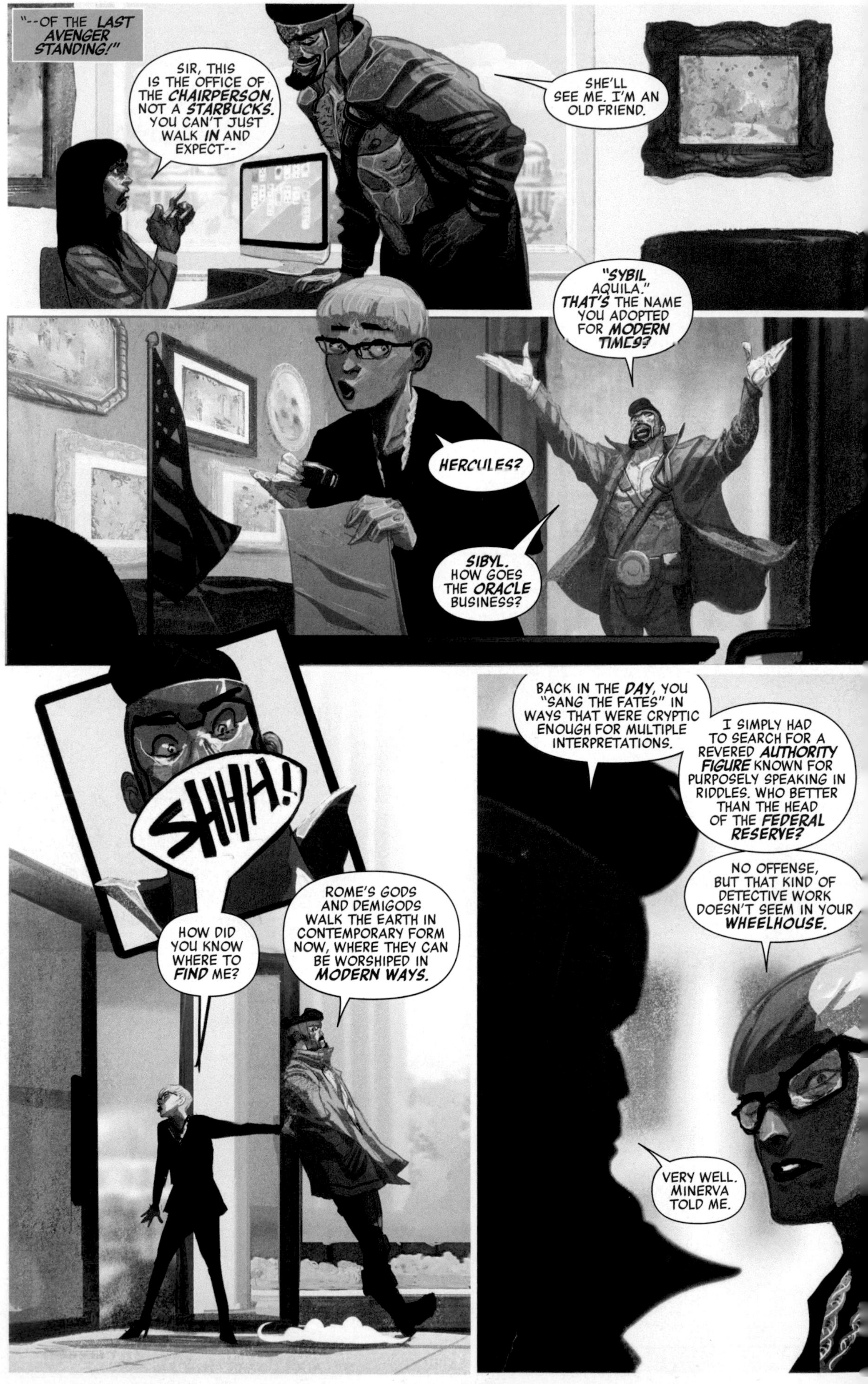
"--OF THE LAST AVENGER STANDING!"
SIR, THIS IS THE OFFICE OF THE CHAIRPERSON, NOT A STARBUCKS. YOU CAN'T JUST WALK IN AND EXPECT--
SHE'LL SEE ME. I'M AN OLD FRIEND.
"SYBIL AQUILA." THAT'S THE NAME YOU ADOPTED FOR MODERN TIMES?
HERCULES?
SIBYL. HOW GOES THE ORACLE BUSINESS?
SHHH!
HOW DID YOU KNOW WHERE TO FIND ME?
ROME'S GODS AND DEMIGODS WALK THE EARTH IN CONTEMPORARY FORM NOW, WHERE THEY CAN BE WORSHIPED IN MODERN WAYS.
BACK IN THE DAY, YOU "SANG THE FATES" IN WAYS THAT WERE CRYPTIC ENOUGH FOR MULTIPLE INTERPRETATIONS.
I SIMPLY HAD TO SEARCH FOR A REVERED AUTHORITY FIGURE KNOWN FOR PURPOSELY SPEAKING IN RIDDLES. WHO BETTER THAN THE HEAD OF THE FEDERAL RESERVE?
NO OFFENSE, BUT THAT KIND OF DETECTIVE WORK DOESN'T SEEM IN YOUR WHEELHOUSE.
VERY WELL. MINERVA TOLD ME.

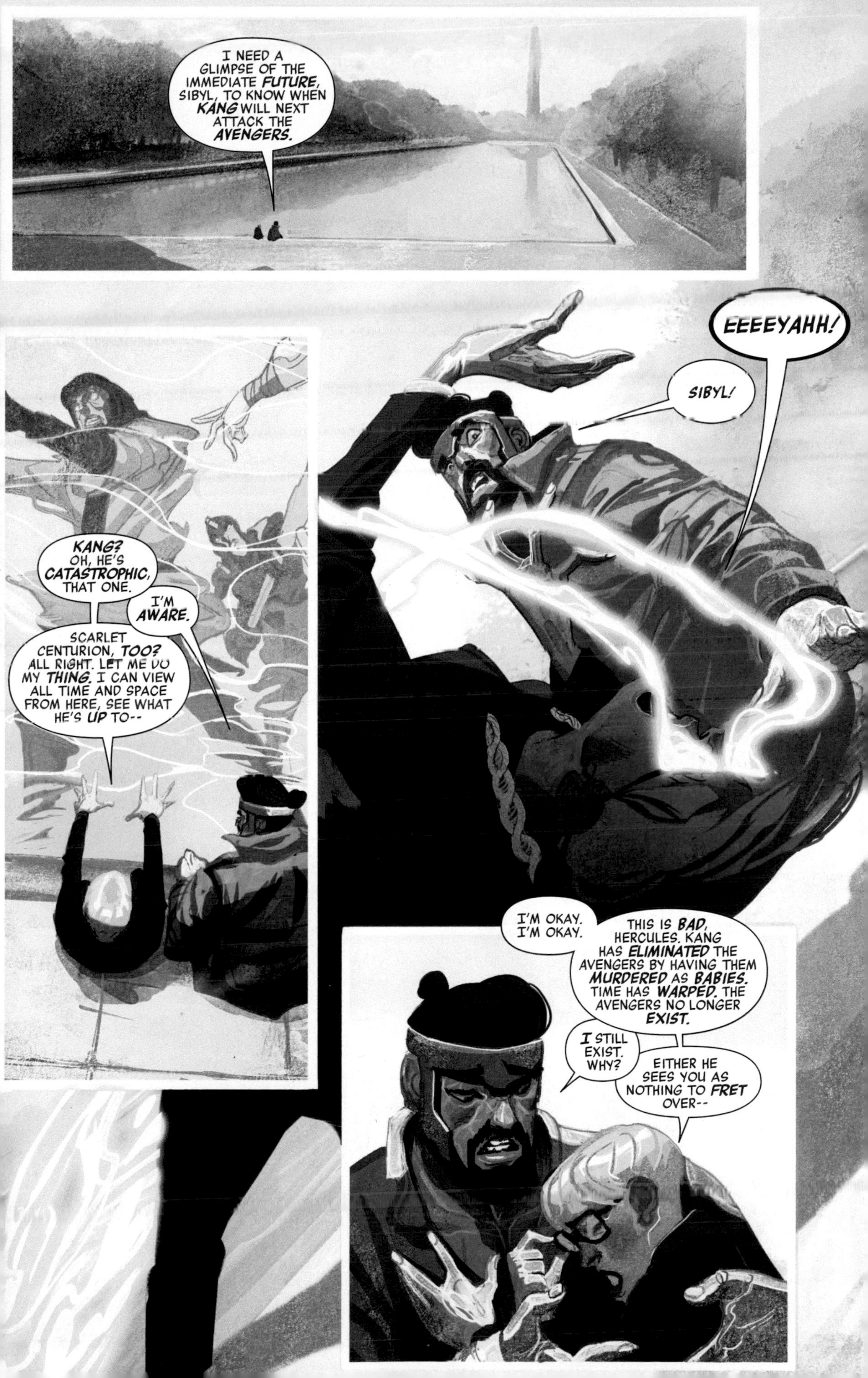
I NEED A GLIMPSE OF THE IMMEDIATE FUTURE, SIBYL, TO KNOW WHEN KANG WILL NEXT ATTACK THE AVENGERS.
KANG? OH, HE'S CATASTROPHIC, THAT ONE.
I'M AWARE.
SCARLET CENTURION, TOO? ALL RIGHT. LET ME DO MY THING. I CAN VIEW ALL TIME AND SPACE FROM HERE, SEE WHAT HE'S UP TO--
EEEEYAHH!
SIBYL!
I'M OKAY. I'M OKAY.
THIS IS BAD, HERCULES. KANG HAS ELIMINATED THE AVENGERS BY HAVING THEM MURDERED AS BABIES. TIME HAS WARPED. THE AVENGERS NO LONGER EXIST.
I STILL EXIST. WHY?
EITHER HE SEES YOU AS NOTHING TO FRET OVER--

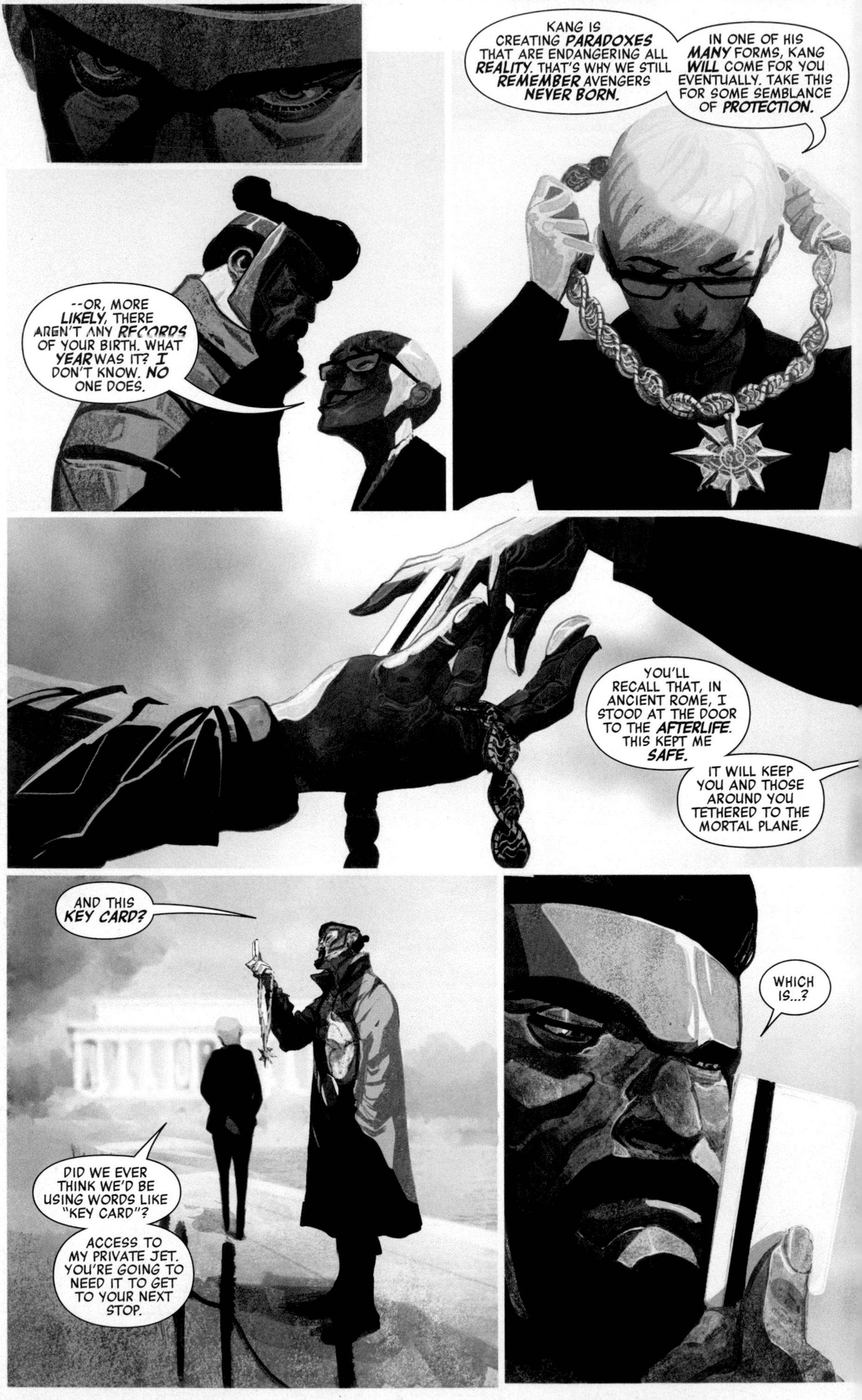
KANG IS CREATING PARADOXES THAT ARE ENDANGERING ALL REALITY. THAT'S WHY WE STILL REMEMBER AVENGERS NEVER BORN.
IN ONE OF HIS MANY FORMS, KANG WILL COME FOR YOU EVENTUALLY. TAKE THIS FOR SOME SEMBLANCE OF PROTECTION.
--OR, MORE LIKELY, THERE AREN'T ANY RECORDS OF YOUR BIRTH. WHAT YEAR WAS IT? I DON'T KNOW. NO ONE DOES.
YOU'LL RECALL THAT, IN ANCIENT ROME, I STOOD AT THE DOOR TO THE AFTERLIFE. THIS KEPT ME SAFE.
IT WILL KEEP YOU AND THOSE AROUND YOU TETHERED TO THE MORTAL PLANE.
AND THIS KEY CARD?
DID WE EVER THINK WE'D BE USING WORDS LIKE "KEY CARD"?
ACCESS TO MY PRIVATE JET. YOU'RE GOING TO NEED IT TO GET TO YOUR NEXT STOP.
WHICH IS...?

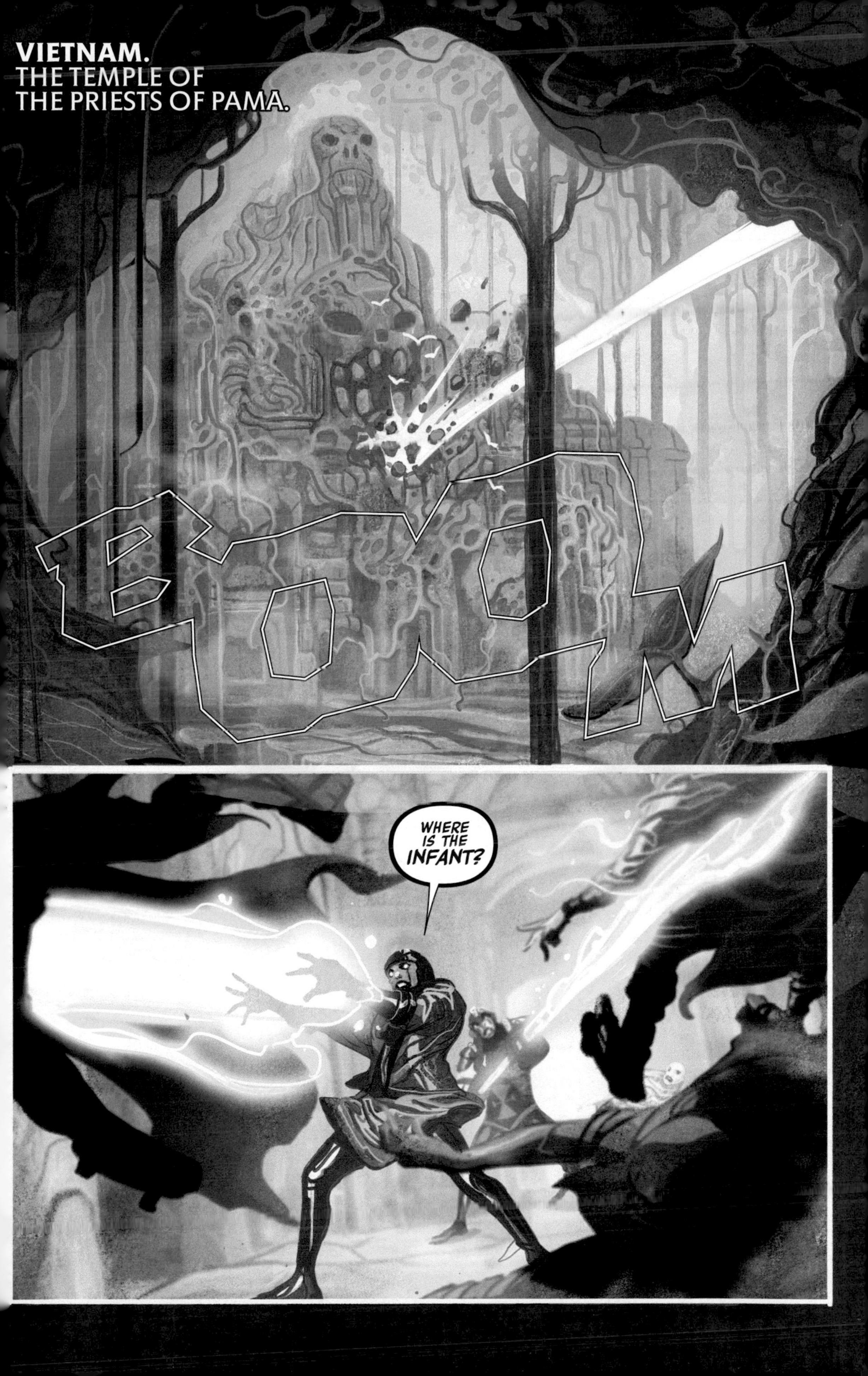
VIETNAM.
THE TEMPLE OF
THE PRIESTS OF PAMA.
BOOM
WHERE IS THE INFANT?

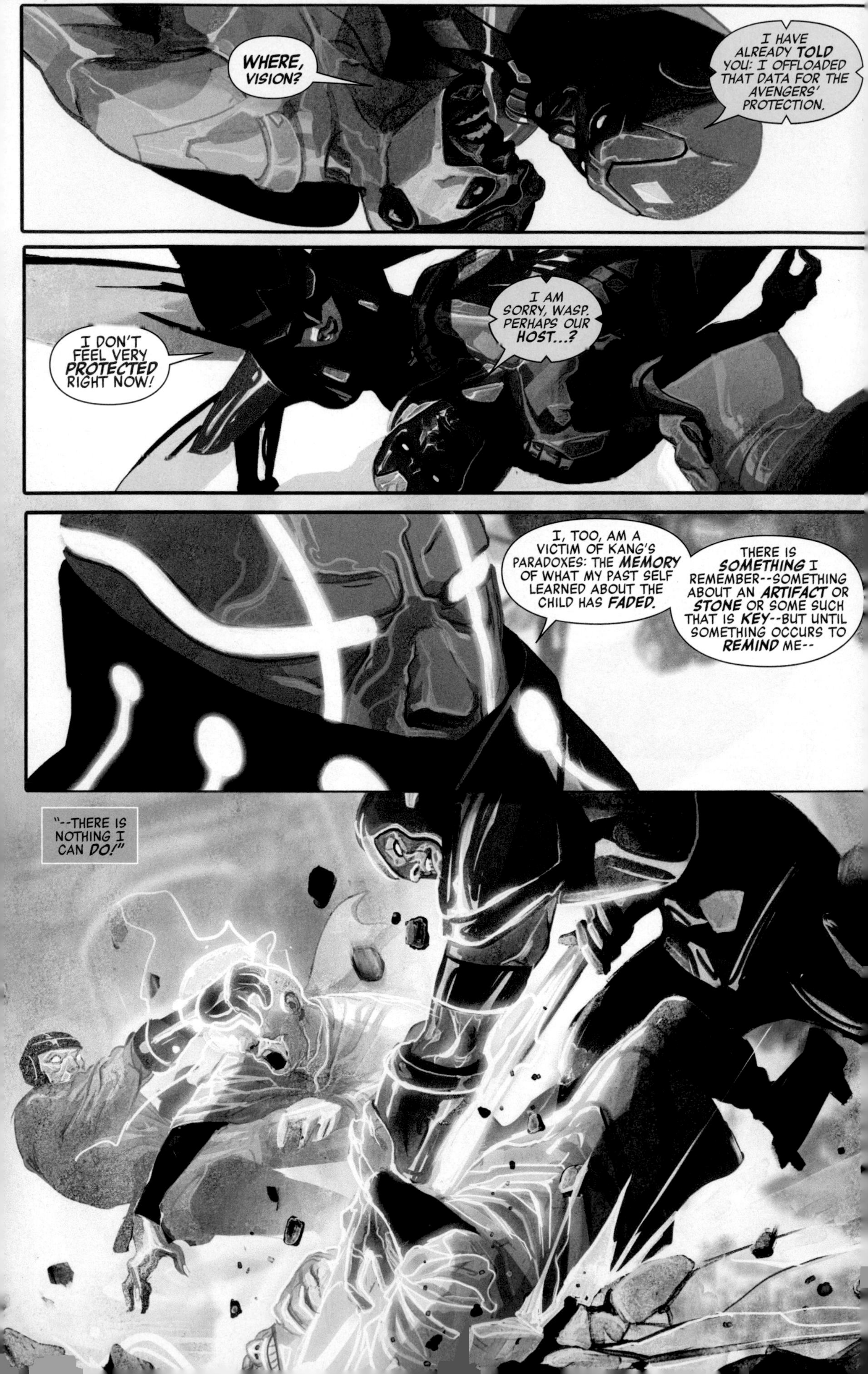
WHERE, VISION?
I HAVE ALREADY TOLD YOU: I OFFLOADED THAT DATA FOR THE AVENGERS' PROTECTION.
I DON'T FEEL VERY PROTECTED RIGHT NOW!
I AM SORRY, WASP. PERHAPS OUR HOST...?
I, TOO, AM A VICTIM OF KANG'S PARADOXES: THE MEMORY OF WHAT MY PAST SELF LEARNED ABOUT THE CHILD HAS FADED.
THERE IS SOMETHING I REMEMBER--SOMETHING ABOUT AN ARTIFACT OR STONE OR SOME SUCH THAT IS KEY--BUT UNTIL SOMETHING OCCURS TO REMIND ME--
"--THERE IS NOTHING I CAN DO!"

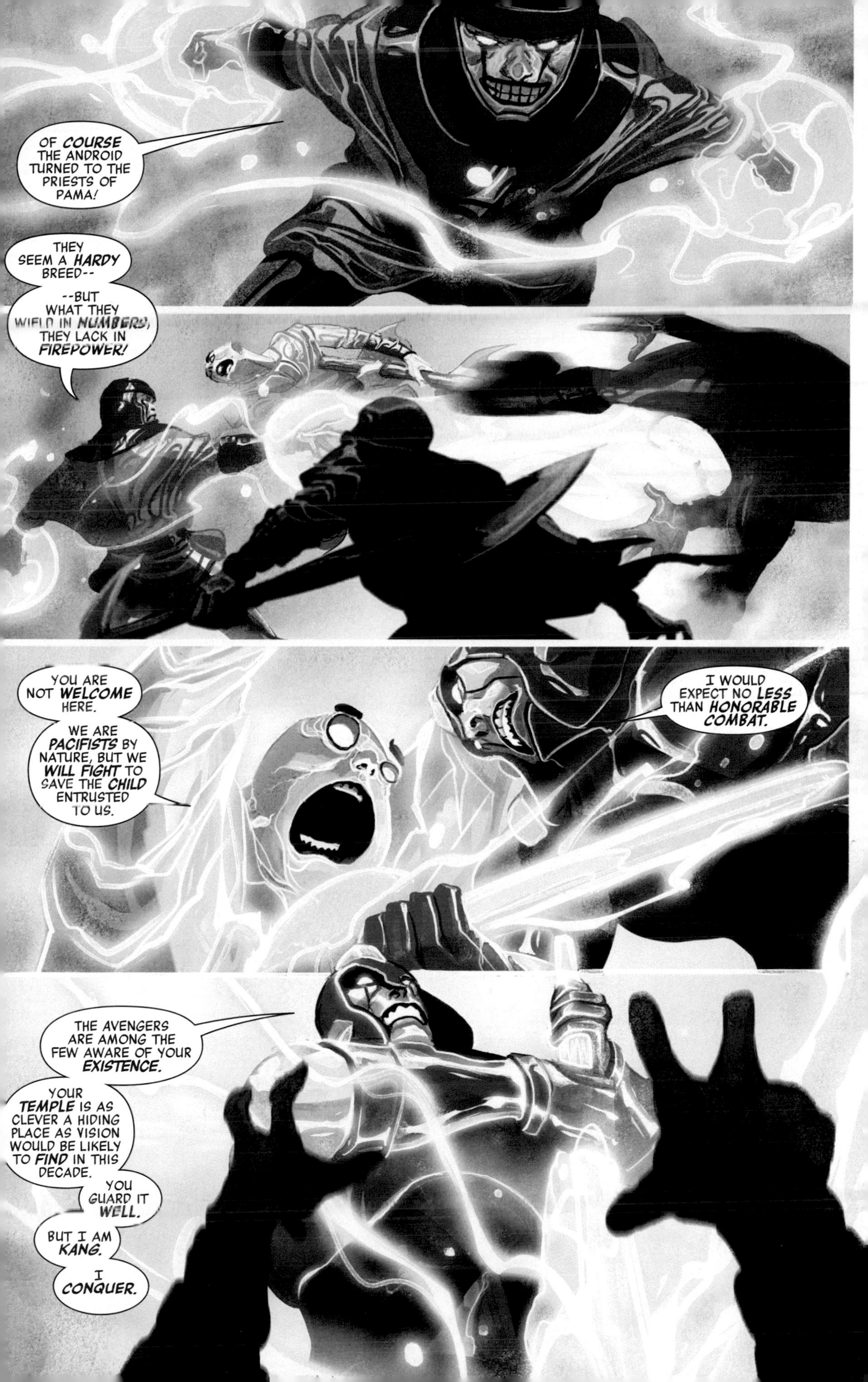
OF COURSE THE ANDROID TURNED TO THE PRIESTS OF PAMA!
THEY SEEM A HARDY BREED--
--BUT WHAT THEY WIELD IN NUMBERS, THEY LACK IN FIREPOWER!
YOU ARE NOT WELCOME HERE.
WE ARE PACIFISTS BY NATURE, BUT WE WILL FIGHT TO SAVE THE CHILD ENTRUSTED TO US.
I WOULD EXPECT NO LESS THAN HONORABLE COMBAT.
THE AVENGERS ARE AMONG THE FEW AWARE OF YOUR EXISTENCE.
YOUR TEMPLE IS AS CLEVER A HIDING PLACE AS VISION WOULD BE LIKELY TO FIND IN THIS DECADE.
YOU GUARD IT WELL.
BUT I AM KANG.
I CONQUER.

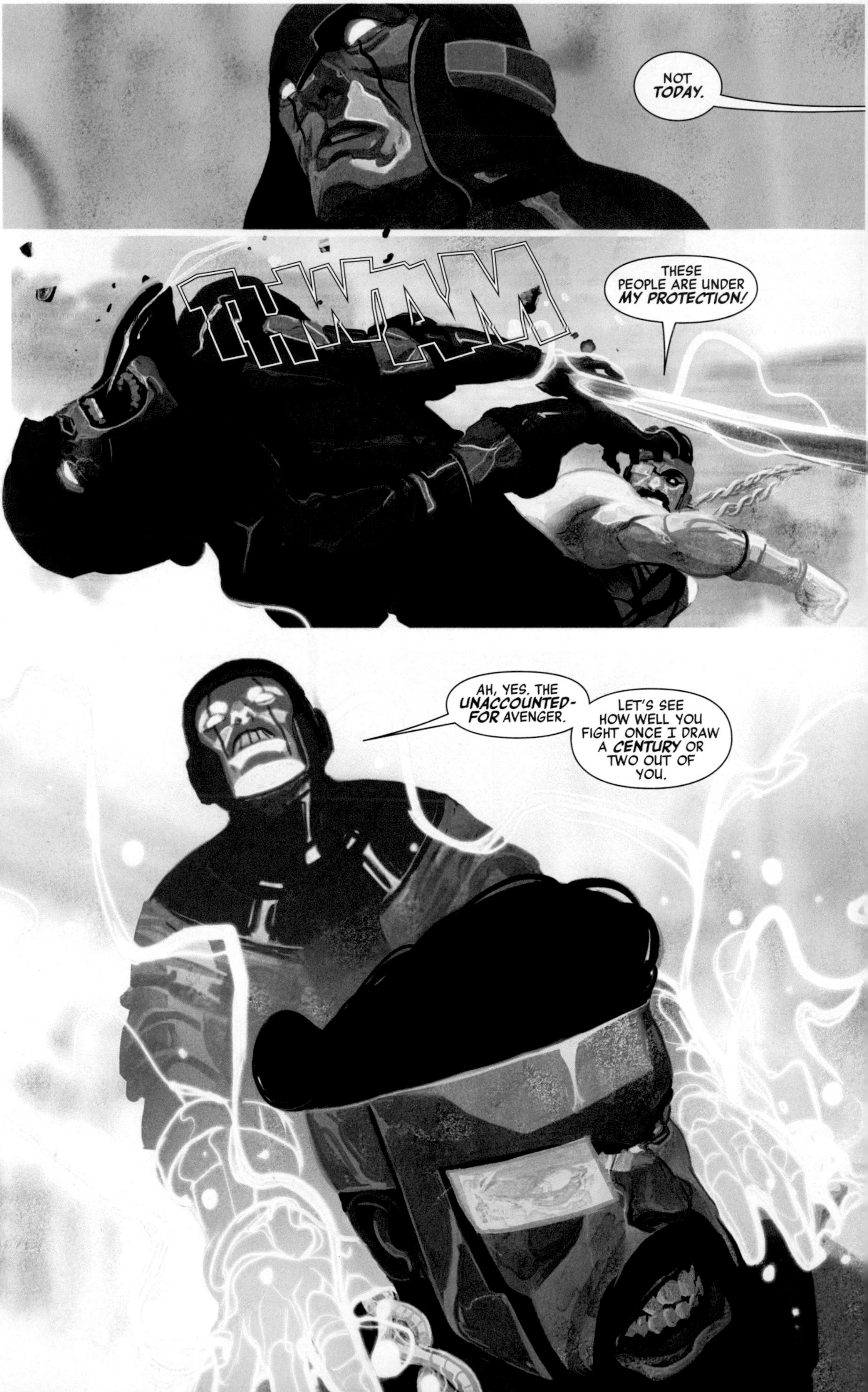
NOT TODAY.
THWAM
THESE PEOPLE ARE UNDER MY PROTECTION!
AH, YES. THE UNACCOUNTED-FOR AVENGER.
LET'S SEE HOW WELL YOU FIGHT ONCE I DRAW A CENTURY OR TWO OUT OF YOU.

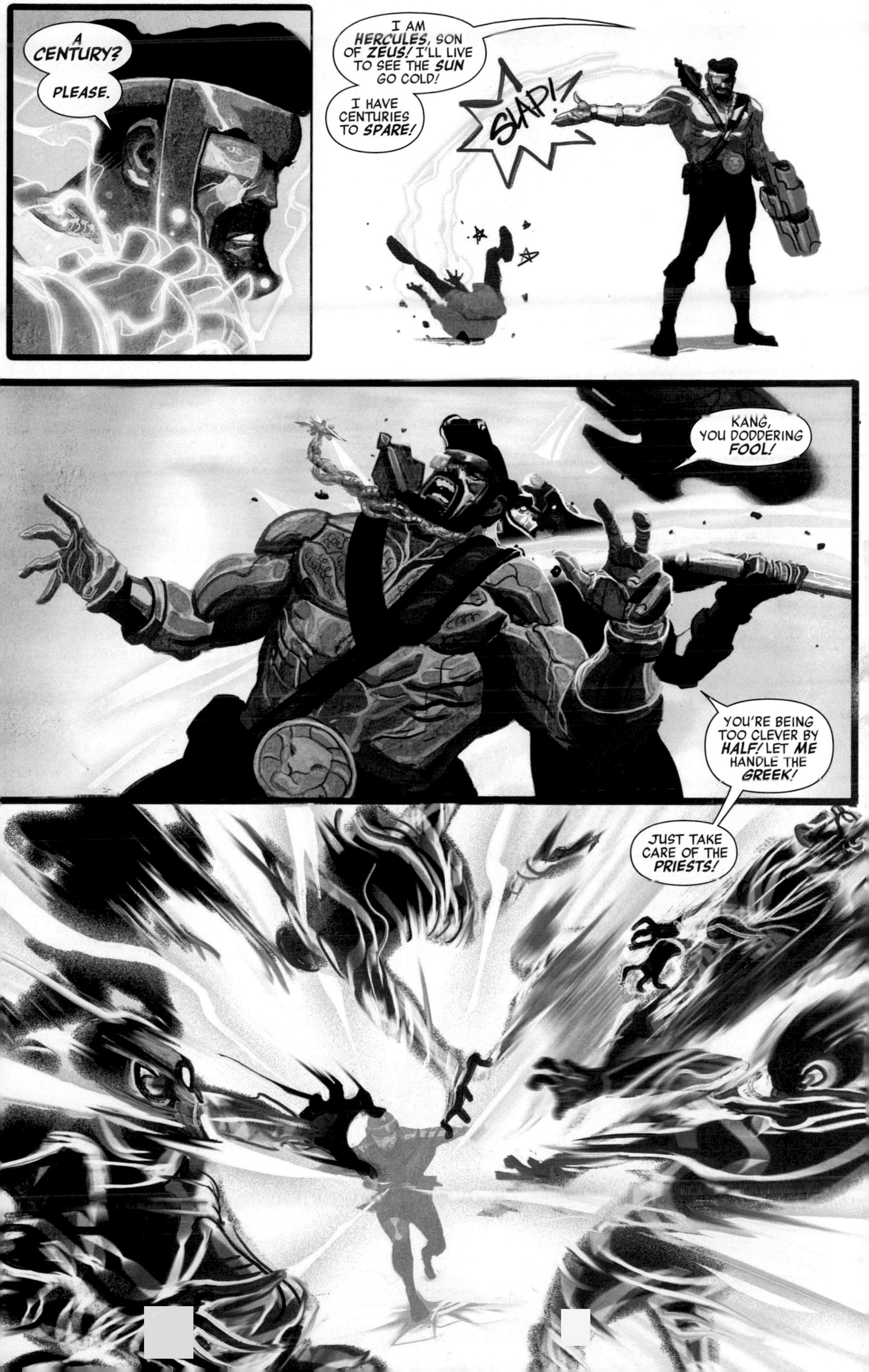
A CENTURY?
PLEASE.
I AM HERCULES, SON OF ZEUS! I'LL LIVE TO SEE THE SUN GO COLD!
I HAVE CENTURIES TO SPARE!
SLAP!!
KANG, YOU DODDERING FOOL!
YOU'RE BEING TOO CLEVER BY HALF! LET ME HANDLE THE GREEK!
JUST TAKE CARE OF THE PRIESTS!

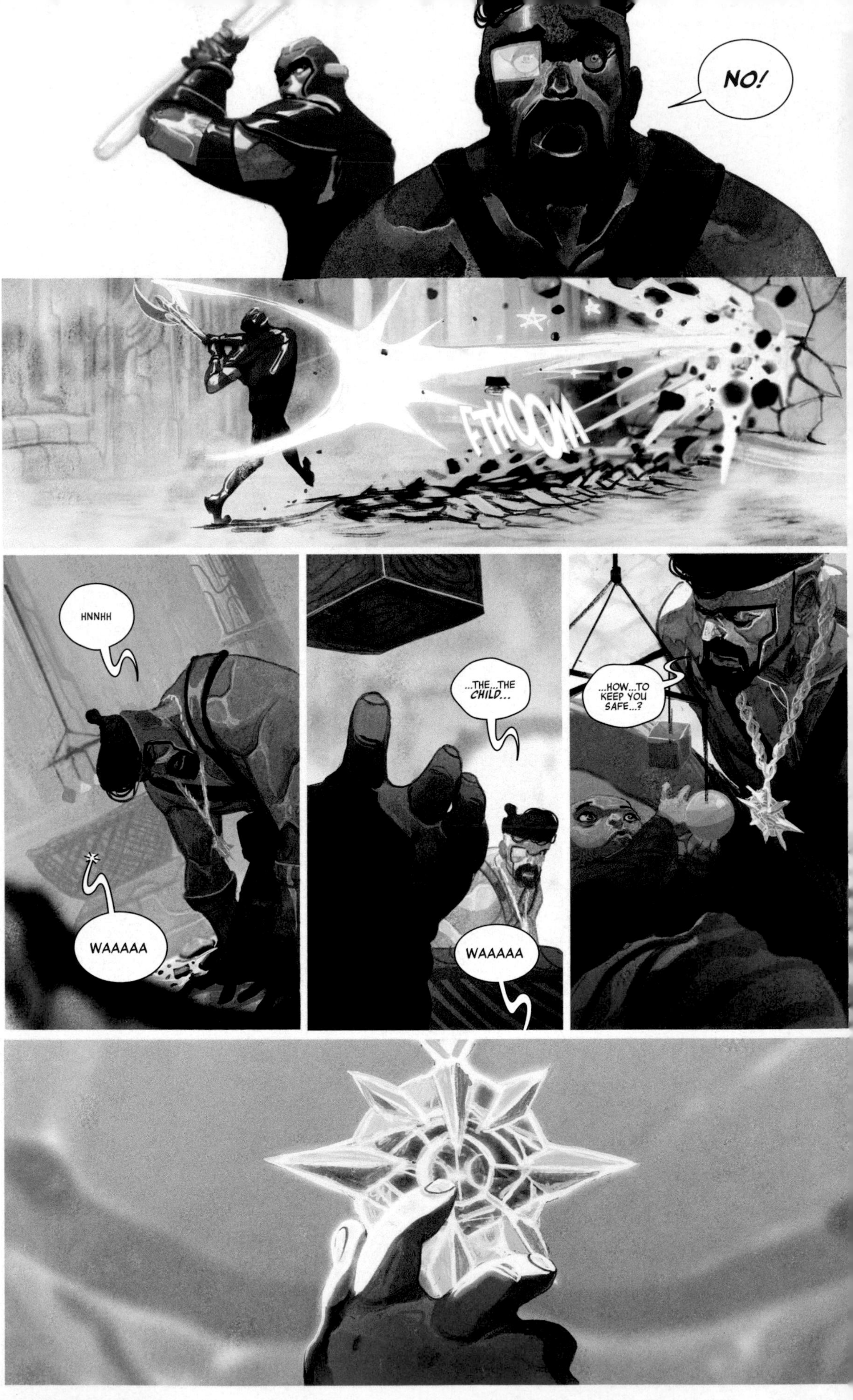
NO!
FTHOOM
HNNHH
WAAAAA
...THE...THE CHILD...
WAAAAA
...HOW...TO KEEP YOU SAFE...?

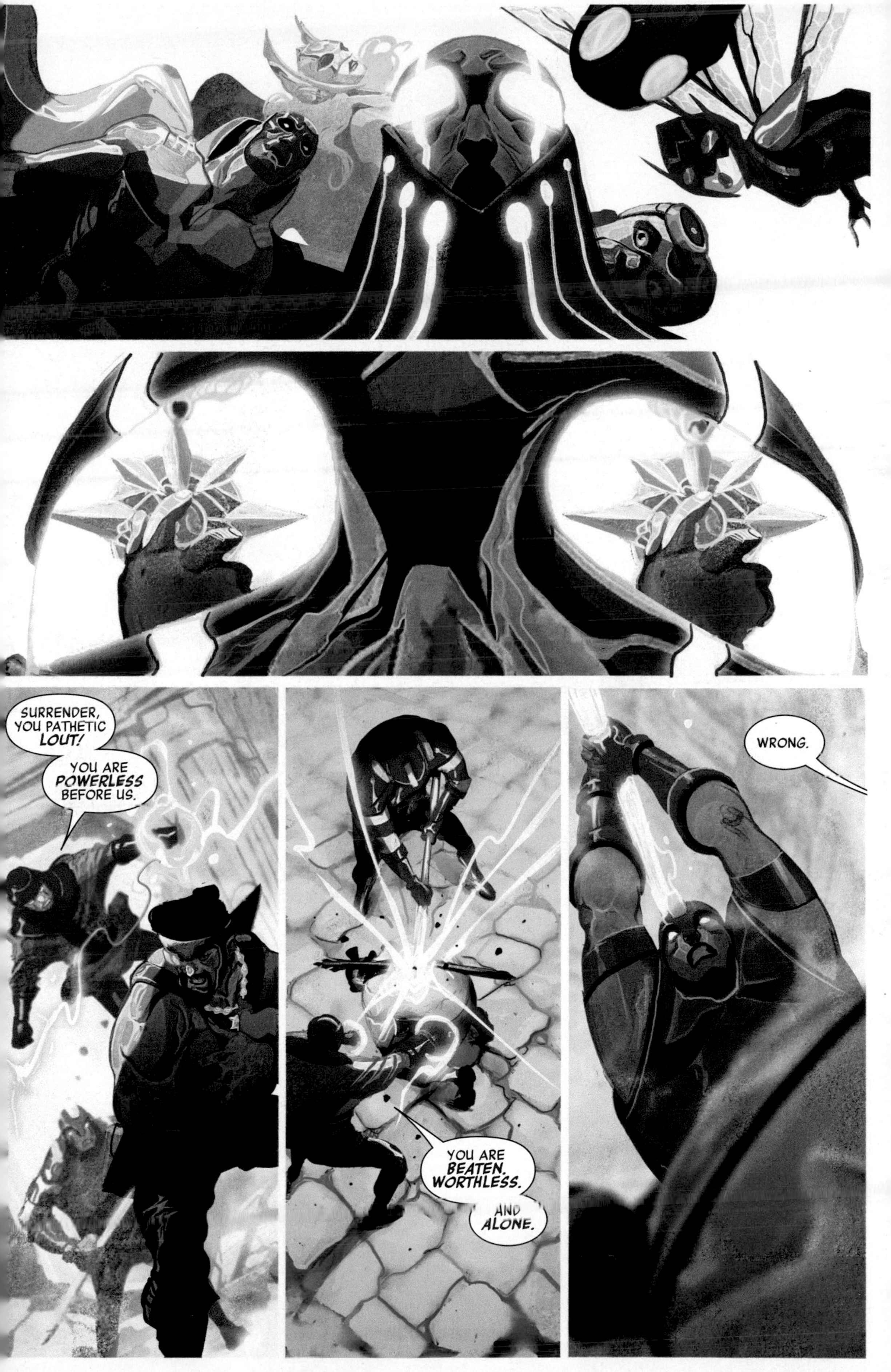
SURRENDER, YOU PATHETIC LOUT!
YOU ARE POWERLESS BEFORE US.
YOU ARE BEATEN. WORTHLESS.
AND ALONE.
WRONG.

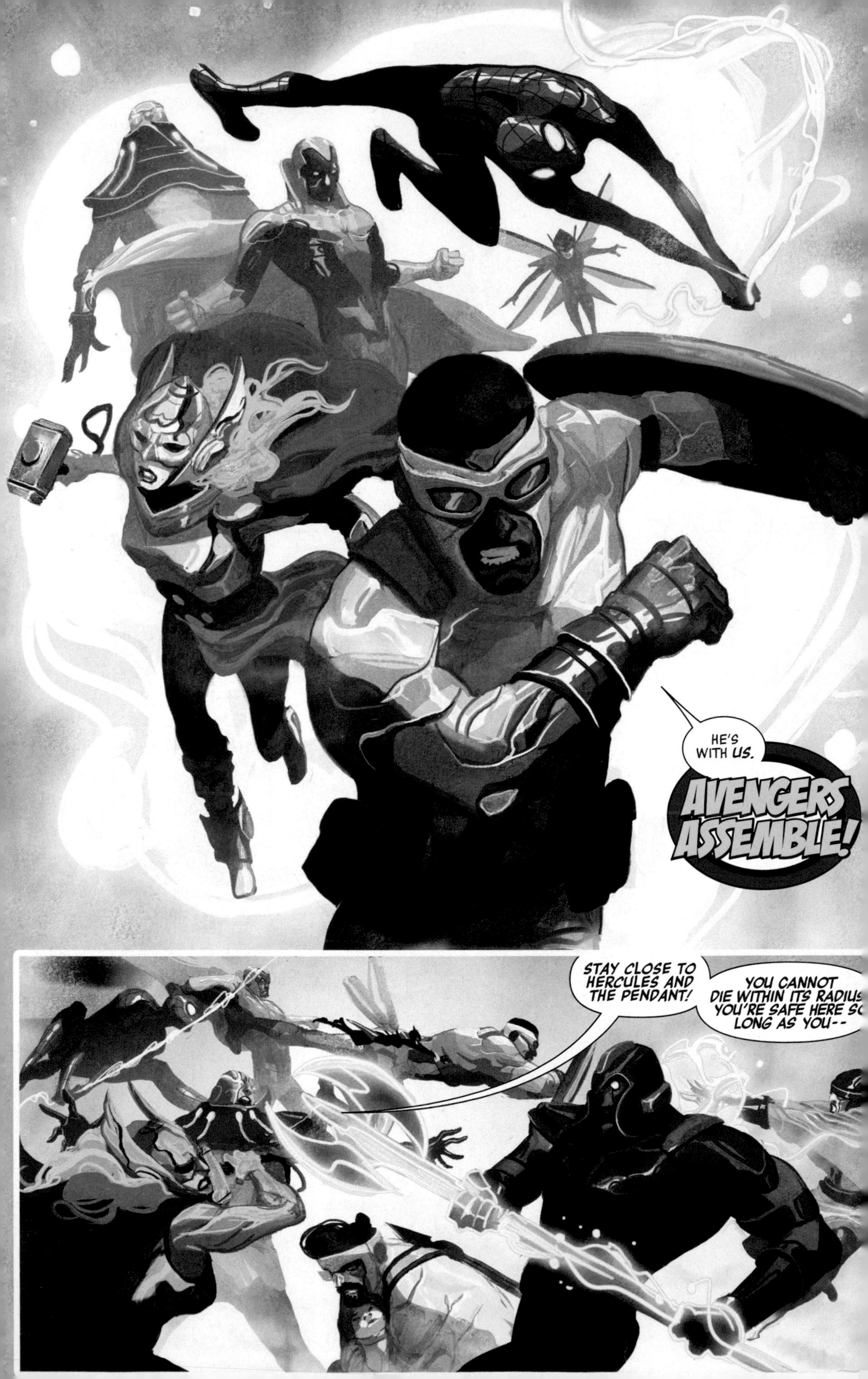
HE'S WITH US.
AVENGERS ASSEMBLE!
STAY CLOSE TO HERCULES AND THE PENDANT!
YOU CANNOT DIE WITHIN ITS RADIUS. YOU'RE SAFE HERE SO LONG AS YOU--

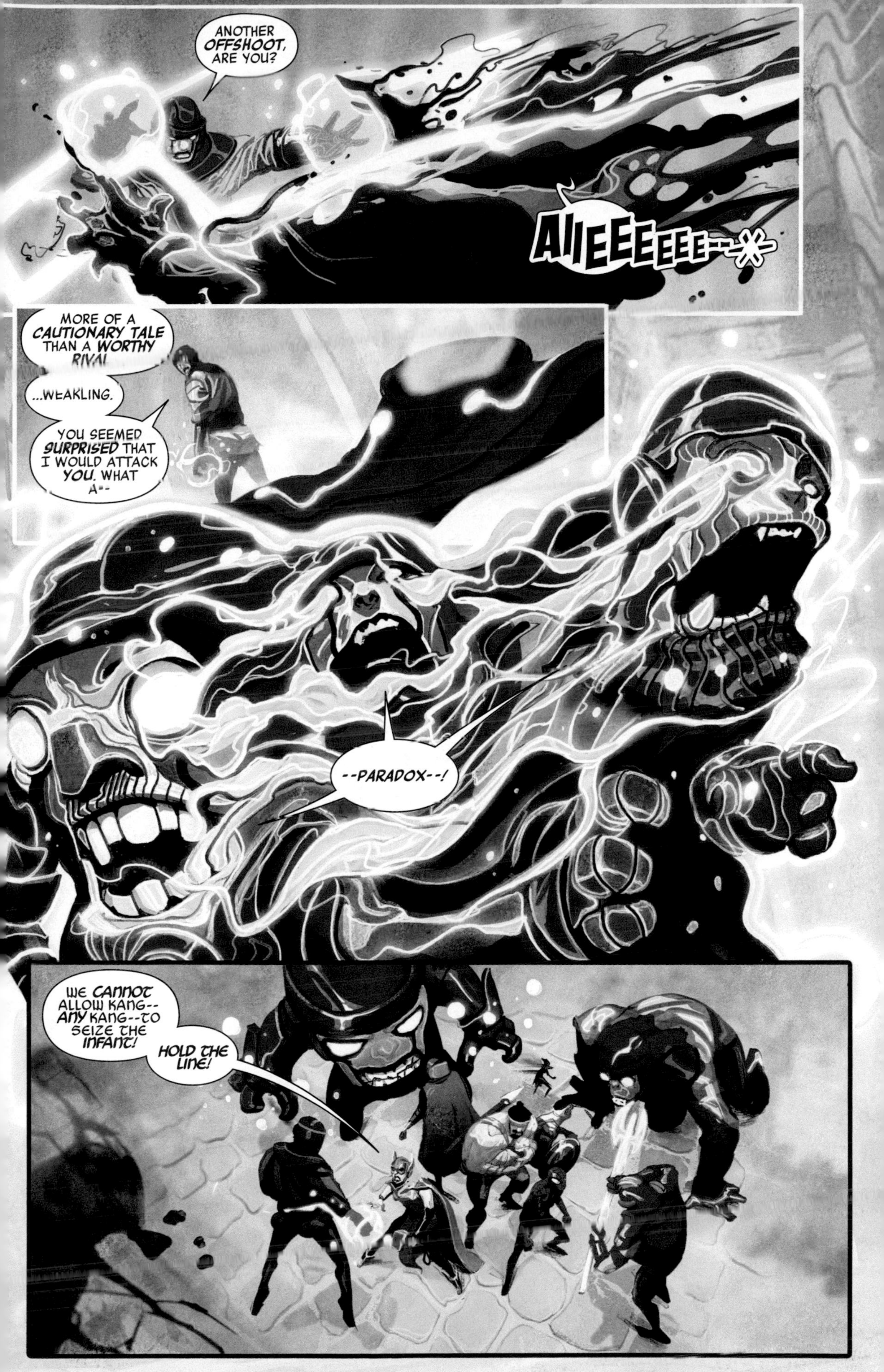

ANOTHER OFFSHOOT, ARE YOU?
AIIEEEEEEE--*
MORE OF A CAUTIONARY TALE THAN A WORTHY RIVAL.
...WEAKLING.
YOU SEEMED SURPRISED THAT I WOULD ATTACK YOU. WHAT A--
--PARADOX--!
WE CANNOT ALLOW KANG-- ANY KANG--TO SEIZE THE INFANT!
HOLD THE LINE!

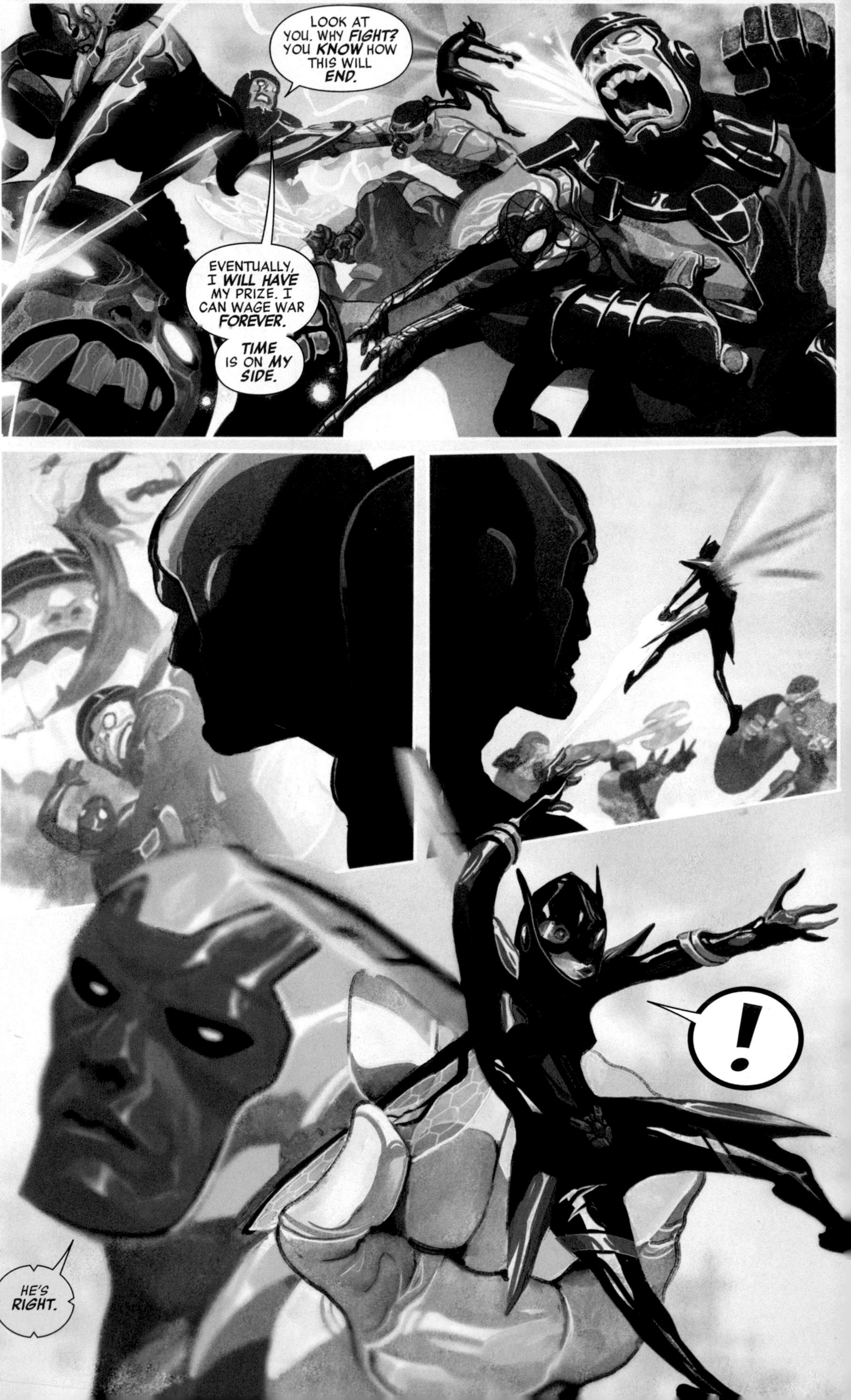
LOOK AT YOU. WHY FIGHT? YOU KNOW HOW THIS WILL END.
EVENTUALLY, I WILL HAVE MY PRIZE. I CAN WAGE WAR FOREVER.
TIME IS ON MY SIDE.
!
HE'S RIGHT.

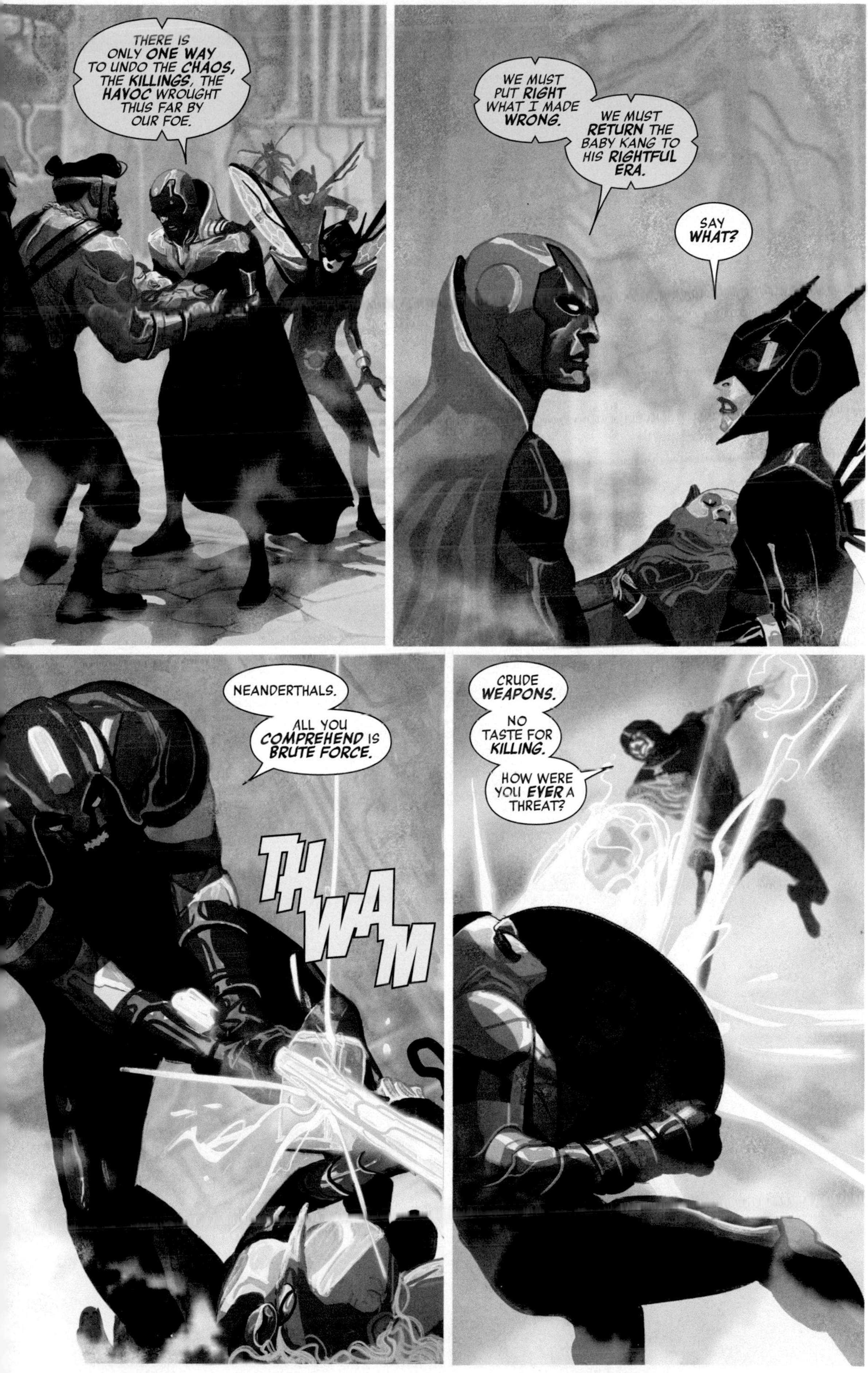
THERE IS ONLY ONE WAY TO UNDO THE CHAOS, THE KILLINGS, THE HAVOC WROUGHT THUS FAR BY OUR FOE.
WE MUST PUT RIGHT WHAT I MADE WRONG.
WE MUST RETURN THE BABY KANG TO HIS RIGHTFUL ERA.
SAY WHAT?
NEANDERTHALS.
ALL YOU COMPREHEND IS BRUTE FORCE.
THWAM
CRUDE WEAPONS.
NO TASTE FOR KILLING.
HOW WERE YOU EVER A THREAT?

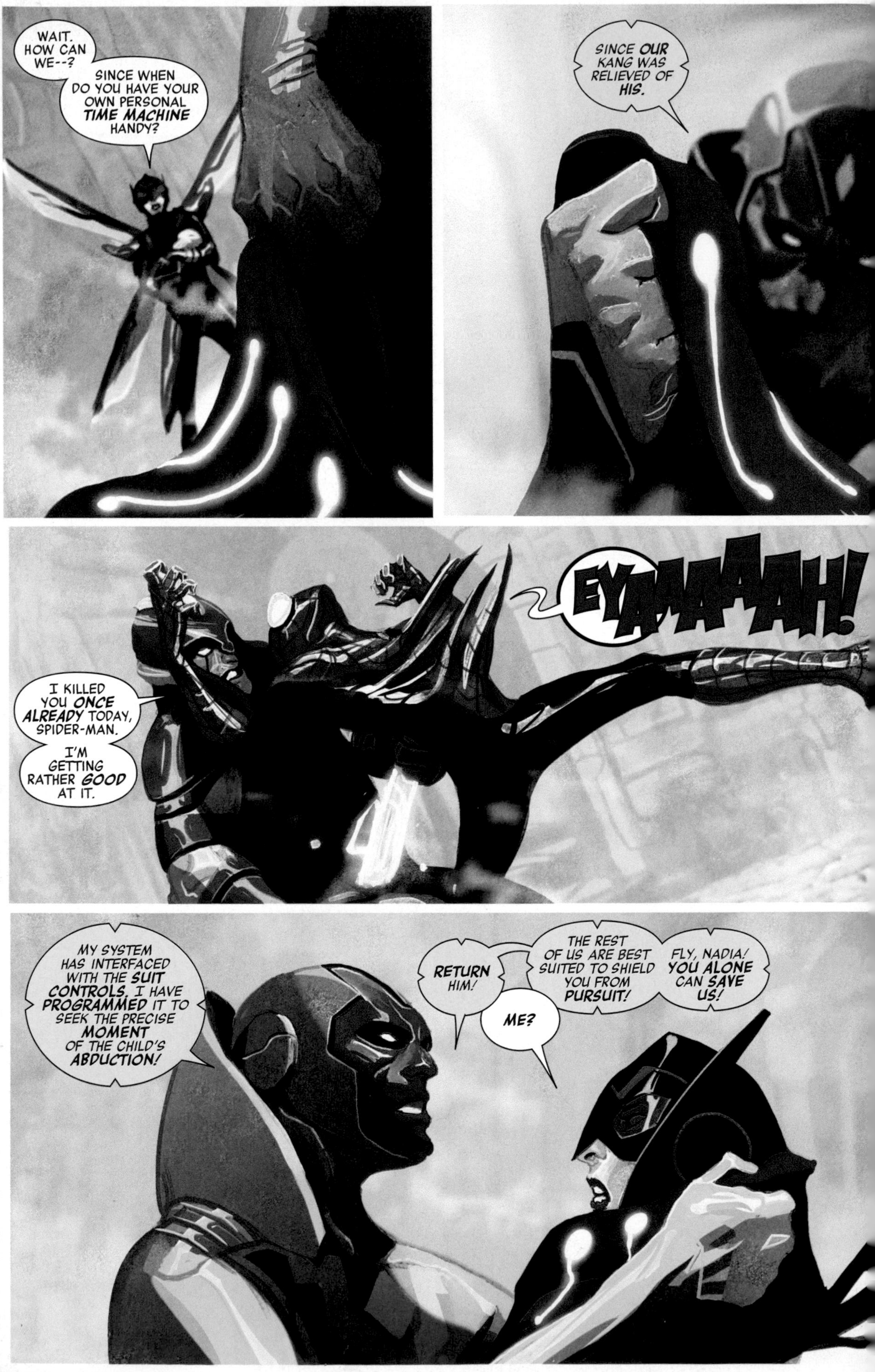
WAIT. HOW CAN WE--?
SINCE WHEN DO YOU HAVE YOUR OWN PERSONAL TIME MACHINE HANDY?
SINCE OUR KANG WAS RELIEVED OF HIS.
EYAAAAAAH!
I KILLED YOU ONCE ALREADY TODAY, SPIDER-MAN.
I'M GETTING RATHER GOOD AT IT.
MY SYSTEM HAS INTERFACED WITH THE SUIT CONTROLS. I HAVE PROGRAMMED IT TO SEEK THE PRECISE MOMENT OF THE CHILD'S ABDUCTION!
RETURN HIM!
ME?
THE REST OF US ARE BEST SUITED TO SHIELD YOU FROM PURSUIT!
FLY, NADIA! YOU ALONE CAN SAVE US!

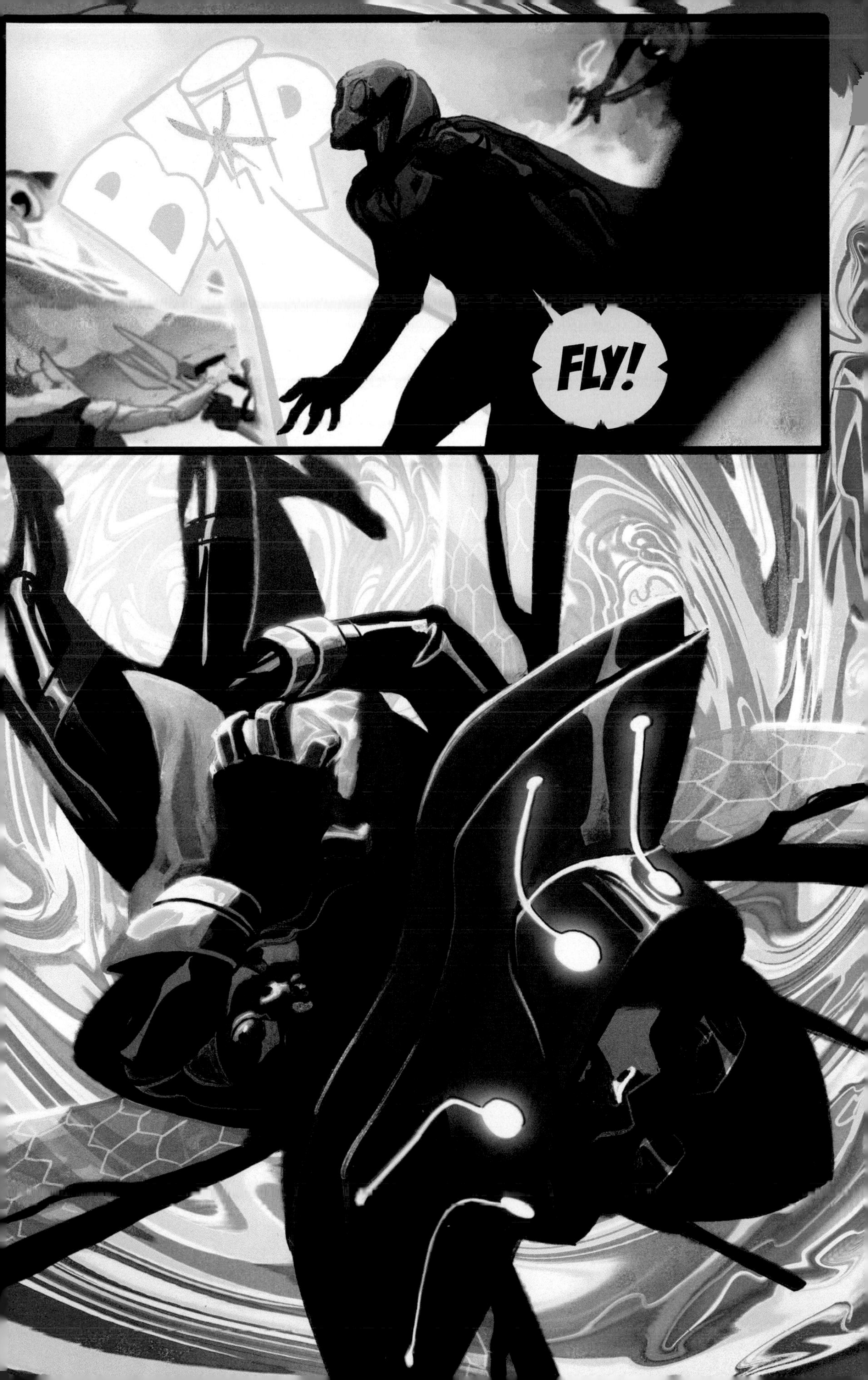
BZAP
FLY!

3

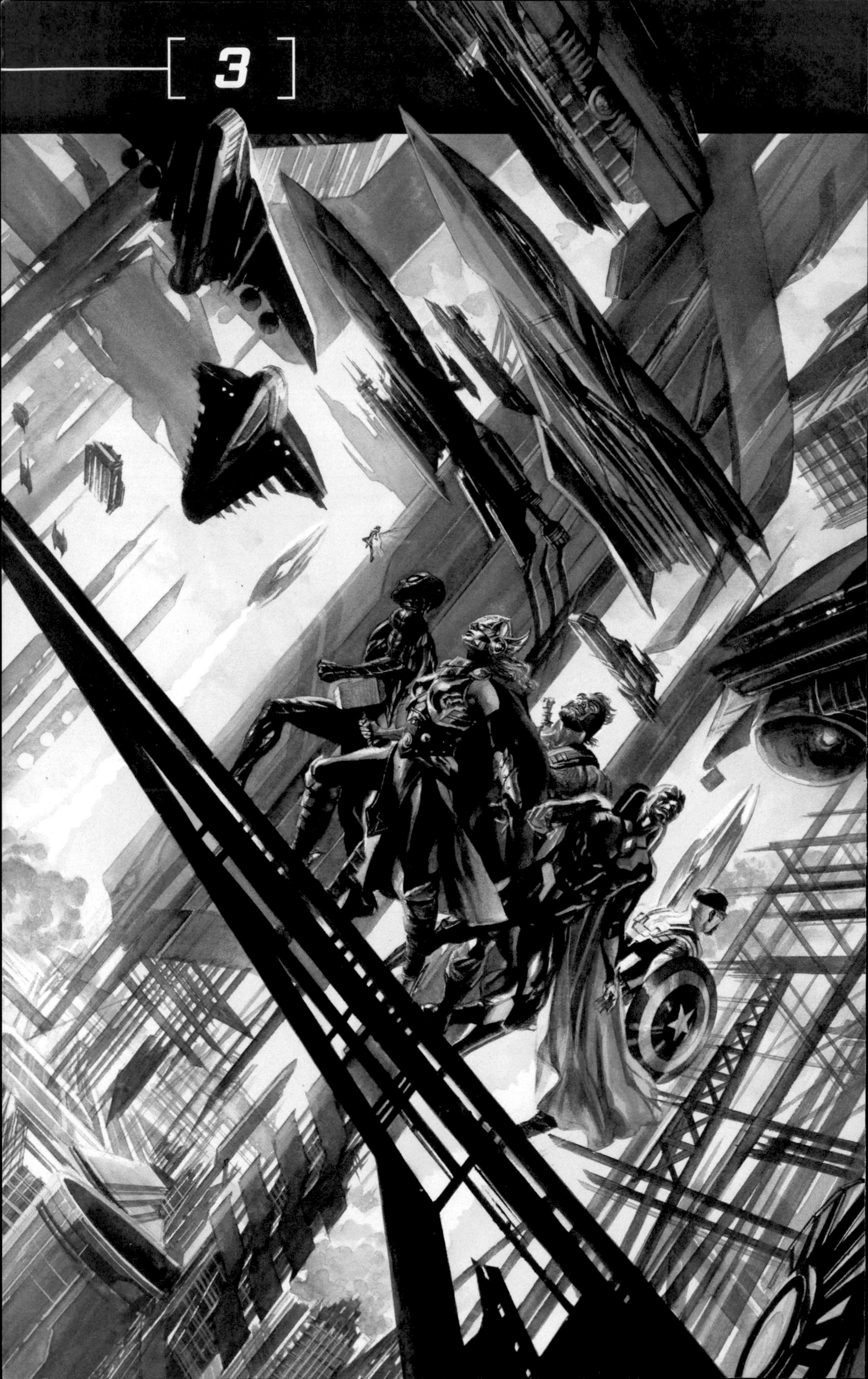

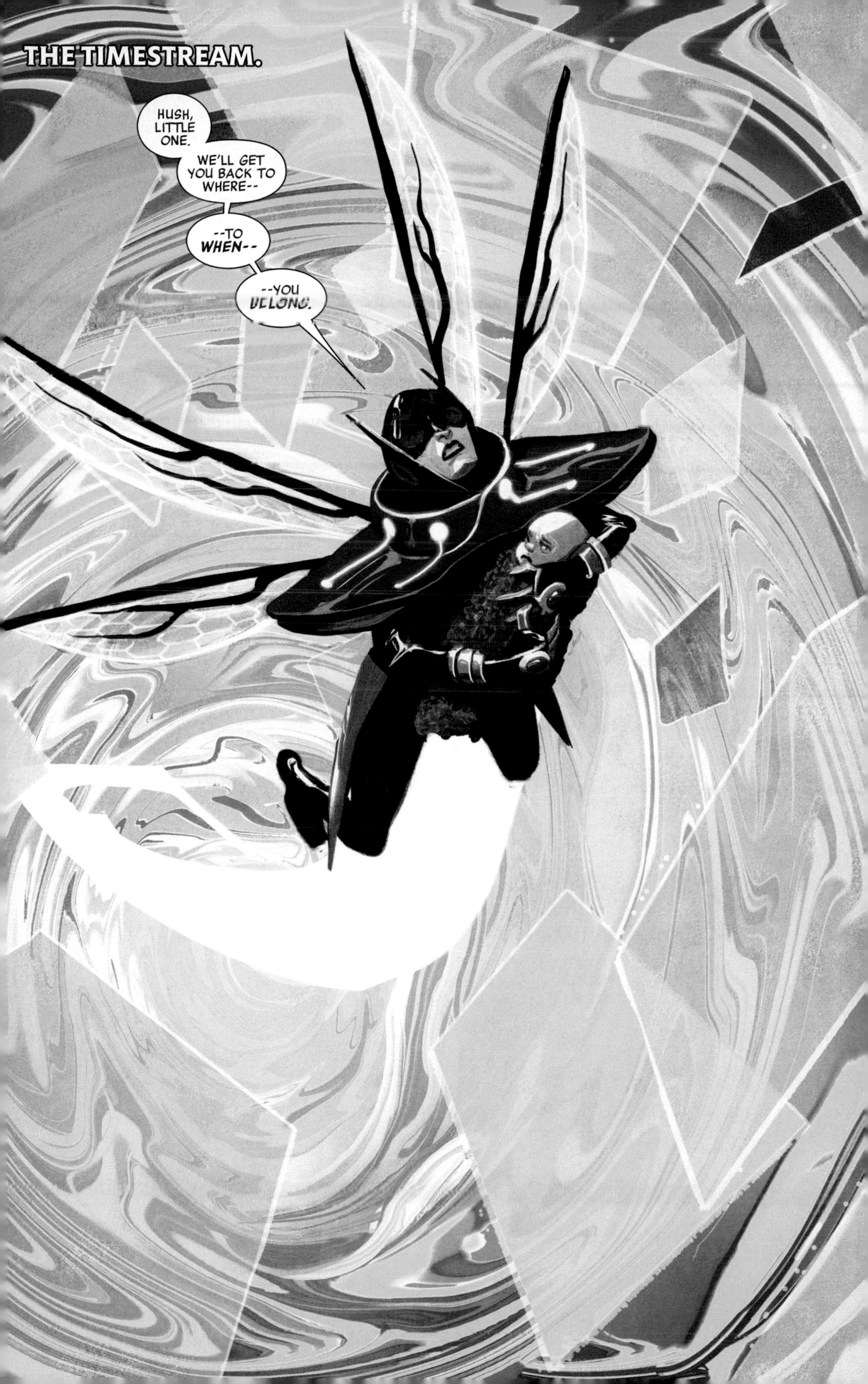
THE TIMESTREAM.
HUSH, LITTLE ONE.
WE'LL GET YOU BACK TO WHERE--
--TO WHEN--
--YOU BELONG.

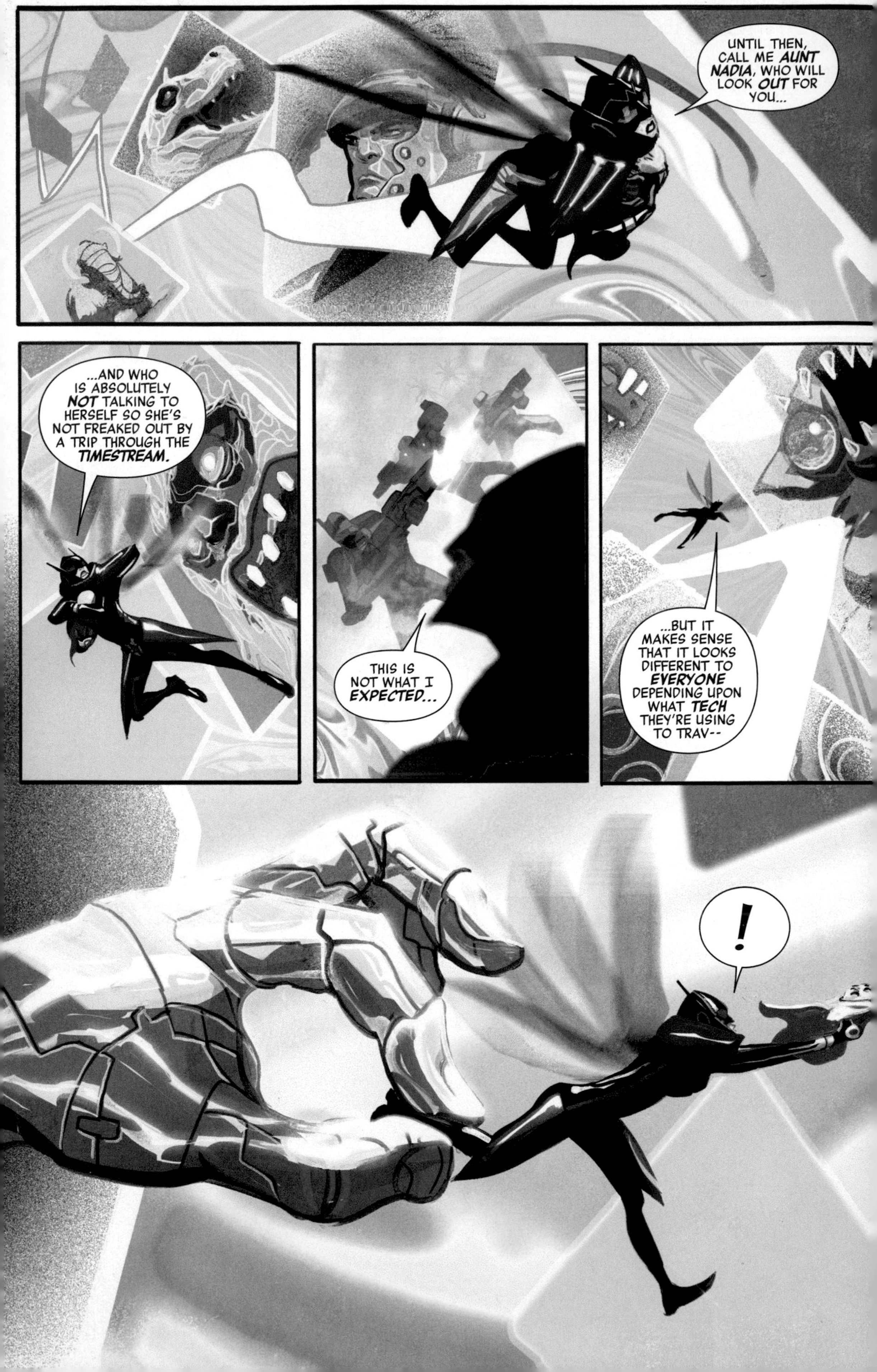
UNTIL THEN, CALL ME AUNT NADIA, WHO WILL LOOK OUT FOR YOU...
...AND WHO IS ABSOLUTELY NOT TALKING TO HERSELF SO SHE'S NOT FREAKED OUT BY A TRIP THROUGH THE TIMESTREAM.
THIS IS NOT WHAT I EXPECTED...
...BUT IT MAKES SENSE THAT IT LOOKS DIFFERENT TO EVERYONE DEPENDING UPON WHAT TECH THEY'RE USING TO TRAV--
!

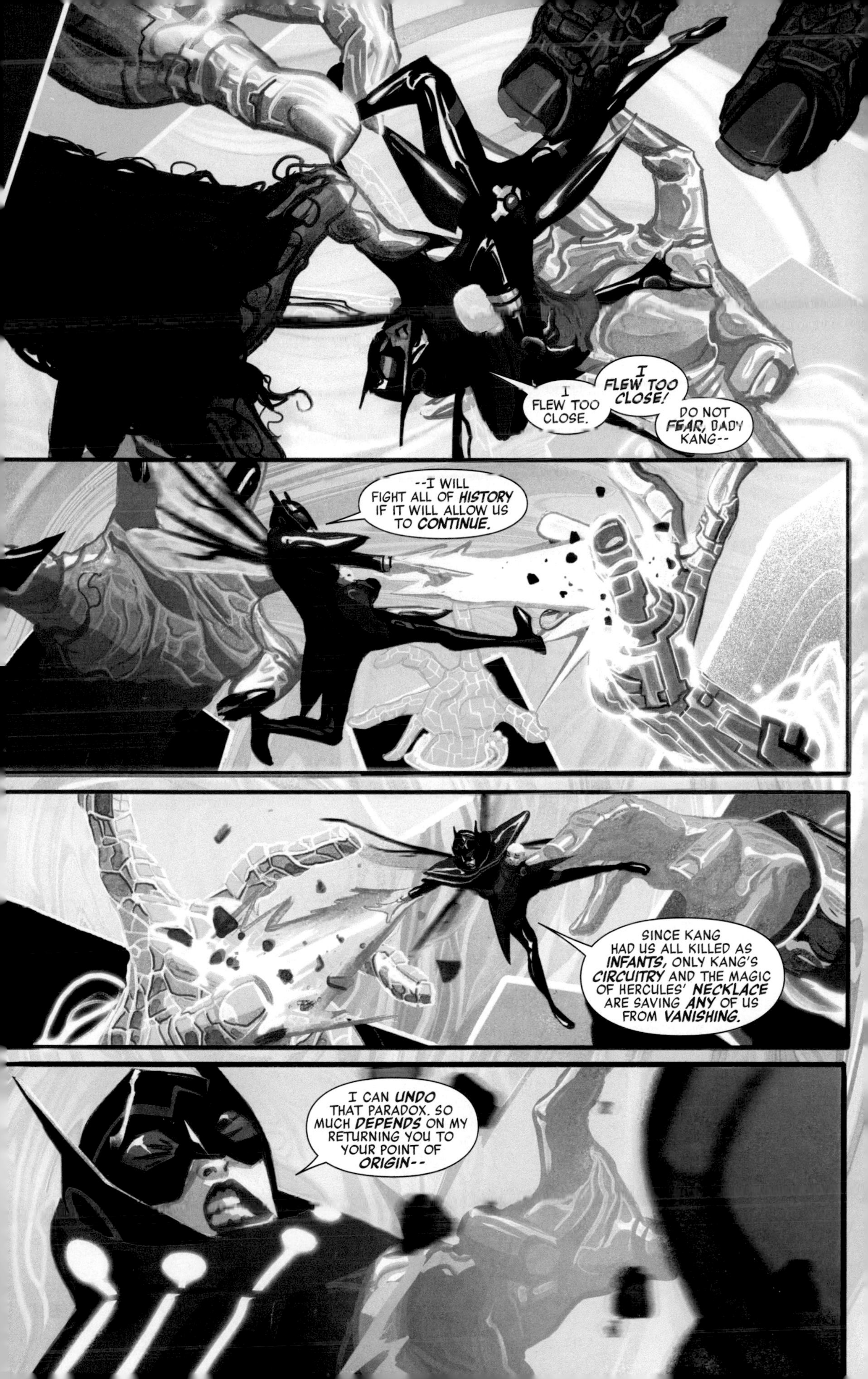
I FLEW TOO CLOSE.
I FLEW TOO CLOSE!
DO NOT FEAR, BADY KANG--
--I WILL FIGHT ALL OF HISTORY IF IT WILL ALLOW US TO CONTINUE.
SINCE KANG HAD US ALL KILLED AS INFANTS, ONLY KANG'S CIRCUITRY AND THE MAGIC OF HERCULES' NECKLACE ARE SAVING ANY OF US FROM VANISHING.
I CAN UNDO THAT PARADOX. SO MUCH DEPENDS ON MY RETURNING YOU TO YOUR POINT OF ORIGIN--

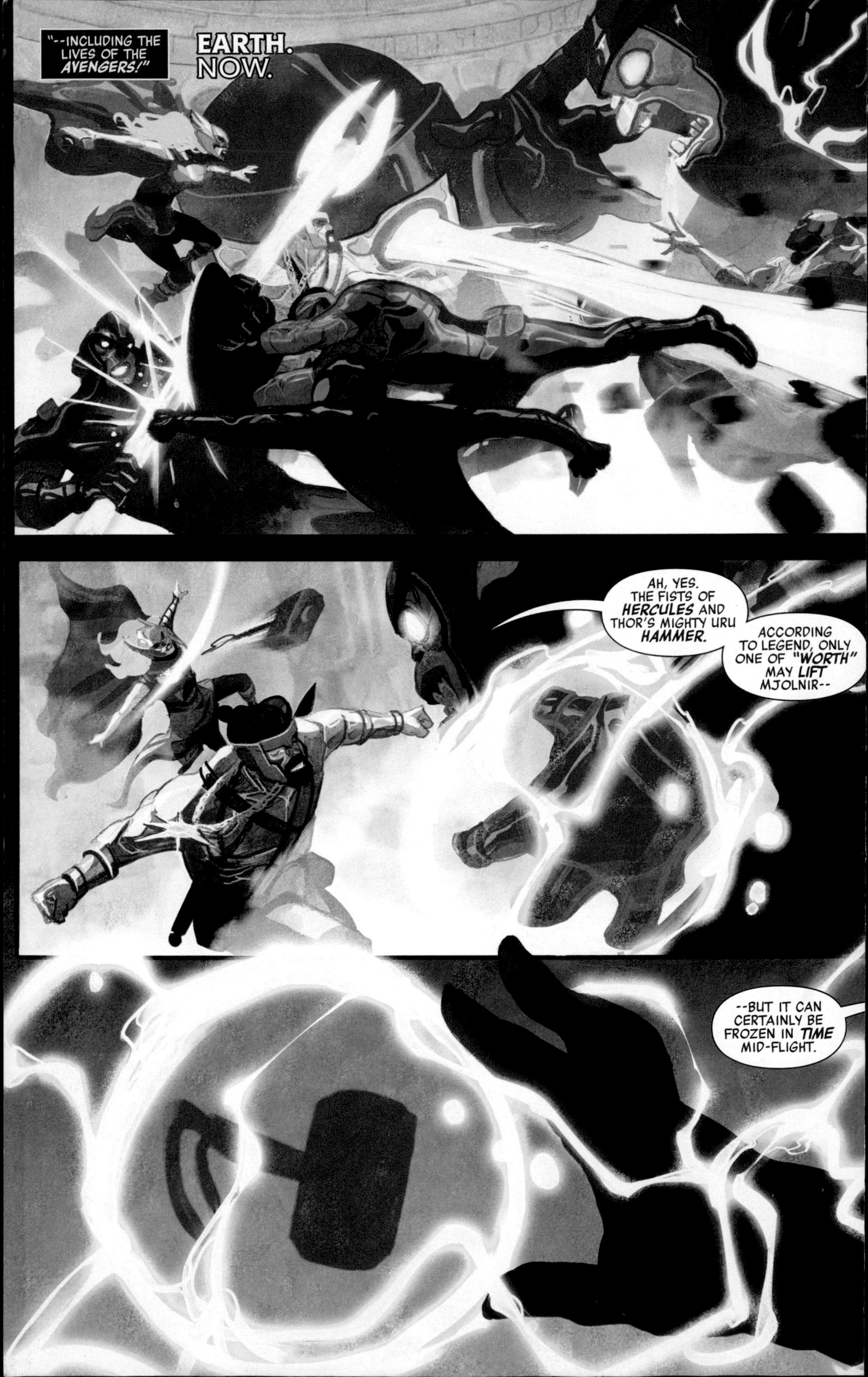
"--INCLUDING THE LIVES OF THE AVENGERS!"
EARTH. NOW.
AH, YES. THE FISTS OF HERCULES AND THOR'S MIGHTY URU HAMMER.
ACCORDING TO LEGEND, ONLY ONE OF "WORTH" MAY LIFT MJOLNIR--
--BUT IT CAN CERTAINLY BE FROZEN IN TIME MID-FLIGHT.

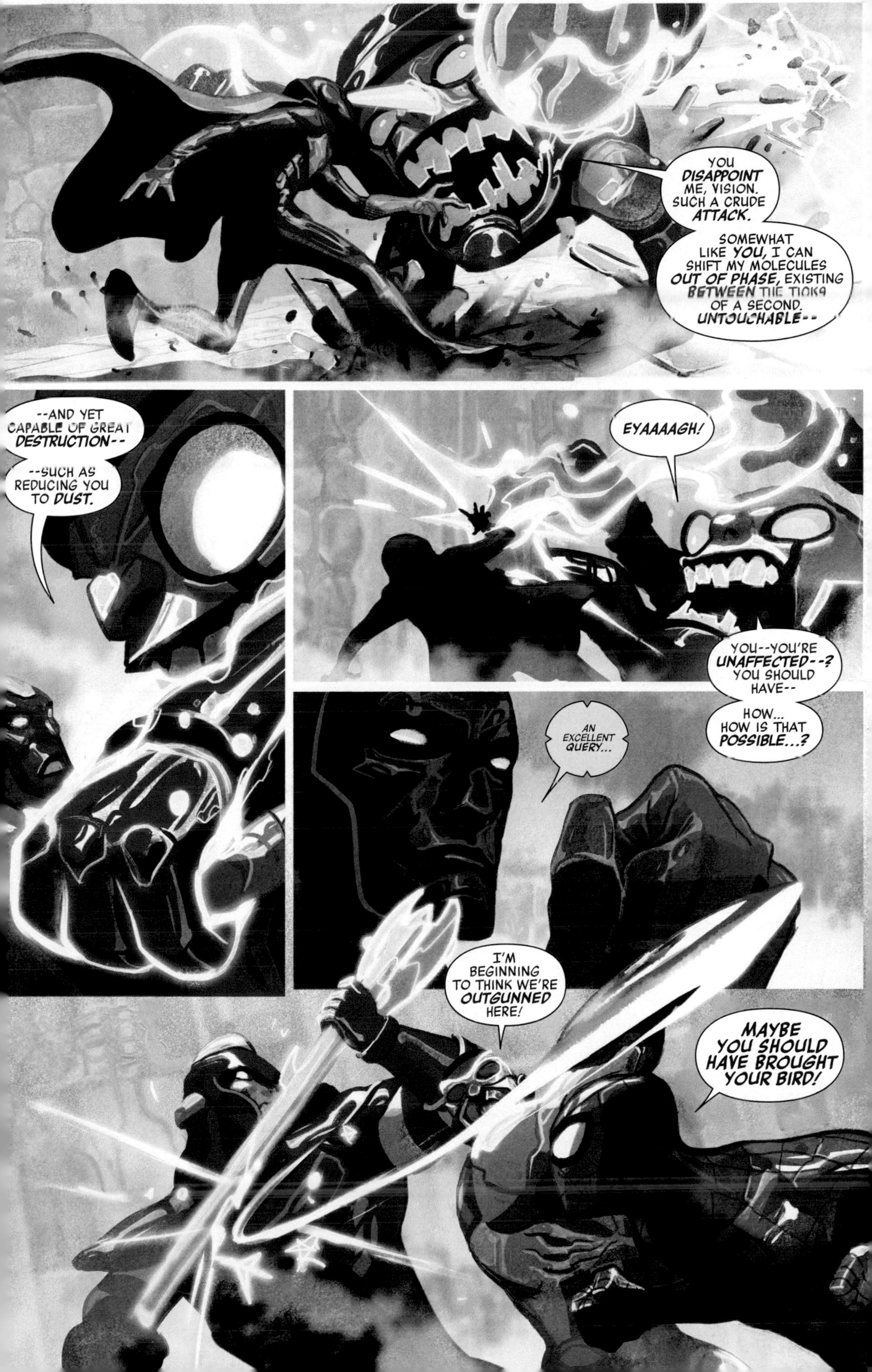

YOU DISAPPOINT ME, VISION. SUCH A CRUDE ATTACK.
SOMEWHAT LIKE YOU, I CAN SHIFT MY MOLECULES OUT OF PHASE, EXISTING BETWEEN THE TICKS OF A SECOND. UNTOUCHABLE--
--AND YET CAPABLE OF GREAT DESTRUCTION--
--SUCH AS REDUCING YOU TO DUST.
EYAAAAGH!
YOU--YOU'RE UNAFFECTED--? YOU SHOULD HAVE--
HOW... HOW IS THAT POSSIBLE...?
AN EXCELLENT QUERY...
I'M BEGINNING TO THINK WE'RE OUTGUNNED HERE!
MAYBE YOU SHOULD HAVE BROUGHT YOUR BIRD!

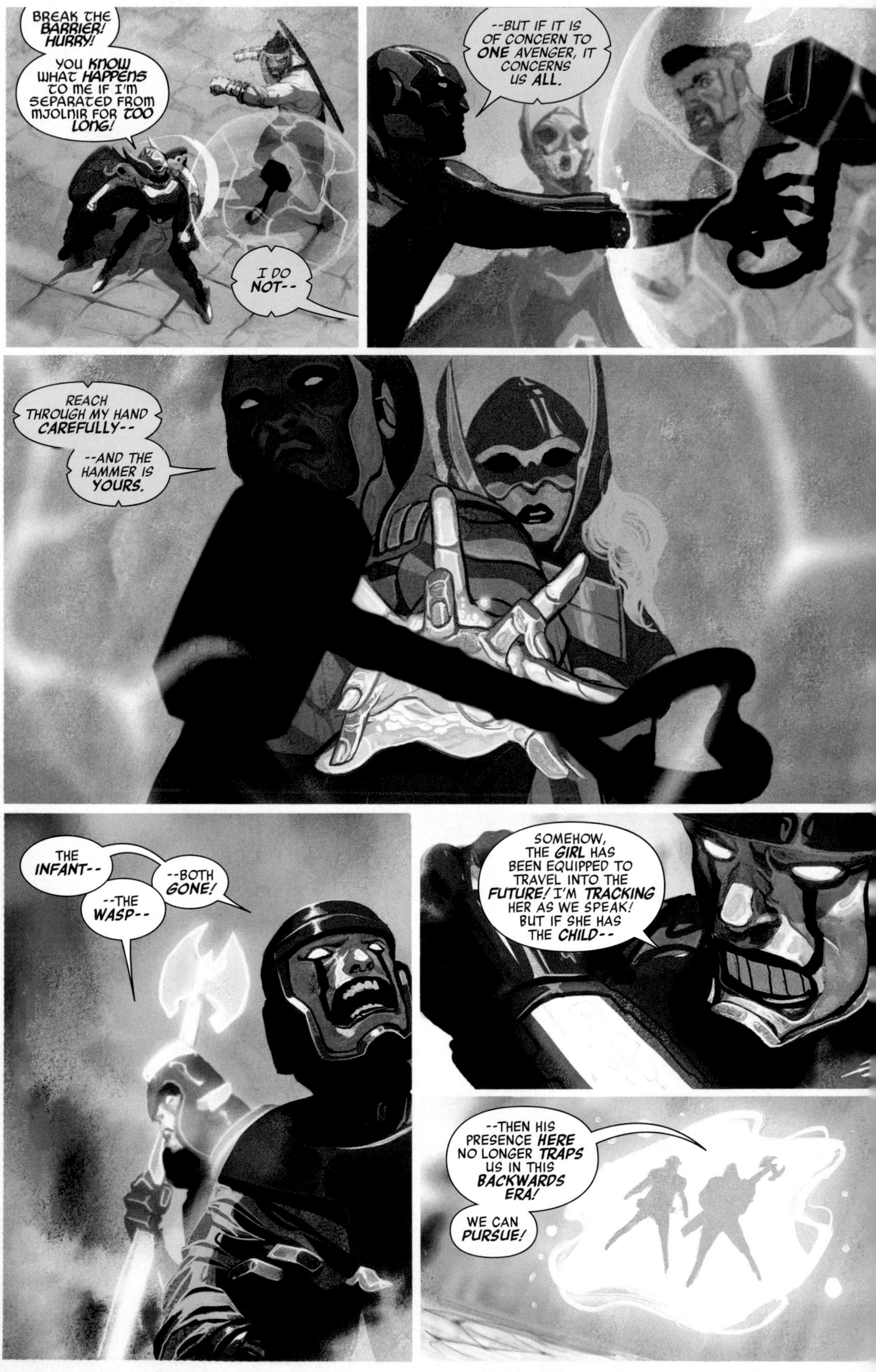
BREAK THE BARRIER! HURRY!
YOU KNOW WHAT HAPPENS TO ME IF I'M SEPARATED FROM MJOLNIR FOR TOO LONG!
I DO NOT--
--BUT IF IT IS OF CONCERN TO ONE AVENGER, IT CONCERNS US ALL.
REACH THROUGH MY HAND CAREFULLY--
--AND THE HAMMER IS YOURS.
THE INFANT--
--THE WASP--
--BOTH GONE!
SOMEHOW, THE GIRL HAS BEEN EQUIPPED TO TRAVEL INTO THE FUTURE! I'M TRACKING HER AS WE SPEAK! BUT IF SHE HAS THE CHILD--
--THEN HIS PRESENCE HERE NO LONGER TRAPS US IN THIS BACKWARDS ERA!
WE CAN PURSUE!

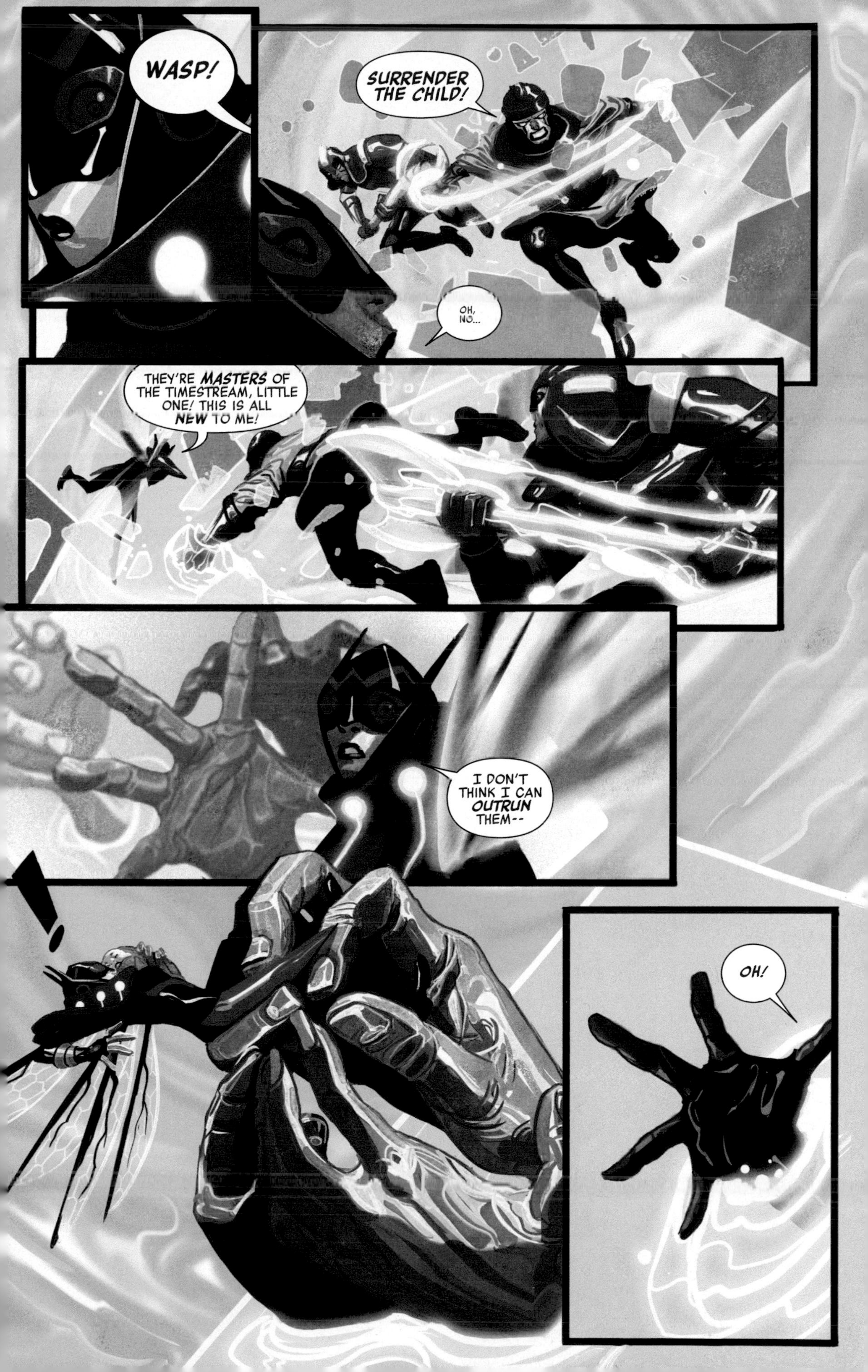

WASP!
SURRENDER THE CHILD!
OH, NO...
THEY'RE MASTERS OF THE TIMESTREAM, LITTLE ONE! THIS IS ALL NEW TO ME!
I DON'T THINK I CAN OUTRUN THEM--
!
OH!

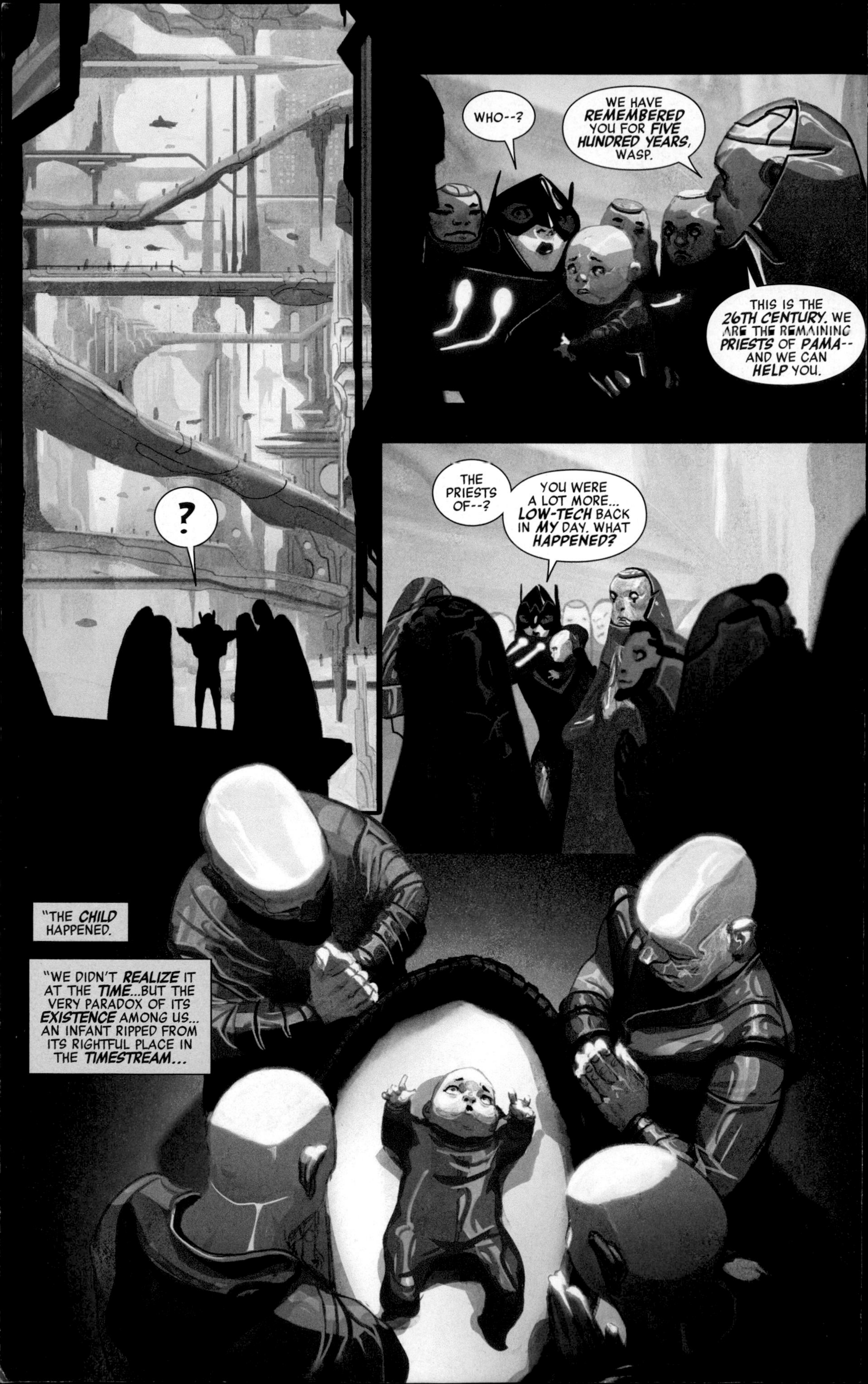
?
WHO--?
WE HAVE REMEMBERED YOU FOR FIVE HUNDRED YEARS, WASP.
THIS IS THE 26TH CENTURY. WE ARE THE REMAINING PRIESTS OF PAMA-- AND WE CAN HELP YOU.
THE PRIESTS OF--?
YOU WERE A LOT MORE... LOW-TECH BACK IN MY DAY. WHAT HAPPENED?
"THE CHILD HAPPENED.
"WE DIDN'T REALIZE IT AT THE TIME...BUT THE VERY PARADOX OF ITS EXISTENCE AMONG US... AN INFANT RIPPED FROM ITS RIGHTFUL PLACE IN THE TIMESTREAM...

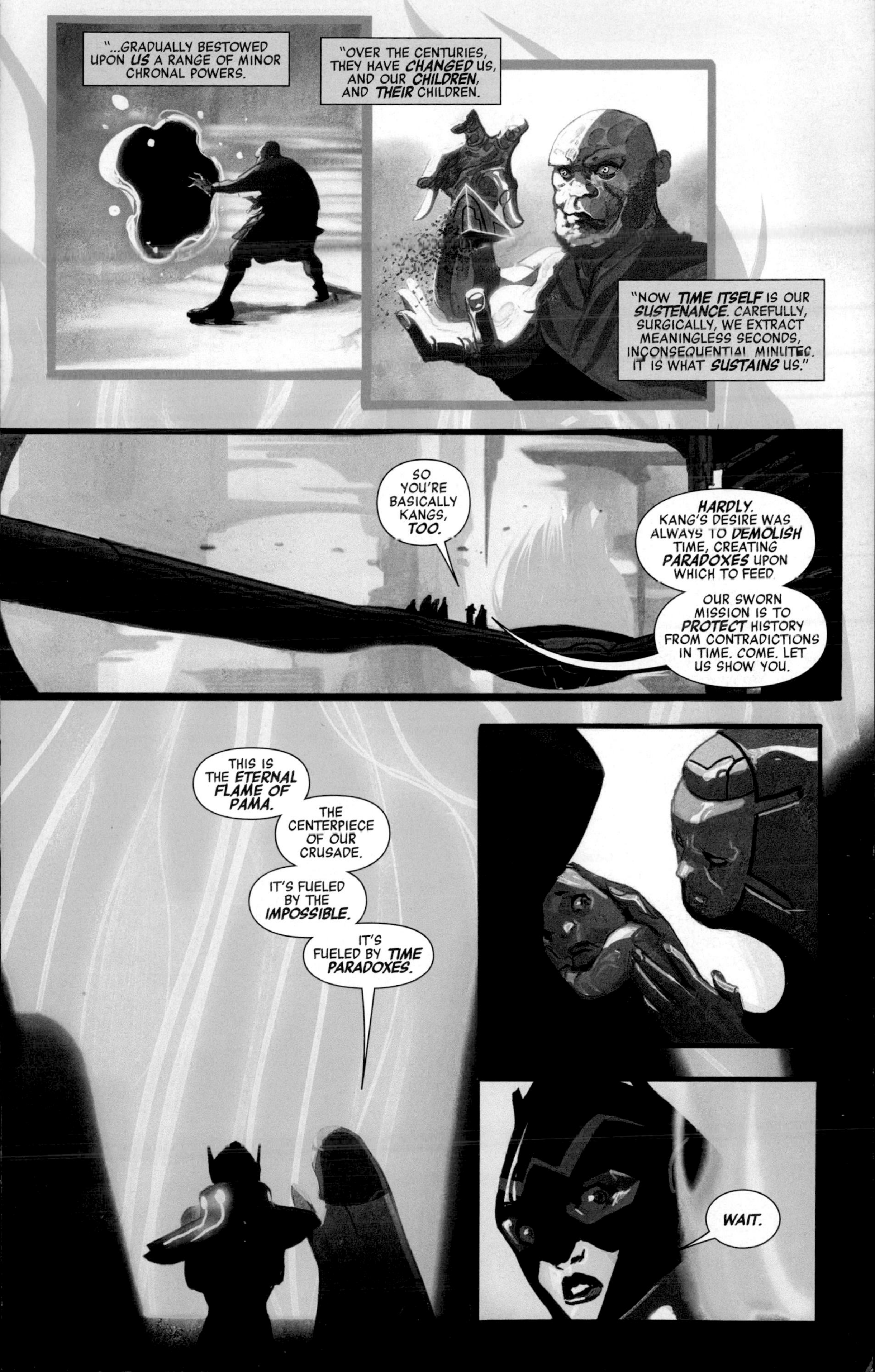
"...GRADUALLY BESTOWED UPON US A RANGE OF MINOR CHRONAL POWERS.
"OVER THE CENTURIES, THEY HAVE CHANGED US, AND OUR CHILDREN, AND THEIR CHILDREN.
"NOW TIME ITSELF IS OUR SUSTENANCE. CAREFULLY, SURGICALLY, WE EXTRACT MEANINGLESS SECONDS, INCONSEQUENTIAL MINUTES. IT IS WHAT SUSTAINS US."
SO YOU'RE BASICALLY KANGS, TOO.
HARDLY. KANG'S DESIRE WAS ALWAYS TO DEMOLISH TIME, CREATING PARADOXES UPON WHICH TO FEED.
OUR SWORN MISSION IS TO PROTECT HISTORY FROM CONTRADICTIONS IN TIME. COME. LET US SHOW YOU.
THIS IS THE ETERNAL FLAME OF PAMA.
THE CENTERPIECE OF OUR CRUSADE.
IT'S FUELED BY THE IMPOSSIBLE.
IT'S FUELED BY TIME PARADOXES.
WAIT.

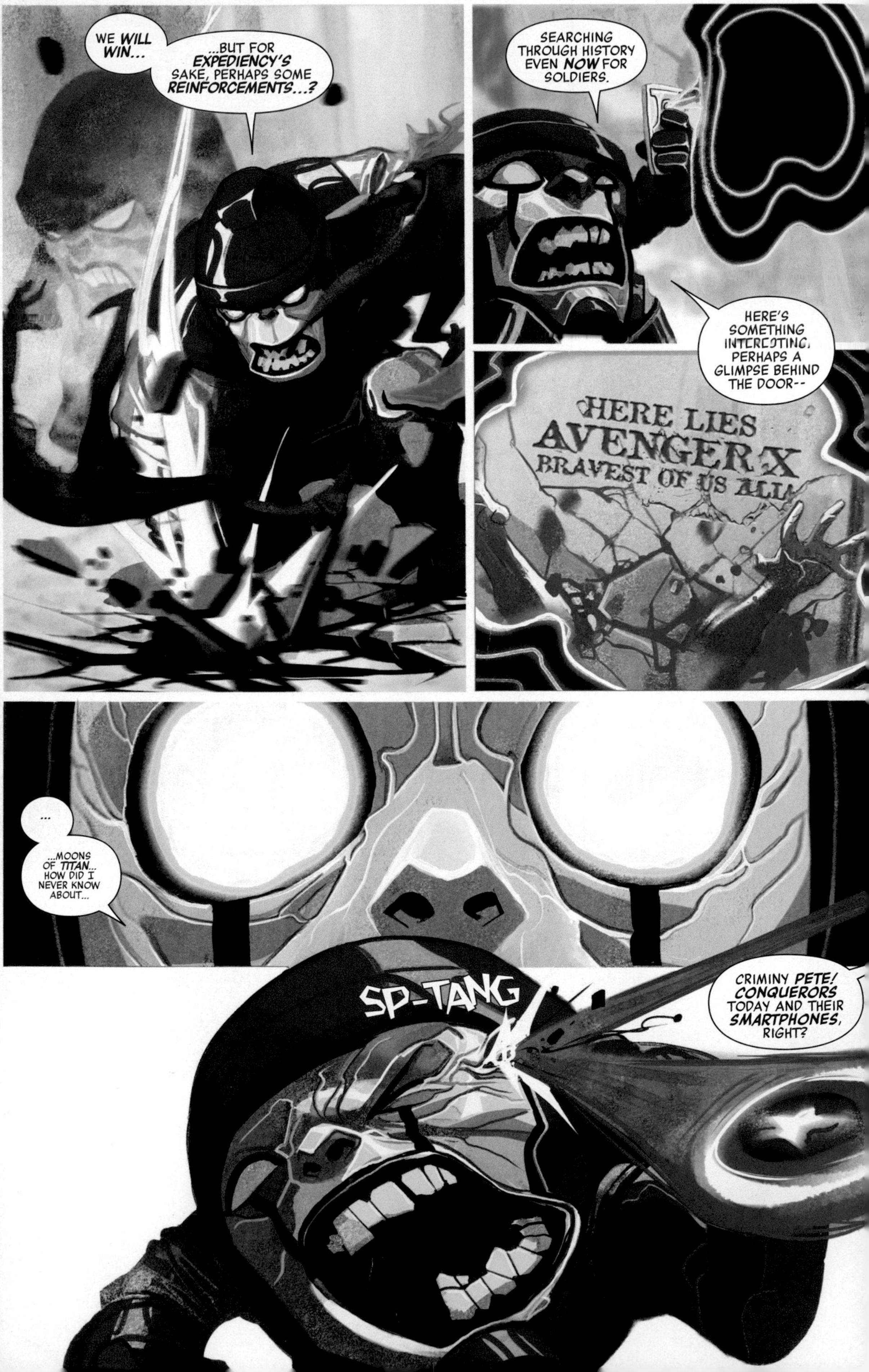
WE WILL WIN...
...BUT FOR EXPEDIENCY'S SAKE, PERHAPS SOME REINFORCEMENTS...?
SEARCHING THROUGH HISTORY EVEN NOW FOR SOLDIERS.
HERE'S SOMETHING INTERESTING, PERHAPS A GLIMPSE BEHIND THE DOOR--
HERE LIES AVENGER X BRAVEST OF US ALL
...
...MOONS OF TITAN... HOW DID I NEVER KNOW ABOUT...
SP-TANG
CRIMINY PETE! CONQUERORS TODAY AND THEIR SMARTPHONES, RIGHT?

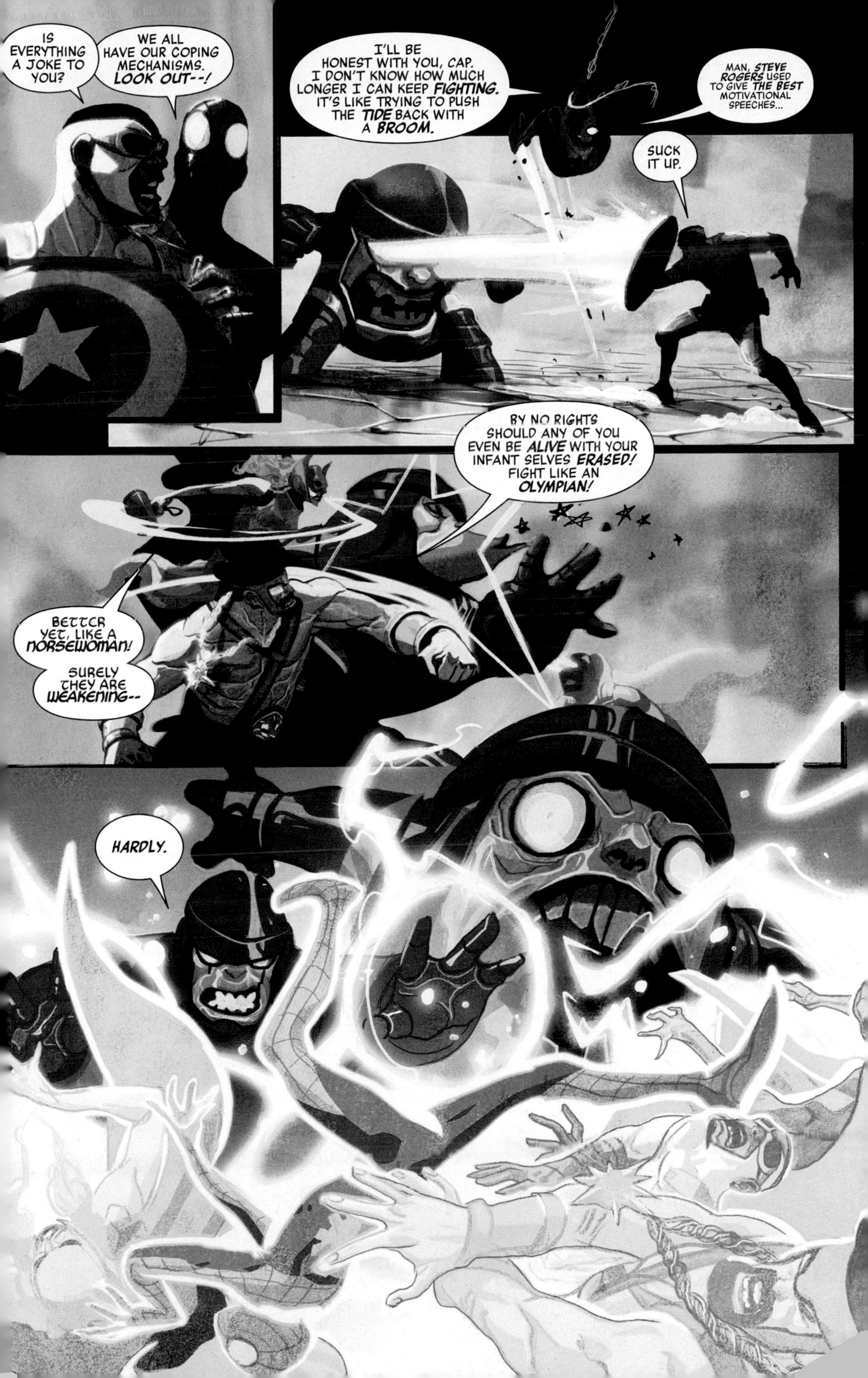
IS EVERYTHING A JOKE TO YOU?
WE ALL HAVE OUR COPING MECHANISMS. LOOK OUT--!
I'LL BE HONEST WITH YOU, CAP. I DON'T KNOW HOW MUCH LONGER I CAN KEEP FIGHTING. IT'S LIKE TRYING TO PUSH THE TIDE BACK WITH A BROOM.
MAN, STEVE ROGERS USED TO GIVE THE BEST MOTIVATIONAL SPEECHES...
SUCK IT UP.
BY NO RIGHTS SHOULD ANY OF YOU EVEN BE ALIVE WITH YOUR INFANT SELVES ERASED! FIGHT LIKE AN OLYMPIAN!
BETTER YET, LIKE A NORSEWOMAN!
SURELY THEY ARE WEAKENING--
HARDLY.

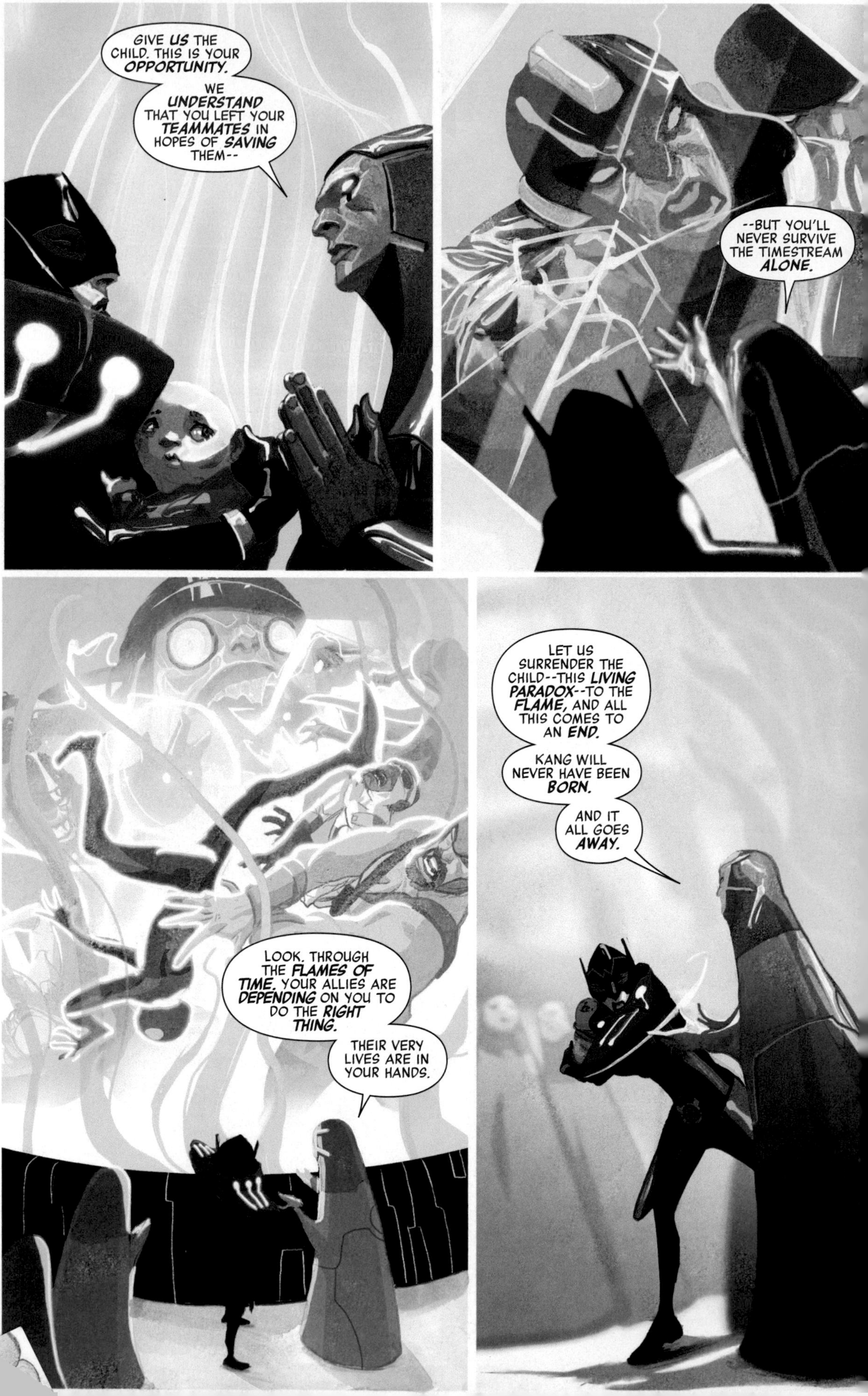
GIVE US THE CHILD. THIS IS YOUR OPPORTUNITY.
WE UNDERSTAND THAT YOU LEFT YOUR TEAMMATES IN HOPES OF SAVING THEM--
--BUT YOU'LL NEVER SURVIVE THE TIMESTREAM ALONE.
LOOK. THROUGH THE FLAMES OF TIME. YOUR ALLIES ARE DEPENDING ON YOU TO DO THE RIGHT THING.
THEIR VERY LIVES ARE IN YOUR HANDS.
LET US SURRENDER THE CHILD--THIS LIVING PARADOX--TO THE FLAME, AND ALL THIS COMES TO AN END.
KANG WILL NEVER HAVE BEEN BORN.
AND IT ALL GOES AWAY.

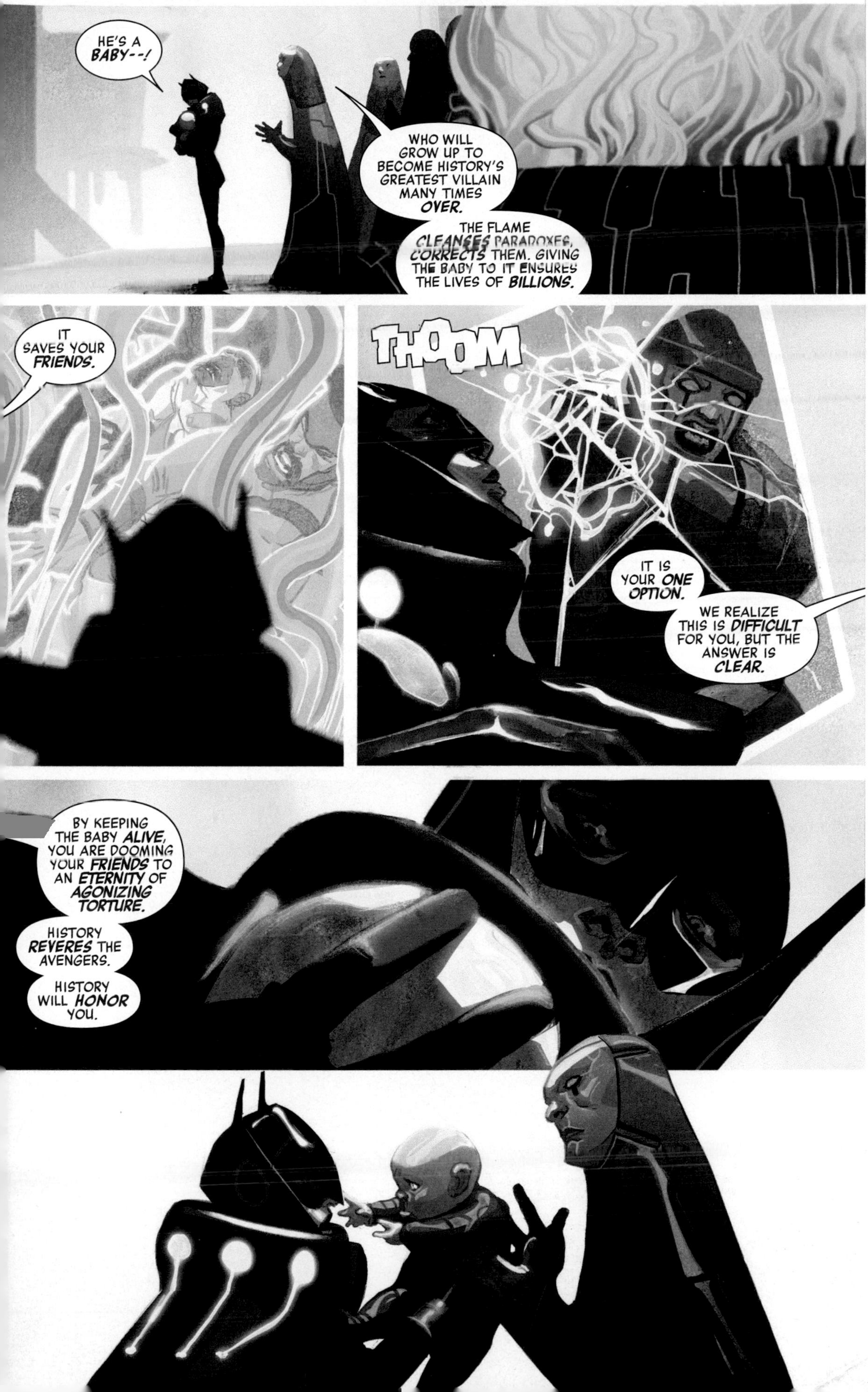

HE'S A BABY--!
WHO WILL GROW UP TO BECOME HISTORY'S GREATEST VILLAIN MANY TIMES OVER.
THE FLAME CLEANSES PARADOXES, CORRECTS THEM. GIVING THE BABY TO IT ENSURES THE LIVES OF BILLIONS.
IT SAVES YOUR FRIENDS.
THOOM
IT IS YOUR ONE OPTION.
WE REALIZE THIS IS DIFFICULT FOR YOU, BUT THE ANSWER IS CLEAR.
BY KEEPING THE BABY ALIVE, YOU ARE DOOMING YOUR FRIENDS TO AN ETERNITY OF AGONIZING TORTURE.
HISTORY REVERES THE AVENGERS.
HISTORY WILL HONOR YOU.

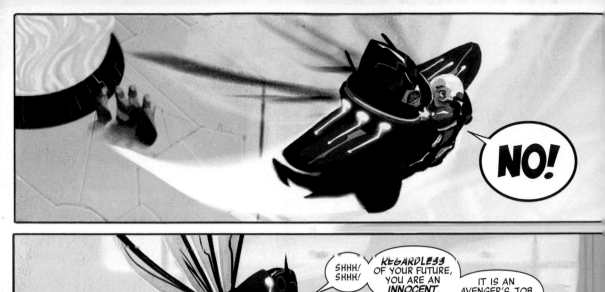

NO!

SHHH! SHHH!

REGARDLESS OF YOUR FUTURE, YOU ARE AN INNOCENT.

IT IS AN AVENGER'S JOB TO PROTECT THE INNOCENT.

SO FORGIVE ME, LITTLE ONE...

...IF I FAIL IN WHAT HAPPENS NEXT.

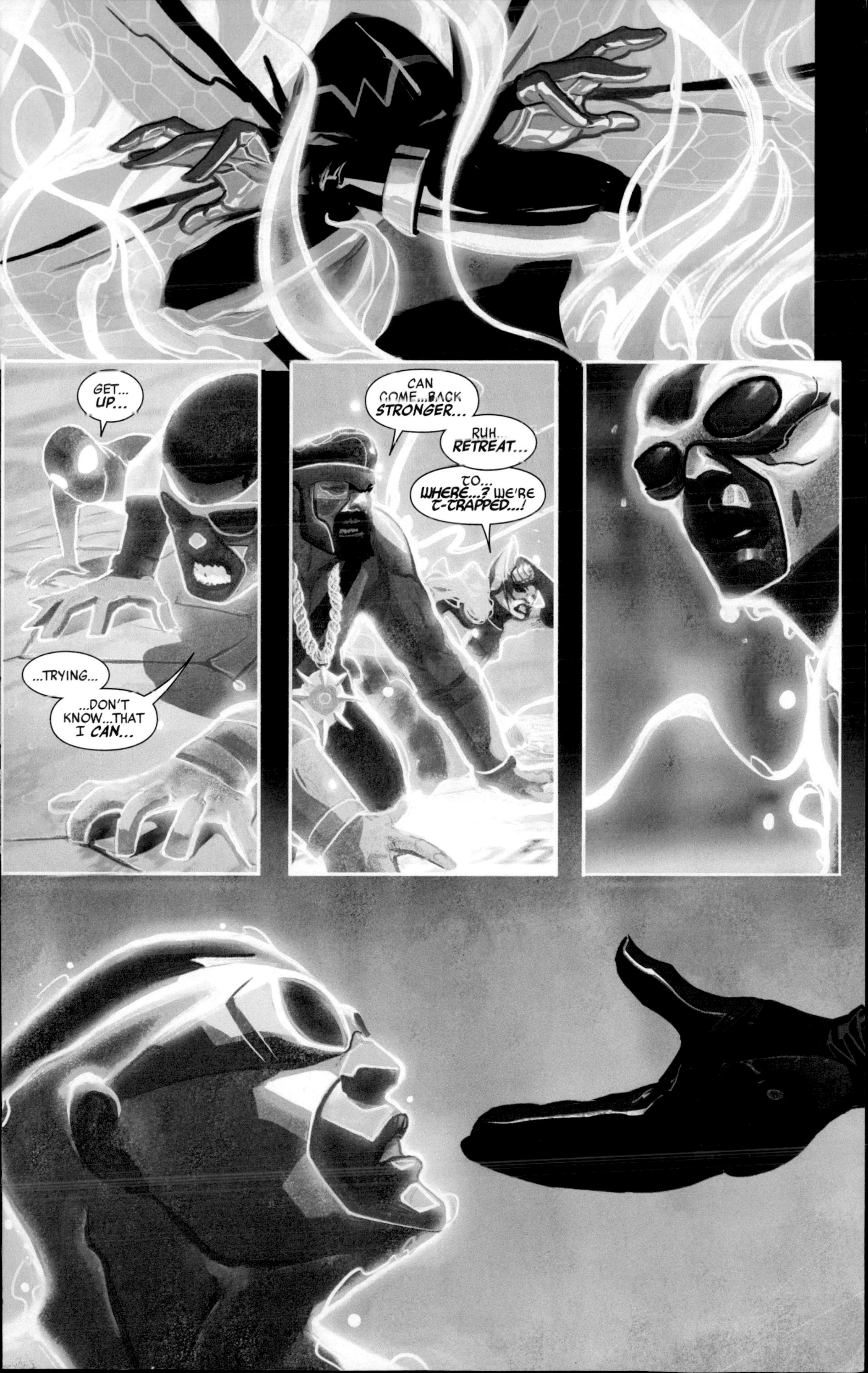
GET... UP...
...TRYING...
...DON'T KNOW...THAT I CAN...
CAN COME...BACK STRONGER...
RUH... RETREAT...
TO... WHERE...? WE'RE T-TRAPPED...!

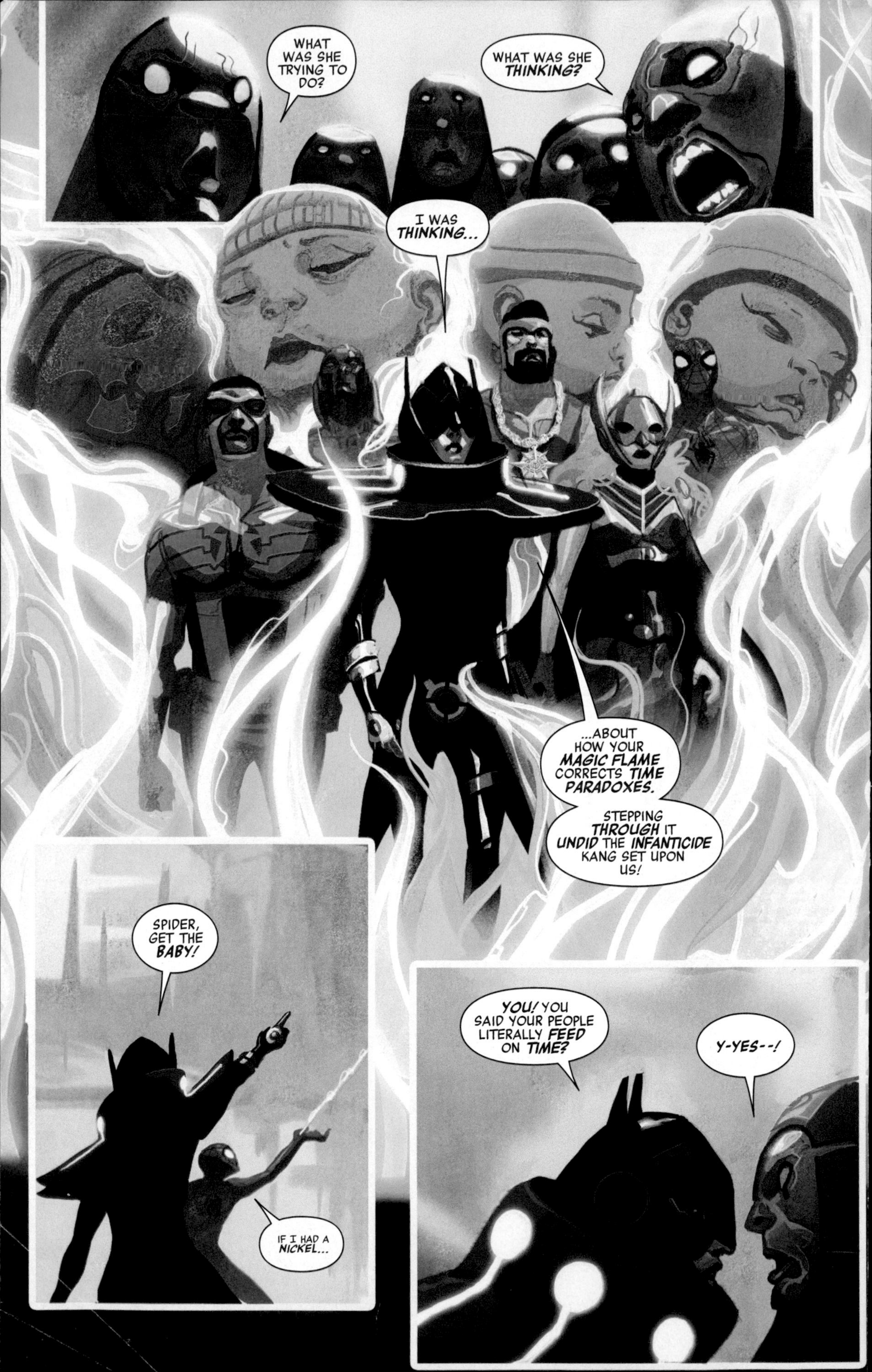
WHAT WAS SHE TRYING TO DO?
WHAT WAS SHE THINKING?
I WAS THINKING...
...ABOUT HOW YOUR MAGIC FLAME CORRECTS TIME PARADOXES.
STEPPING THROUGH IT UNDID THE INFANTICIDE KANG SET UPON US!
SPIDER, GET THE BABY!
IF I HAD A NICKEL...
YOU! YOU SAID YOUR PEOPLE LITERALLY FEED ON TIME?
Y-YES--!

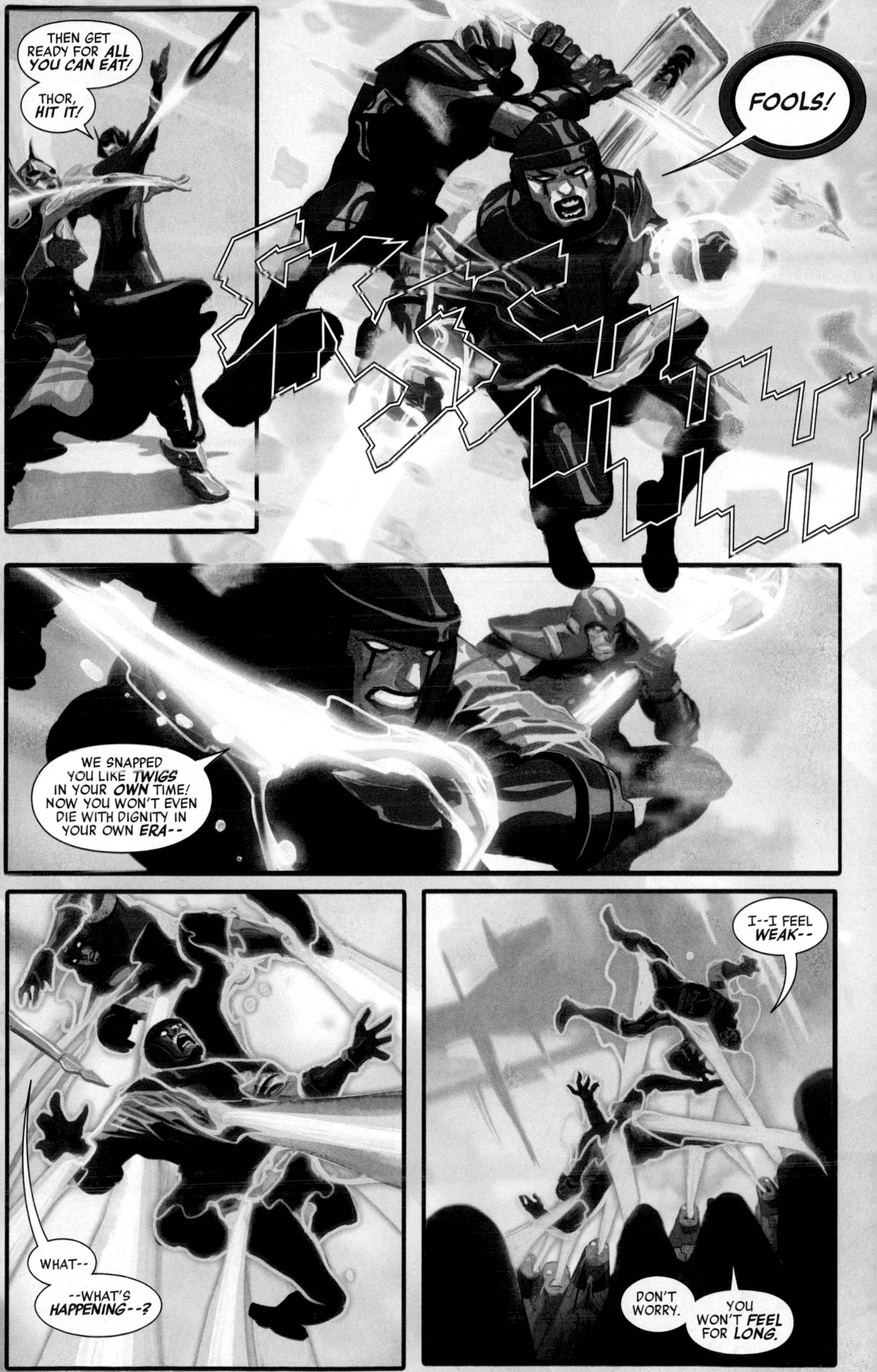
THEN GET READY FOR ALL YOU CAN EAT!
THOR, HIT IT!
FOOLS!
WE SNAPPED YOU LIKE TWIGS IN YOUR OWN TIME! NOW YOU WON'T EVEN DIE WITH DIGNITY IN YOUR OWN ERA--
WHAT--
--WHAT'S HAPPENING--?
I--I FEEL WEAK--
DON'T WORRY.
YOU WON'T FEEL FOR LONG.

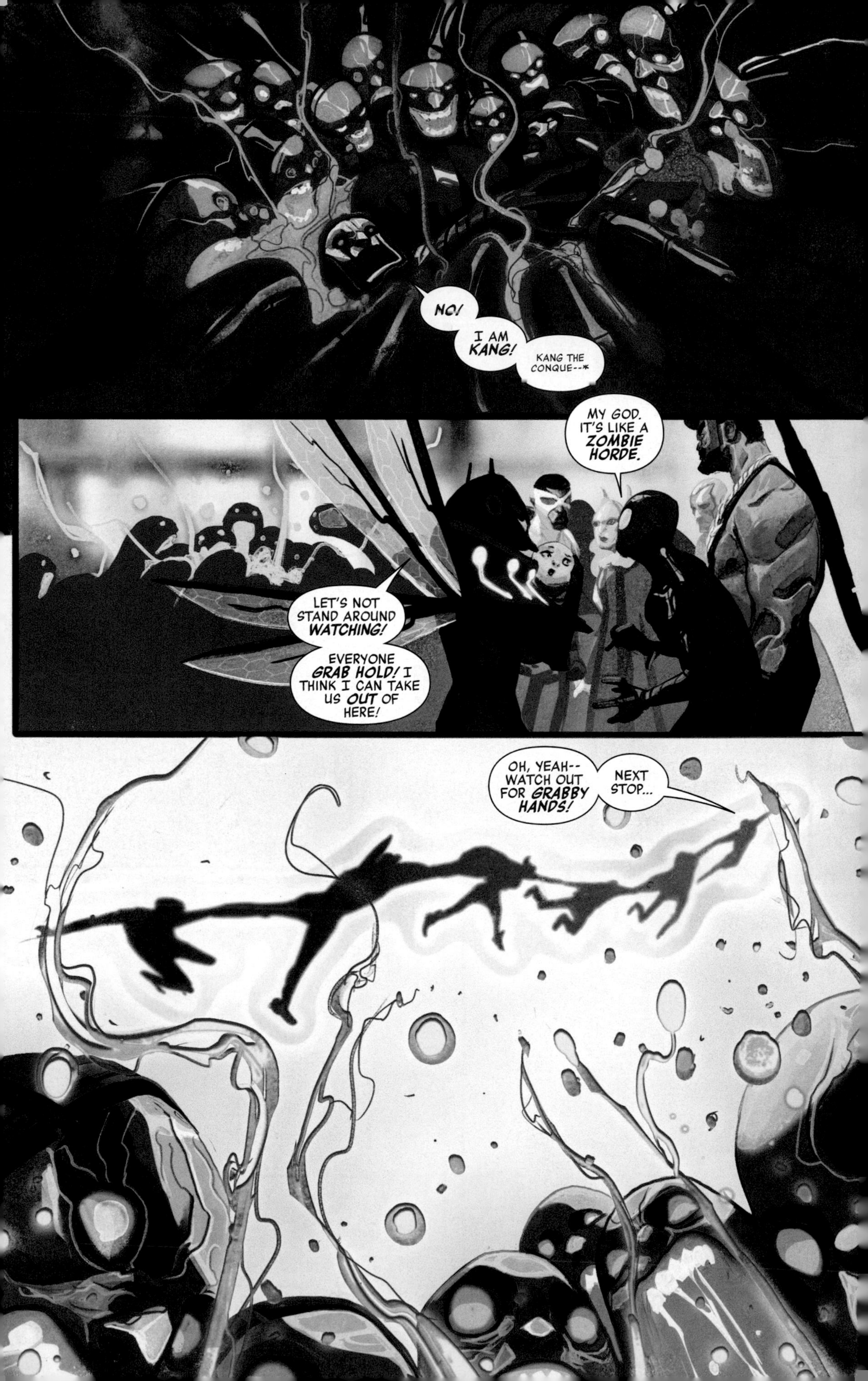
NO!
I AM KANG!
KANG THE CONQUE--*
MY GOD. IT'S LIKE A ZOMBIE HORDE.
LET'S NOT STAND AROUND WATCHING!
EVERYONE GRAB HOLD! I THINK I CAN TAKE US OUT OF HERE!
NEXT STOP...
OH, YEAH--WATCH OUT FOR GRABBY HANDS!

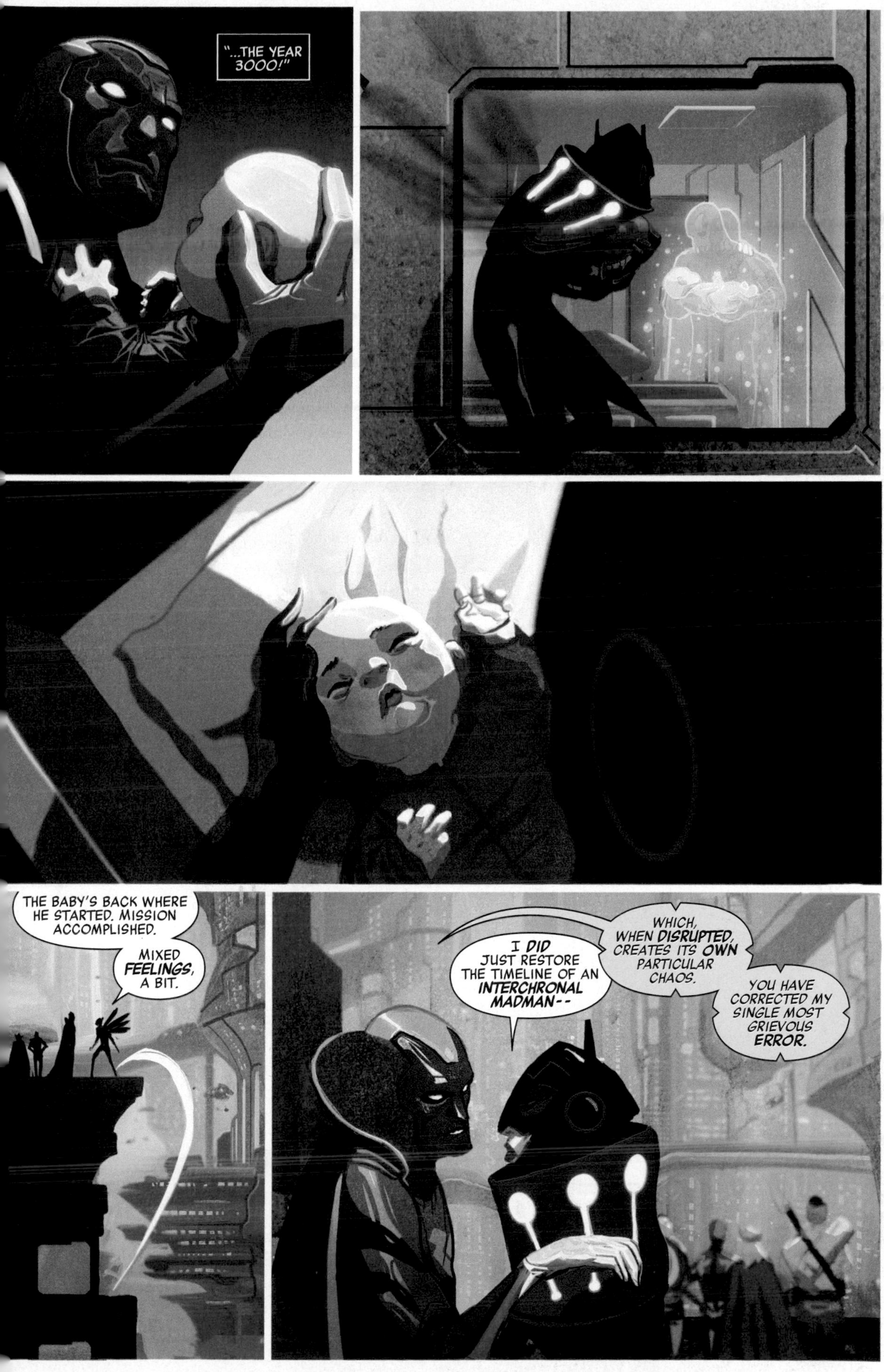
"...THE YEAR 3000!"
THE BABY'S BACK WHERE HE STARTED. MISSION ACCOMPLISHED.
MIXED FEELINGS, A BIT.
I DID JUST RESTORE THE TIMELINE OF AN INTERCHRONAL MADMAN--
WHICH, WHEN DISRUPTED, CREATES ITS OWN PARTICULAR CHAOS.
YOU HAVE CORRECTED MY SINGLE MOST GRIEVOUS ERROR.

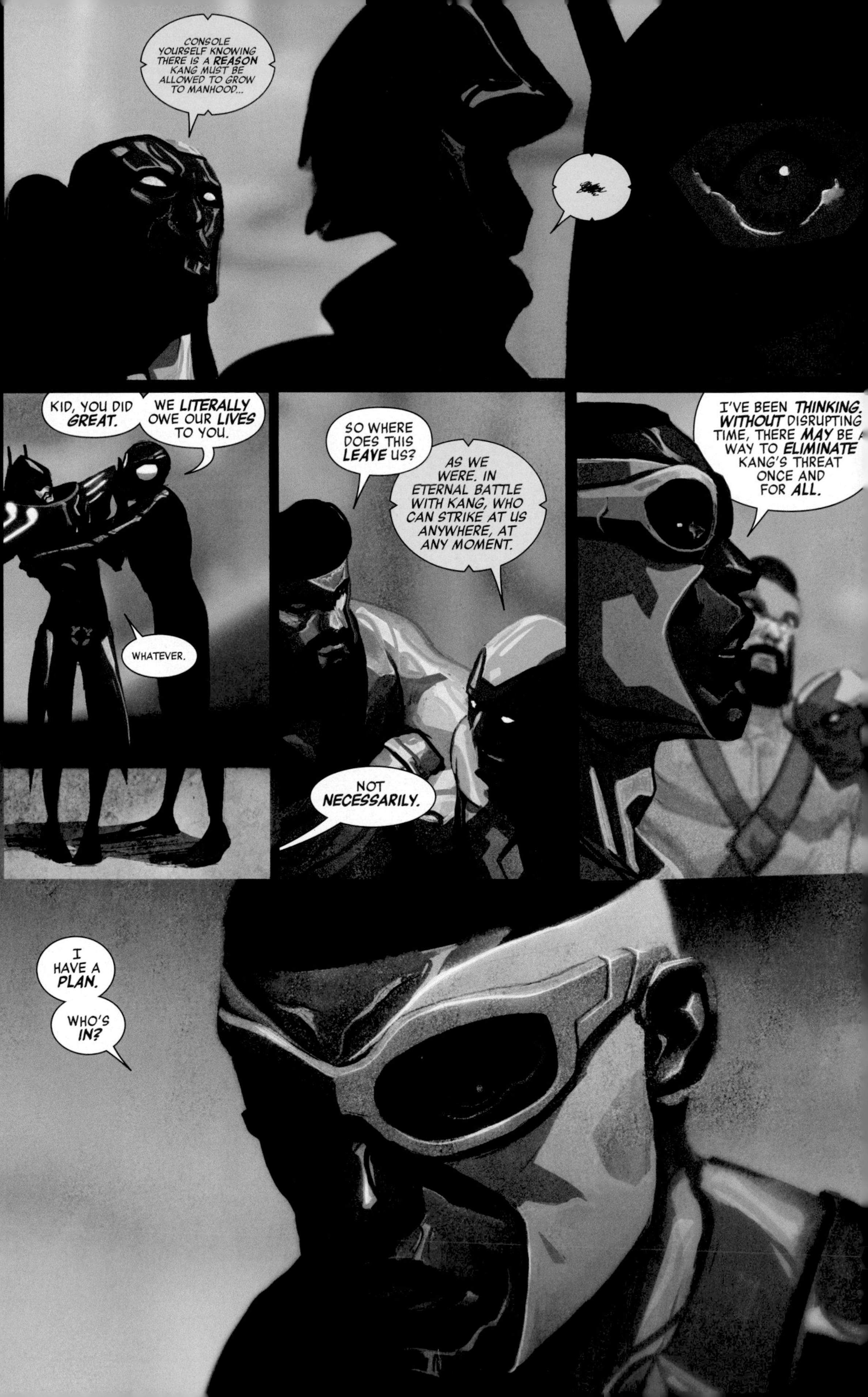
CONSOLE YOURSELF KNOWING THERE IS A REASON KANG MUST BE ALLOWED TO GROW TO MANHOOD...
KID, YOU DID GREAT.
WE LITERALLY OWE OUR LIVES TO YOU.
WHATEVER.
SO WHERE DOES THIS LEAVE US?
AS WE WERE. IN ETERNAL BATTLE WITH KANG, WHO CAN STRIKE AT US ANYWHERE, AT ANY MOMENT.
NOT NECESSARILY.
I'VE BEEN THINKING. WITHOUT DISRUPTING TIME, THERE MAY BE A WAY TO ELIMINATE KANG'S THREAT ONCE AND FOR ALL.
I HAVE A PLAN.
WHO'S IN?

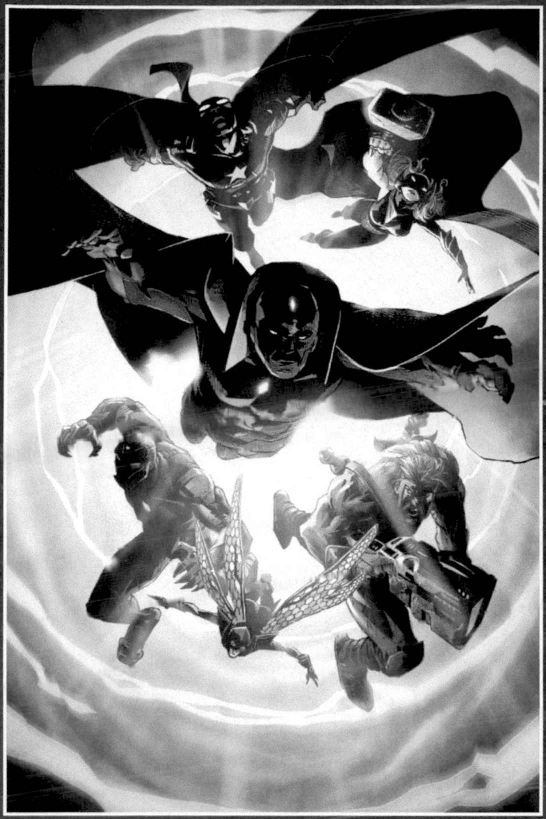

#1 VARIANT BY
ADAM KUBERT & SONIA OBACK

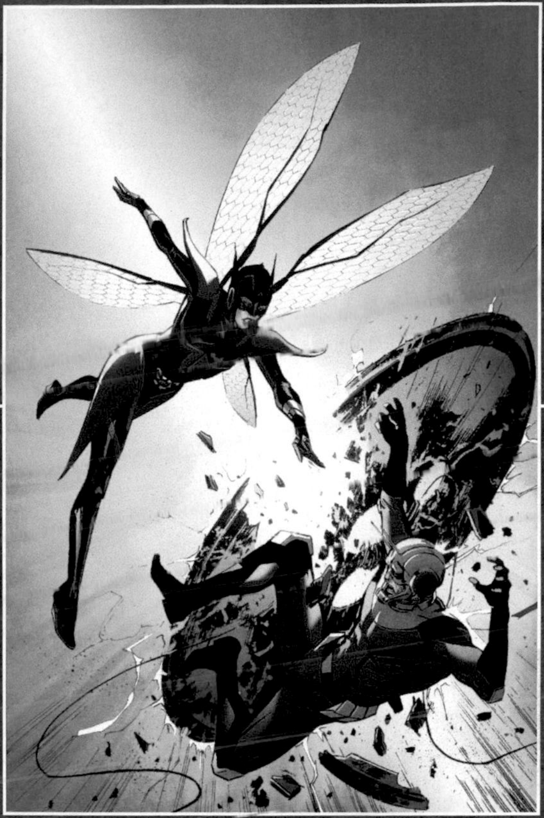

#1 DIVIDED WE STAND VARIANT BY
BUTCH GUICE & RACHELLE ROSENBERG

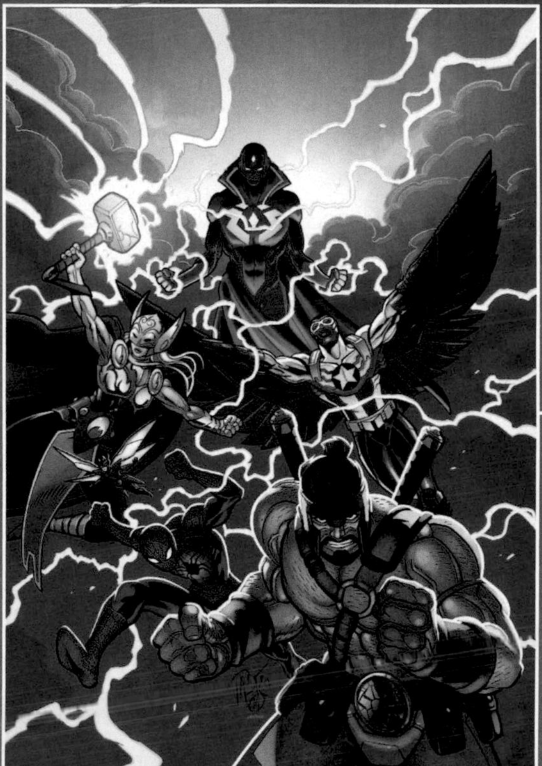

#1 DISNEY VARIANT BY
LORENZO PASTROVICCHIO & CHRIS SOTOMAYOR

4

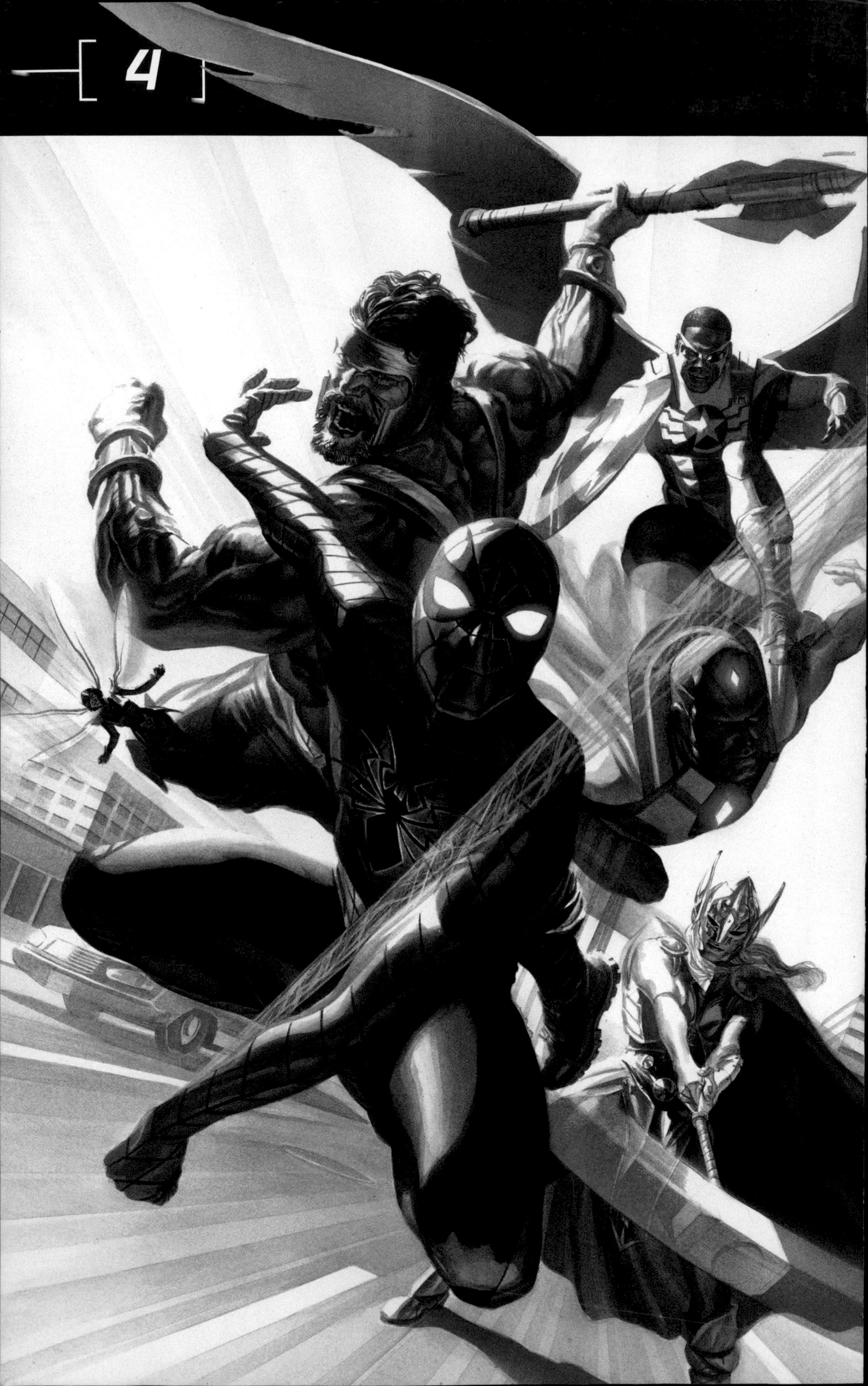

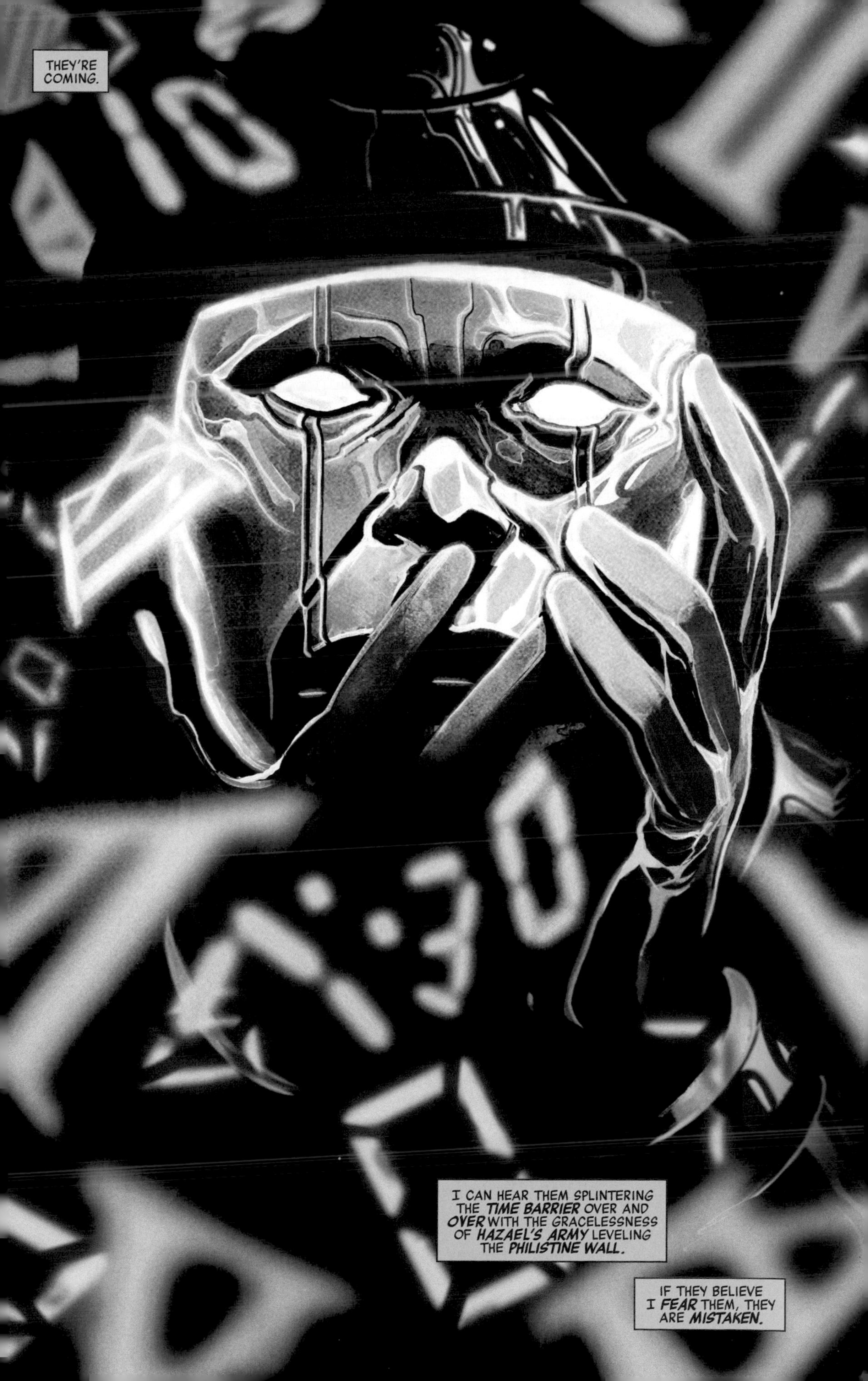
THEY'RE COMING.
I CAN HEAR THEM SPLINTERING THE TIME BARRIER OVER AND OVER WITH THE GRACELESSNESS OF HAZAEL'S ARMY LEVELING THE PHILISTINE WALL.
IF THEY BELIEVE I FEAR THEM, THEY ARE MISTAKEN.

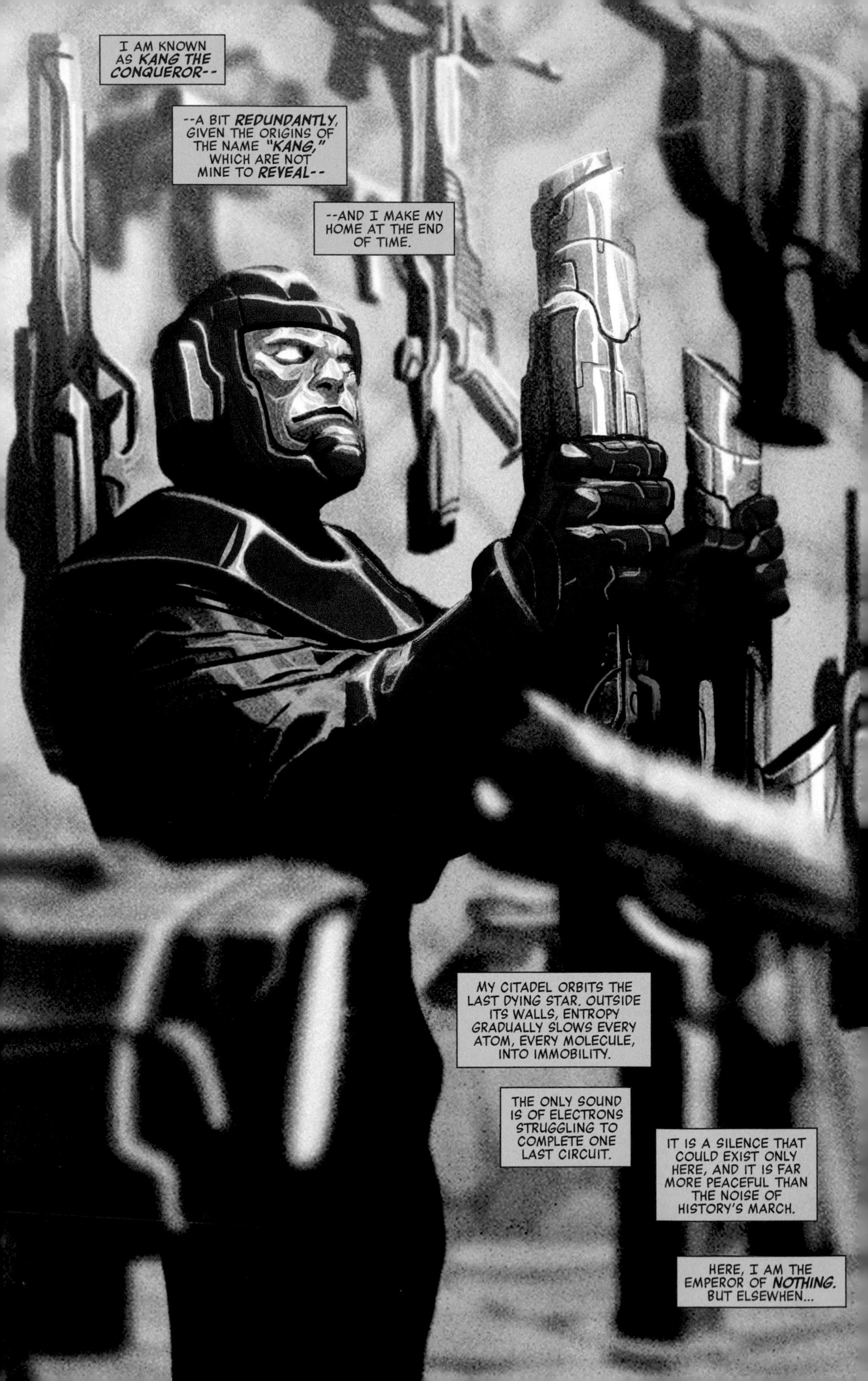
I AM KNOWN AS *KANG THE CONQUEROR*--
--A BIT *REDUNDANTLY*, GIVEN THE ORIGINS OF THE NAME *"KANG,"* WHICH ARE NOT MINE TO *REVEAL*--
--AND I MAKE MY HOME AT THE END OF TIME.
MY CITADEL ORBITS THE LAST DYING STAR. OUTSIDE ITS WALLS, ENTROPY GRADUALLY SLOWS EVERY ATOM, EVERY MOLECULE, INTO IMMOBILITY.
THE ONLY SOUND IS OF ELECTRONS STRUGGLING TO COMPLETE ONE LAST CIRCUIT.
IT IS A SILENCE THAT COULD EXIST ONLY HERE, AND IT IS FAR MORE PEACEFUL THAN THE NOISE OF HISTORY'S MARCH.
HERE, I AM THE EMPEROR OF *NOTHING*. BUT ELSEWHEN...

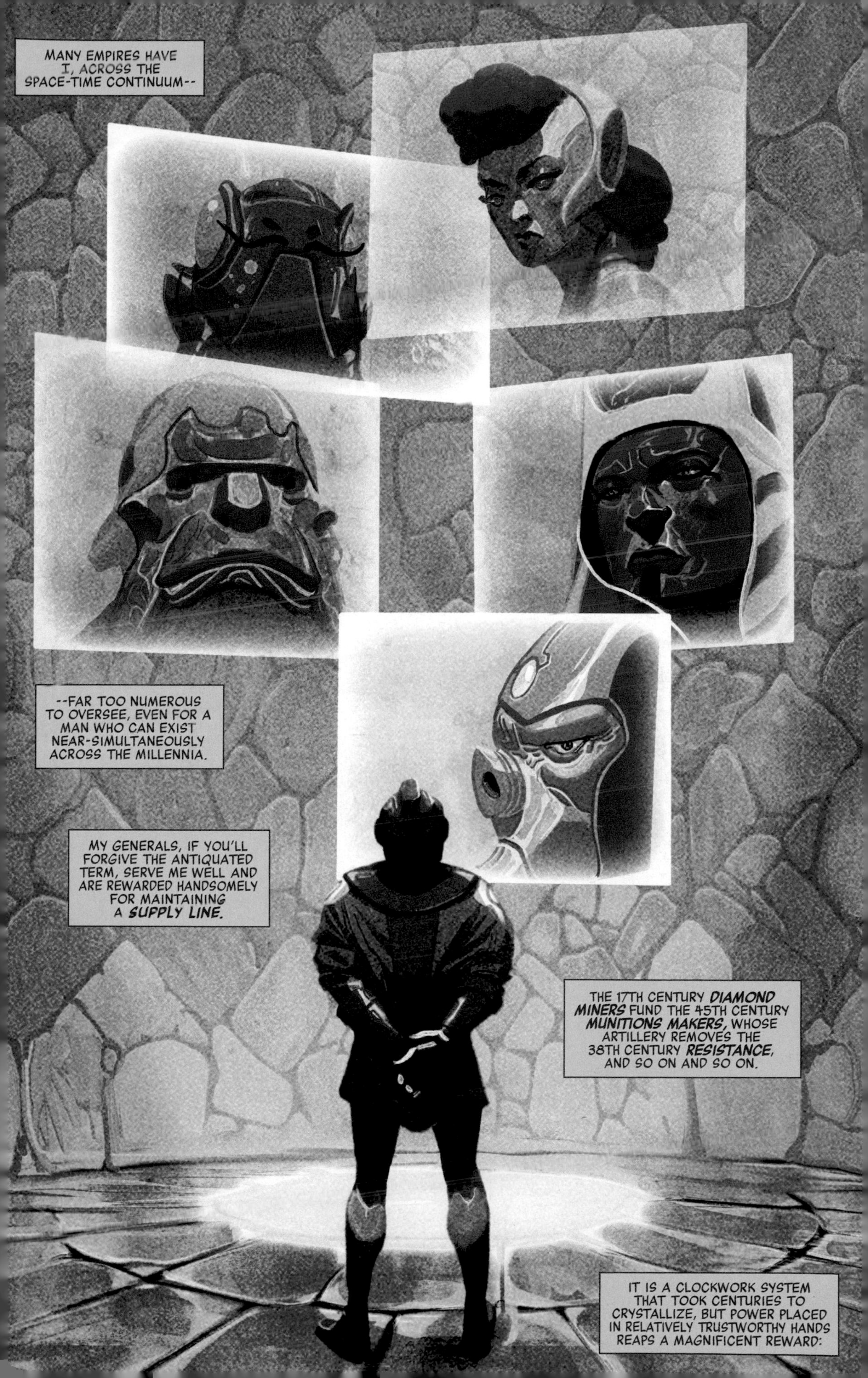
MANY EMPIRES HAVE I, ACROSS THE SPACE-TIME CONTINUUM--
--FAR TOO NUMEROUS TO OVERSEE, EVEN FOR A MAN WHO CAN EXIST NEAR-SIMULTANEOUSLY ACROSS THE MILLENNIA.
MY GENERALS, IF YOU'LL FORGIVE THE ANTIQUATED TERM, SERVE ME WELL AND ARE REWARDED HANDSOMELY FOR MAINTAINING A SUPPLY LINE.
THE 17TH CENTURY DIAMOND MINERS FUND THE 45TH CENTURY MUNITIONS MAKERS, WHOSE ARTILLERY REMOVES THE 38TH CENTURY RESISTANCE, AND SO ON AND SO ON.
IT IS A CLOCKWORK SYSTEM THAT TOOK CENTURIES TO CRYSTALLIZE, BUT POWER PLACED IN RELATIVELY TRUSTWORTHY HANDS REAPS A MAGNIFICENT REWARD:

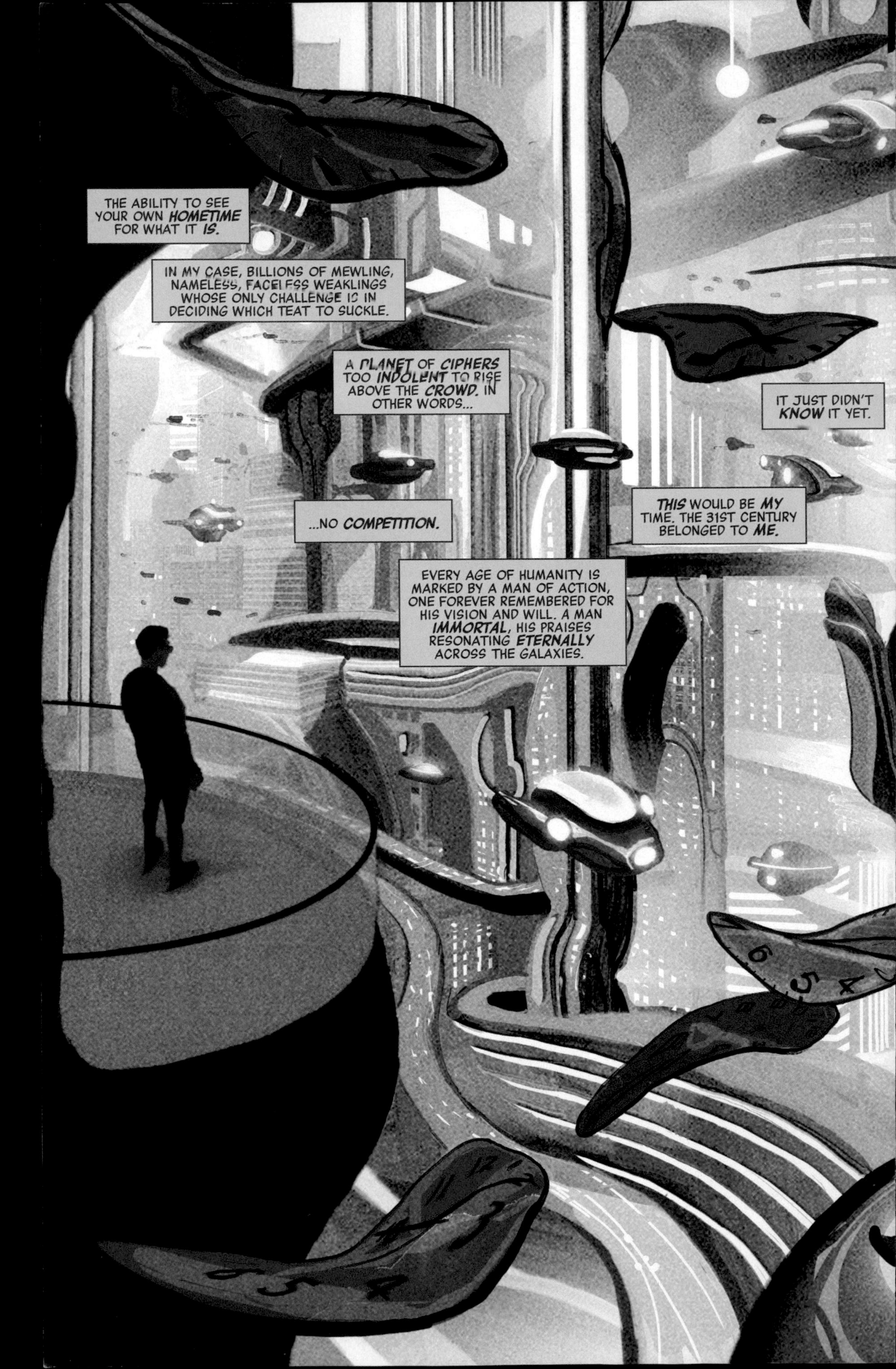

THE ABILITY TO SEE YOUR OWN HOMETIME FOR WHAT IT IS.
IN MY CASE, BILLIONS OF MEWLING, NAMELESS, FACELESS WEAKLINGS WHOSE ONLY CHALLENGE IS IN DECIDING WHICH TEAT TO SUCKLE.
A PLANET OF CIPHERS TOO INDOLENT TO RISE ABOVE THE CROWD. IN OTHER WORDS...
...NO COMPETITION.
IT JUST DIDN'T KNOW IT YET.
THIS WOULD BE MY TIME. THE 31ST CENTURY BELONGED TO ME.
EVERY AGE OF HUMANITY IS MARKED BY A MAN OF ACTION, ONE FOREVER REMEMBERED FOR HIS VISION AND WILL. A MAN IMMORTAL, HIS PRAISES RESONATING ETERNALLY ACROSS THE GALAXIES.

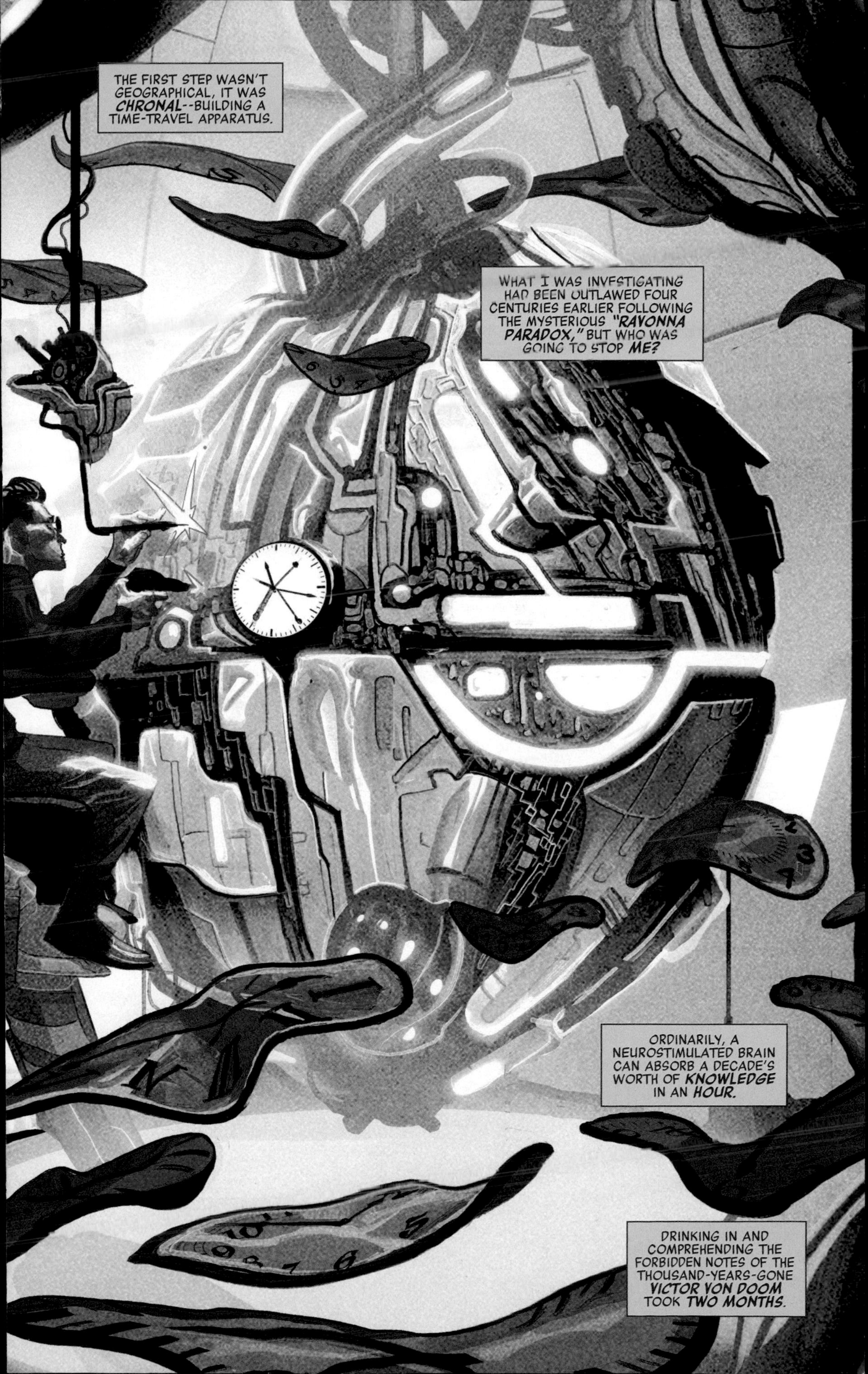

THE FIRST STEP WASN'T GEOGRAPHICAL, IT WAS CHRONAL--BUILDING A TIME-TRAVEL APPARATUS.
WHAT I WAS INVESTIGATING HAD BEEN OUTLAWED FOUR CENTURIES EARLIER FOLLOWING THE MYSTERIOUS "RAVONNA PARADOX," BUT WHO WAS GOING TO STOP ME?
ORDINARILY, A NEUROSTIMULATED BRAIN CAN ABSORB A DECADE'S WORTH OF KNOWLEDGE IN AN HOUR.
DRINKING IN AND COMPREHENDING THE FORBIDDEN NOTES OF THE THOUSAND-YEARS-GONE VICTOR VON DOOM TOOK TWO MONTHS.

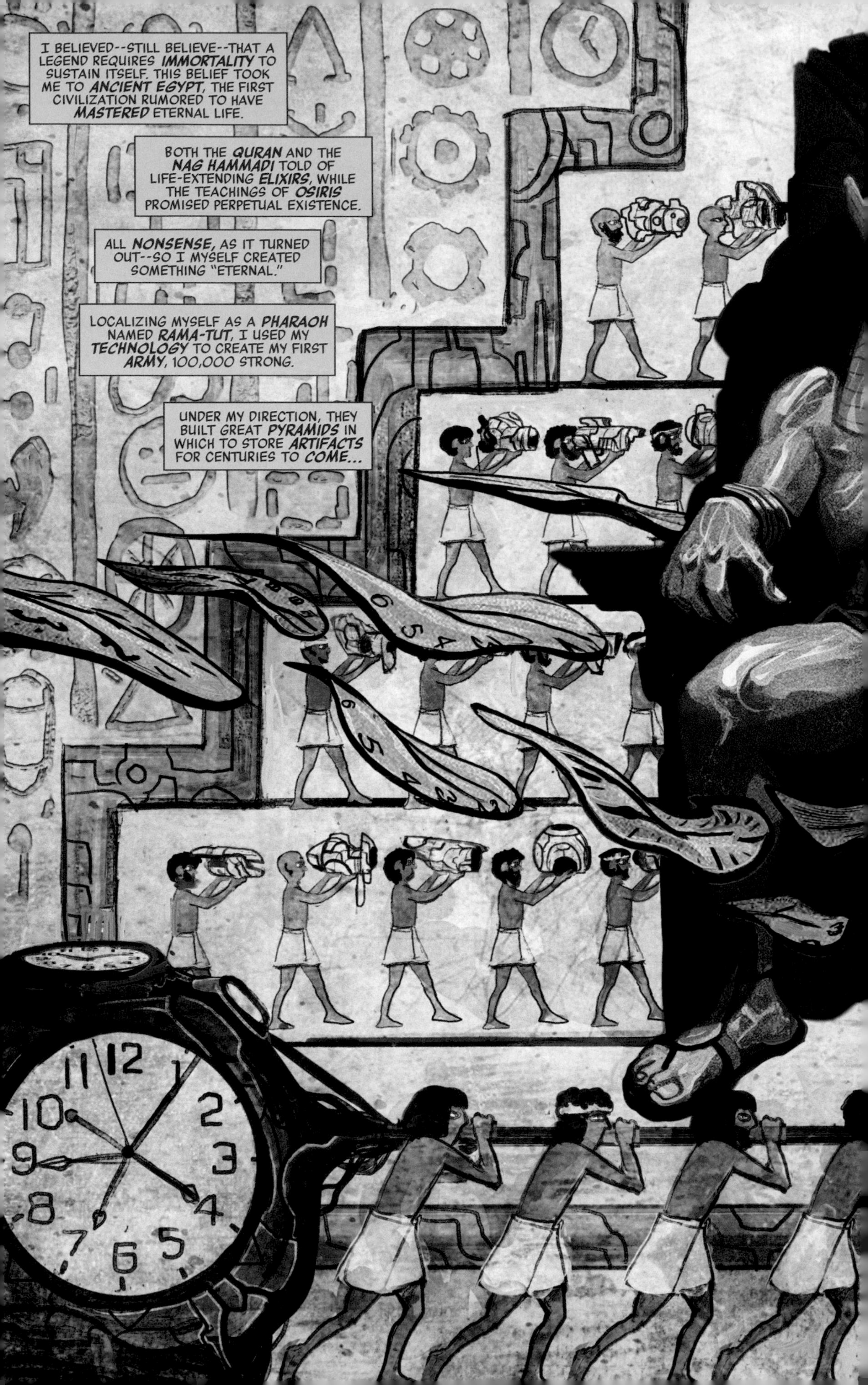
I BELIEVED--STILL BELIEVE--THAT A LEGEND REQUIRES IMMORTALITY TO SUSTAIN ITSELF. THIS BELIEF TOOK ME TO ANCIENT EGYPT, THE FIRST CIVILIZATION RUMORED TO HAVE MASTERED ETERNAL LIFE.
BOTH THE QURAN AND THE NAG HAMMADI TOLD OF LIFE-EXTENDING ELIXIRS, WHILE THE TEACHINGS OF OSIRIS PROMISED PERPETUAL EXISTENCE.
ALL NONSENSE, AS IT TURNED OUT--SO I MYSELF CREATED SOMETHING "ETERNAL."
LOCALIZING MYSELF AS A PHARAOH NAMED RAMA-TUT, I USED MY TECHNOLOGY TO CREATE MY FIRST ARMY, 100,000 STRONG.
UNDER MY DIRECTION, THEY BUILT GREAT PYRAMIDS IN WHICH TO STORE ARTIFACTS FOR CENTURIES TO COME...

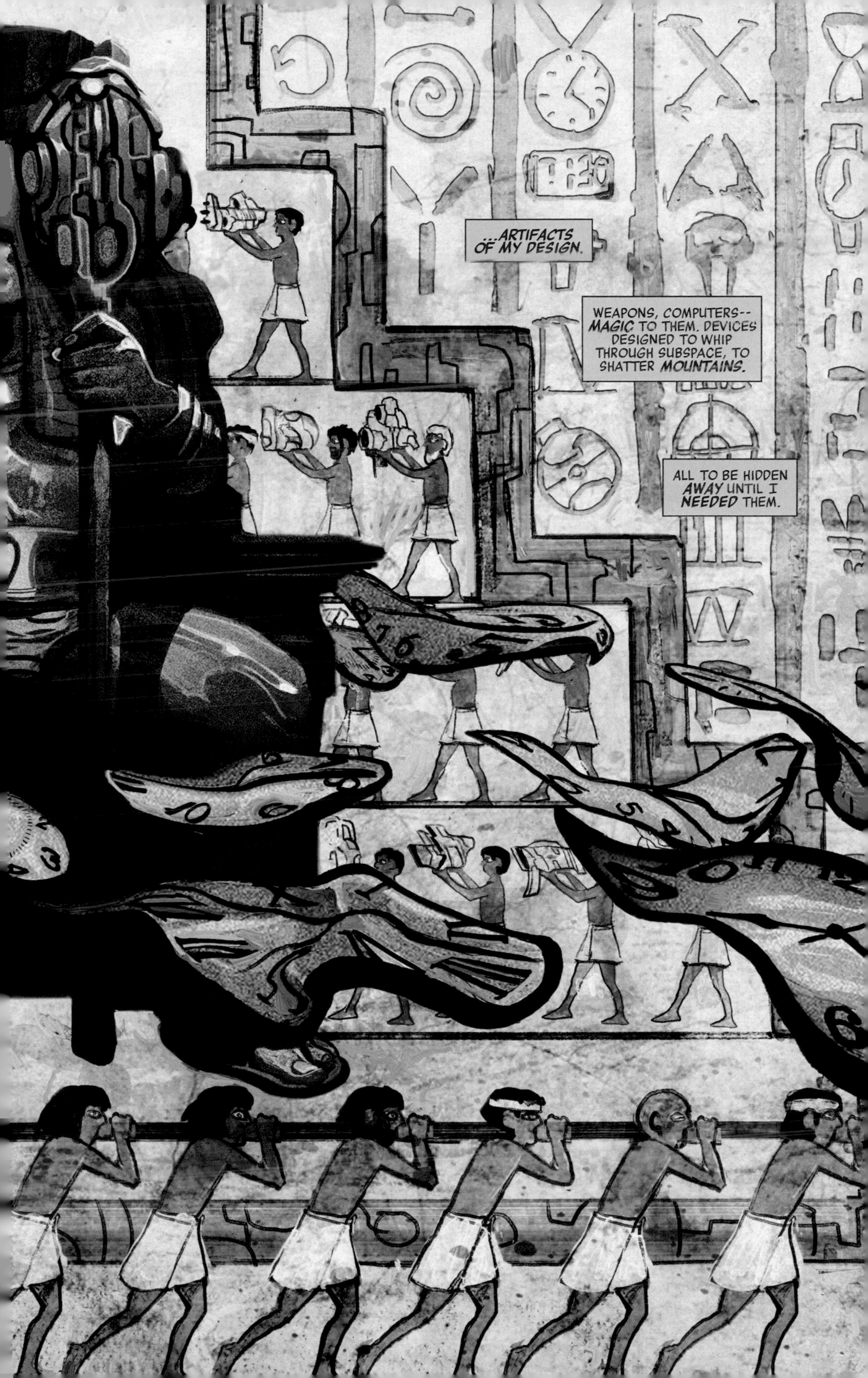
...ARTIFACTS OF MY DESIGN.
WEAPONS, COMPUTERS-- MAGIC TO THEM. DEVICES DESIGNED TO WHIP THROUGH SUBSPACE, TO SHATTER MOUNTAINS.
ALL TO BE HIDDEN AWAY UNTIL I NEEDED THEM.

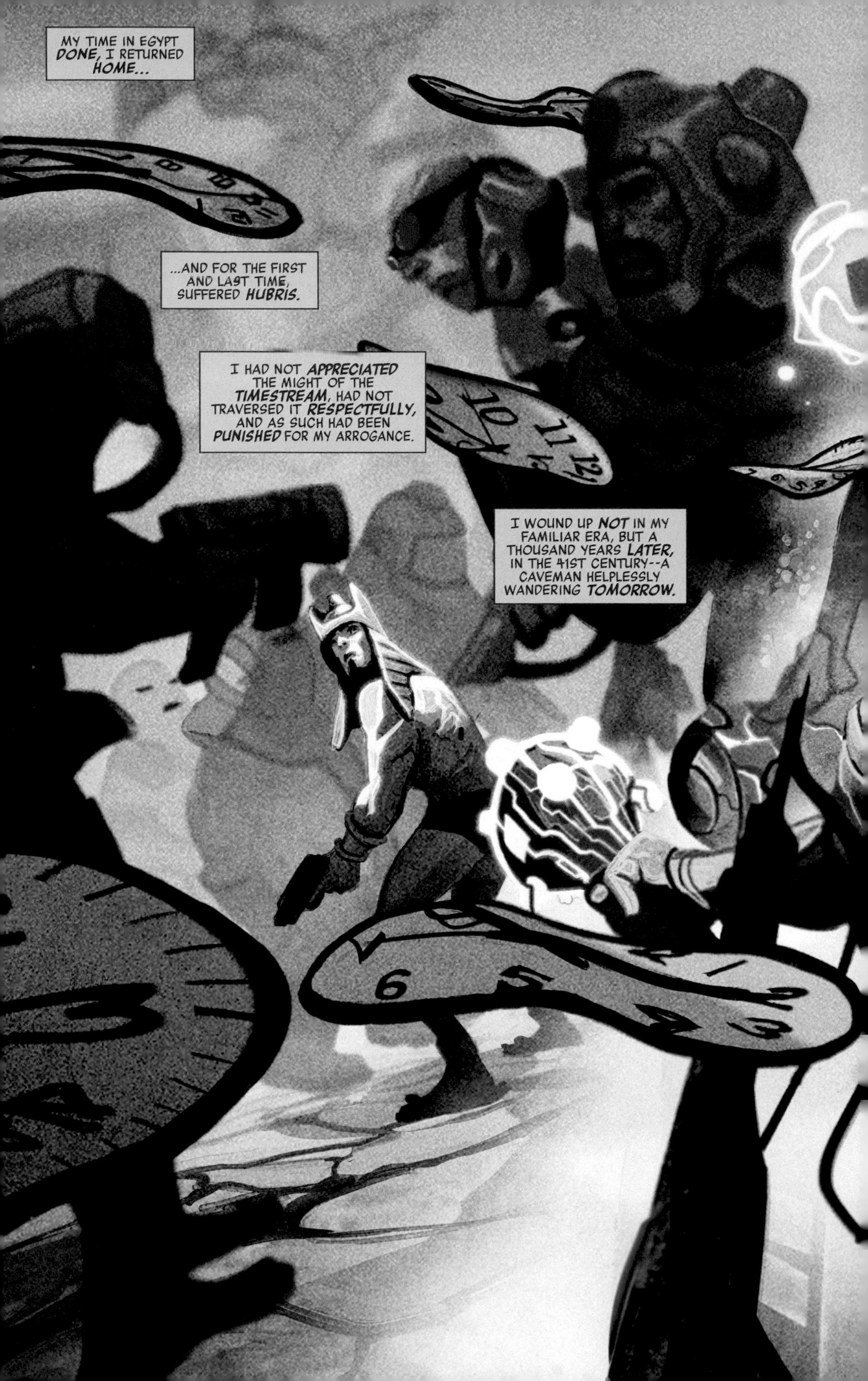
MY TIME IN EGYPT DONE, I RETURNED HOME...
...AND FOR THE FIRST AND LAST TIME, SUFFERED HUBRIS.
I HAD NOT APPRECIATED THE MIGHT OF THE TIMESTREAM, HAD NOT TRAVERSED IT RESPECTFULLY, AND AS SUCH HAD BEEN PUNISHED FOR MY ARROGANCE.
I WOUND UP NOT IN MY FAMILIAR ERA, BUT A THOUSAND YEARS LATER, IN THE 41ST CENTURY--A CAVEMAN HELPLESSLY WANDERING TOMORROW.

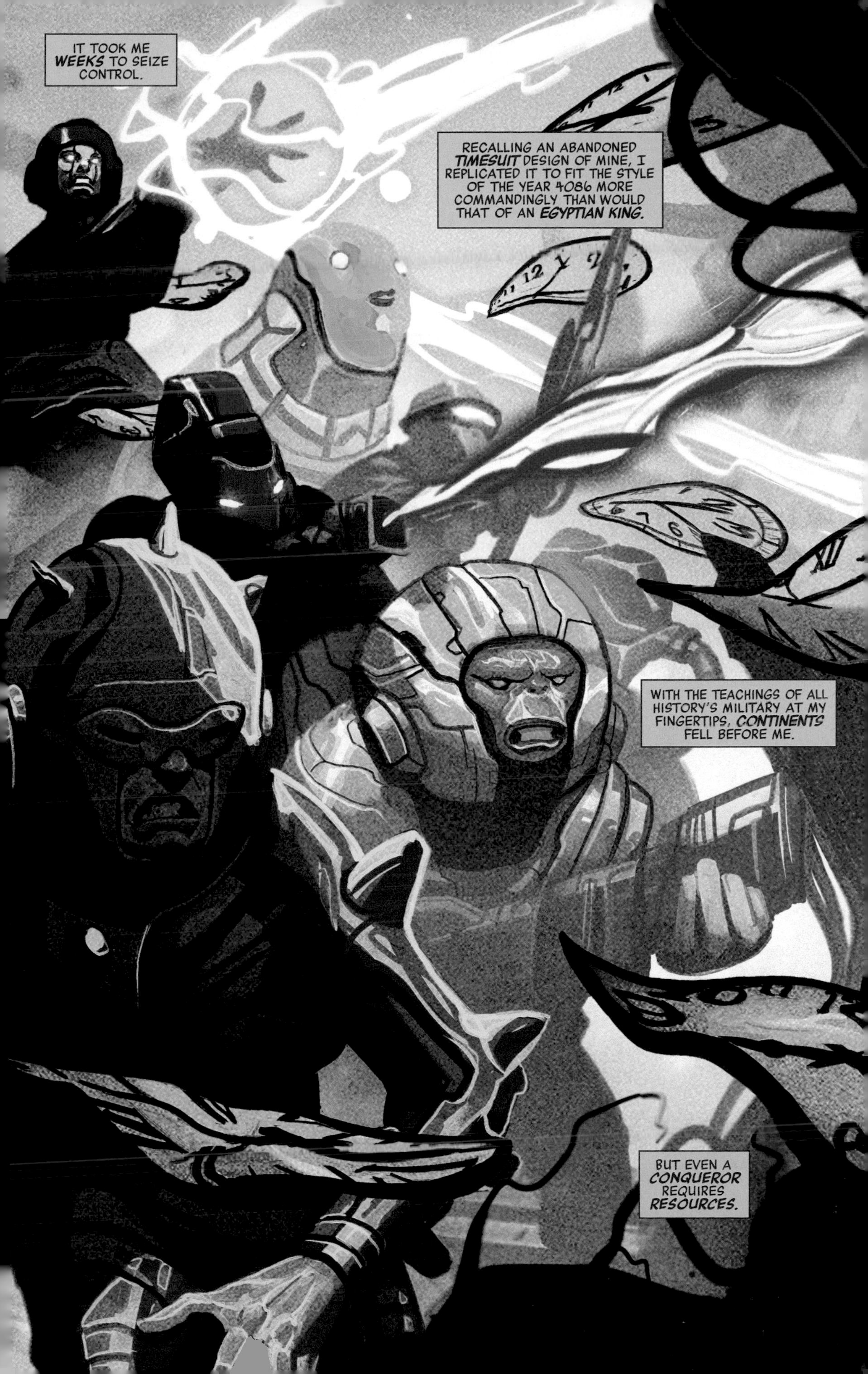
IT TOOK ME WEEKS TO SEIZE CONTROL.
RECALLING AN ABANDONED TIMESUIT DESIGN OF MINE, I REPLICATED IT TO FIT THE STYLE OF THE YEAR 4086 MORE COMMANDINGLY THAN WOULD THAT OF AN EGYPTIAN KING.
WITH THE TEACHINGS OF ALL HISTORY'S MILITARY AT MY FINGERTIPS, CONTINENTS FELL BEFORE ME.
BUT EVEN A CONQUEROR REQUIRES RESOURCES.

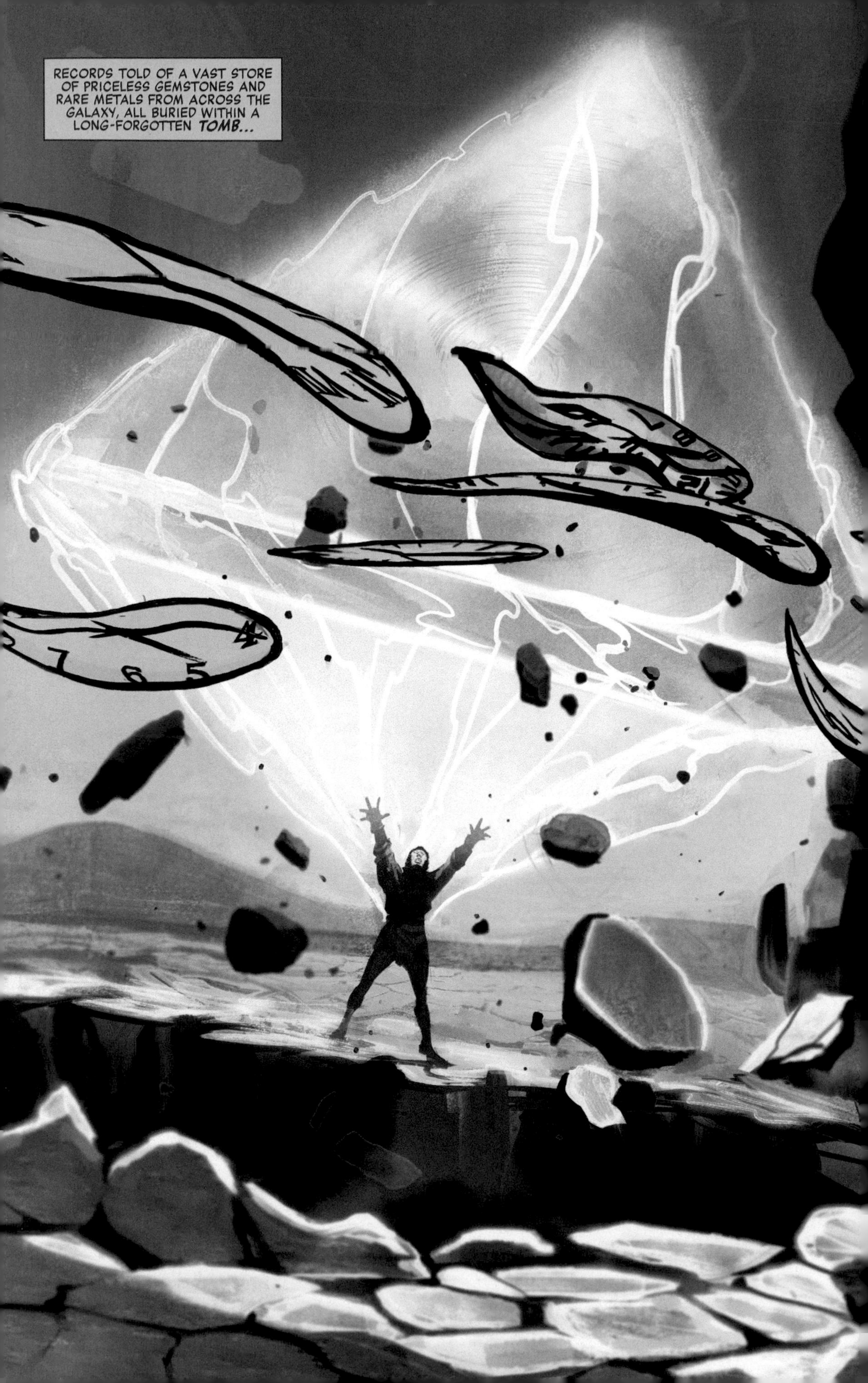
RECORDS TOLD OF A VAST STORE OF PRICELESS GEMSTONES AND RARE METALS FROM ACROSS THE GALAXY, ALL BURIED WITHIN A LONG-FORGOTTEN TOMB...

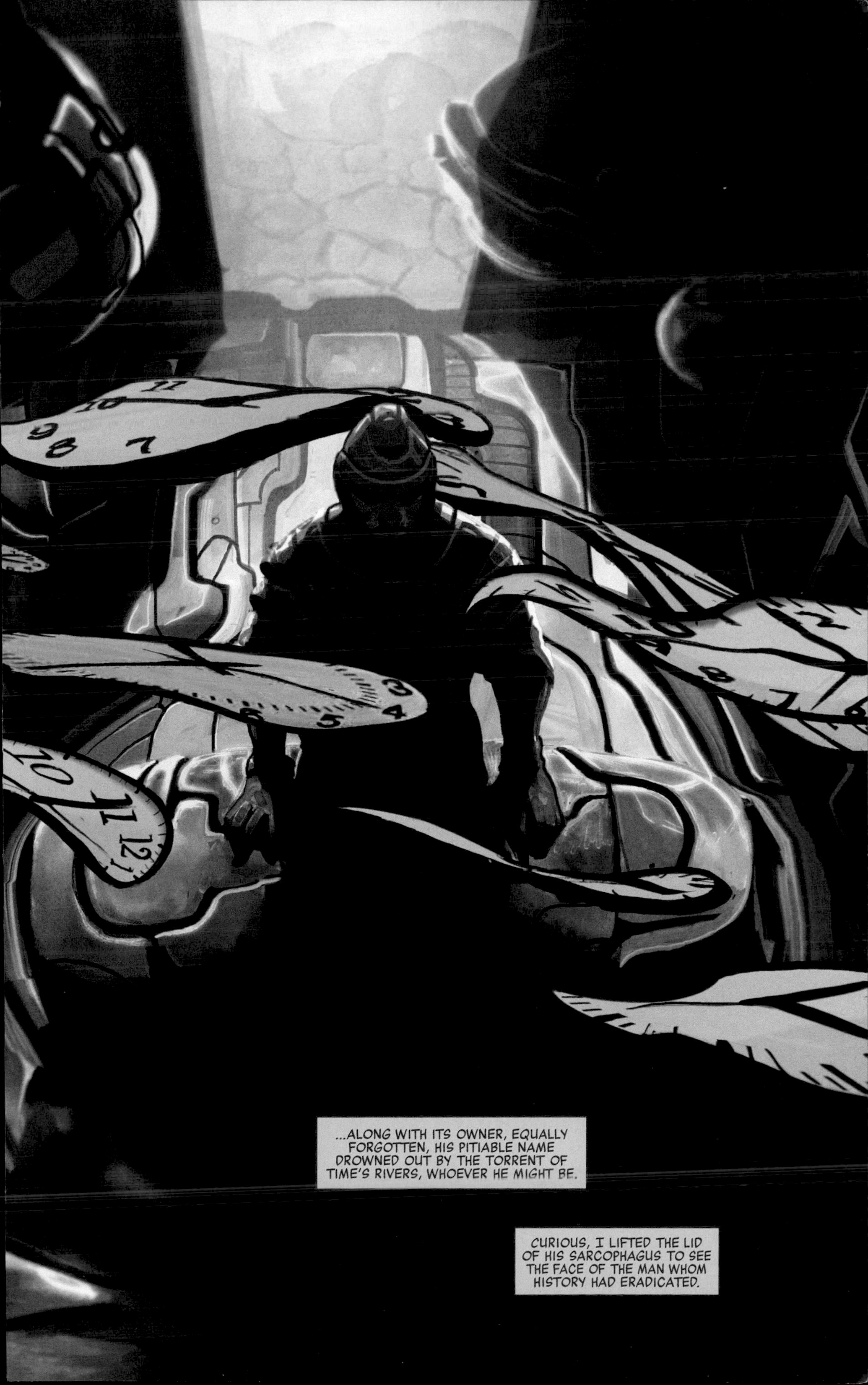
...ALONG WITH ITS OWNER, EQUALLY FORGOTTEN, HIS PITIABLE NAME DROWNED OUT BY THE TORRENT OF TIME'S RIVERS, WHOEVER HE MIGHT BE.
CURIOUS, I LIFTED THE LID OF HIS SARCOPHAGUS TO SEE THE FACE OF THE MAN WHOM HISTORY HAD ERADICATED.

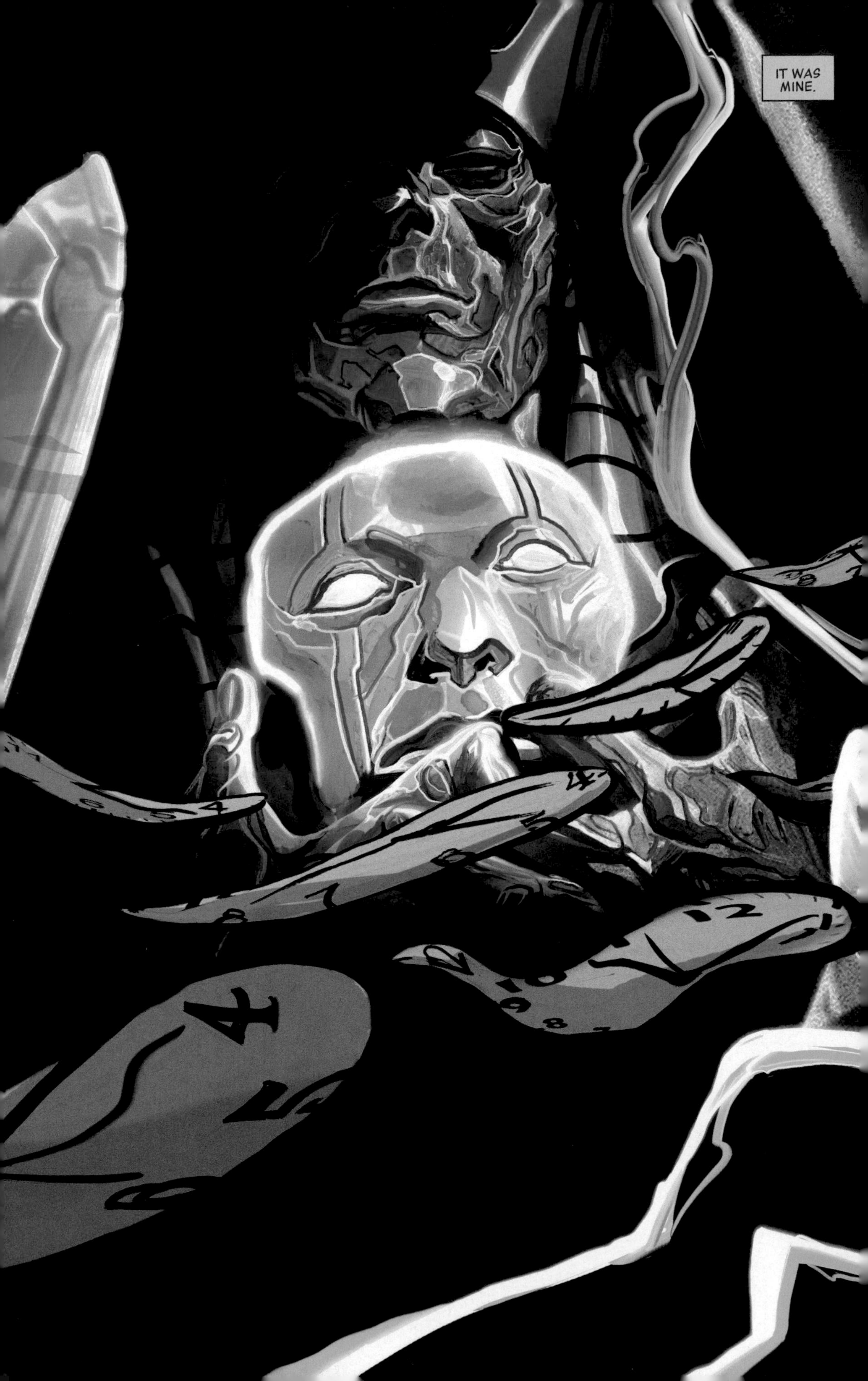
IT WAS MINE.

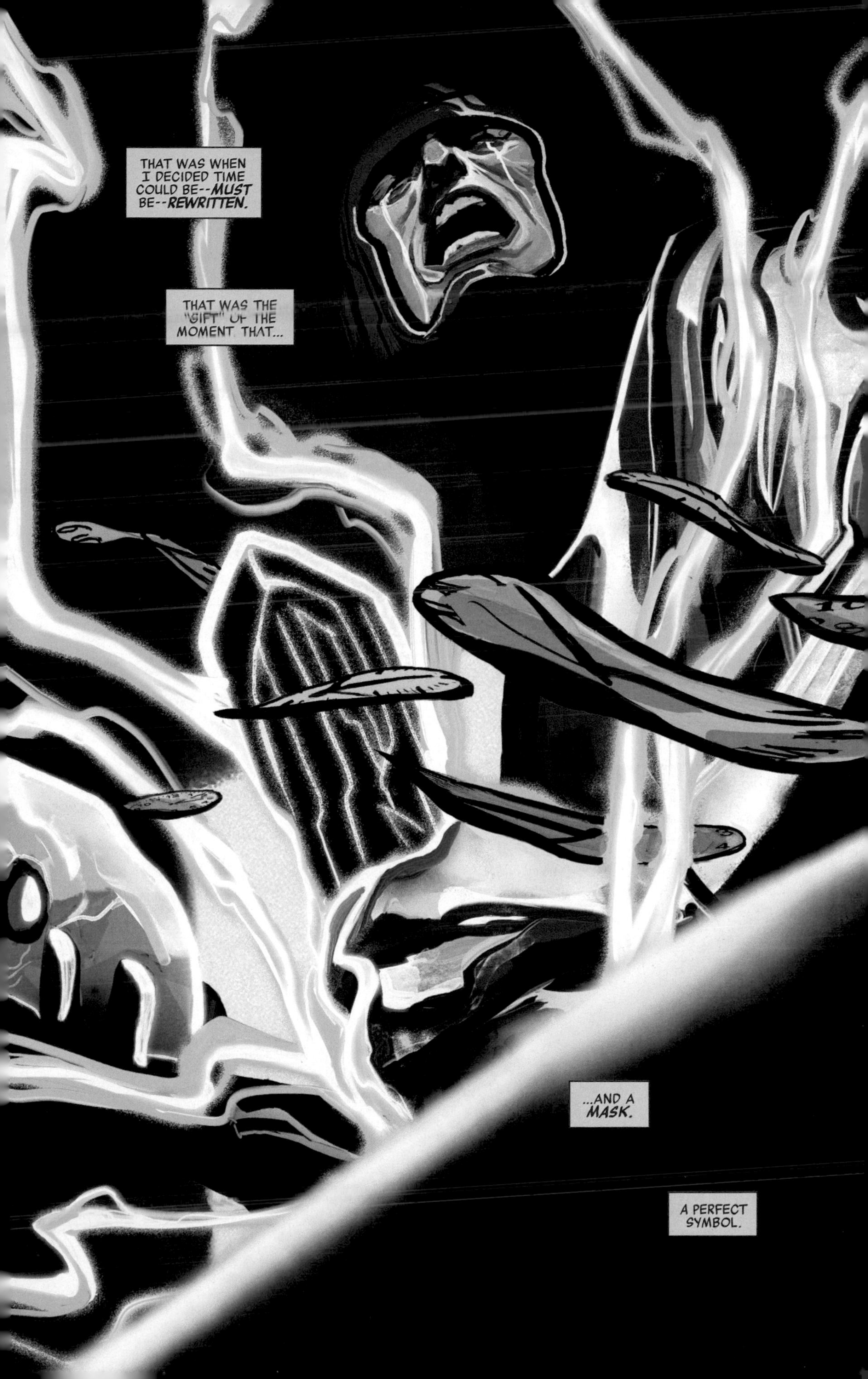
THAT WAS WHEN I DECIDED TIME COULD BE--MUST BE--REWRITTEN.
THAT WAS THE "GIFT" OF THE MOMENT THAT...
...AND A MASK.
A PERFECT SYMBOL.

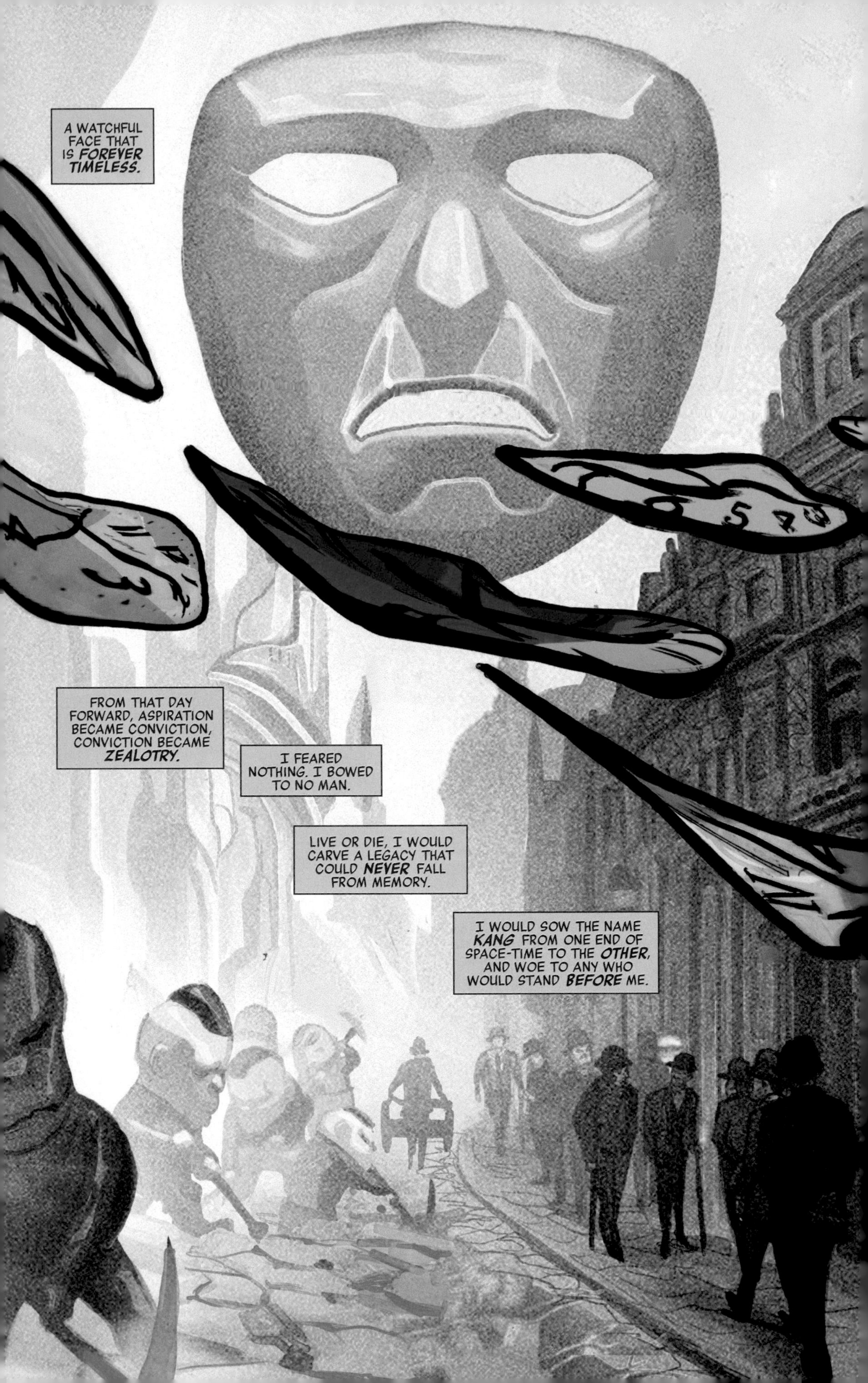
A WATCHFUL FACE THAT IS FOREVER TIMELESS.
FROM THAT DAY FORWARD, ASPIRATION BECAME CONVICTION, CONVICTION BECAME ZEALOTRY.
I FEARED NOTHING. I BOWED TO NO MAN.
LIVE OR DIE, I WOULD CARVE A LEGACY THAT COULD NEVER FALL FROM MEMORY.
I WOULD SOW THE NAME KANG FROM ONE END OF SPACE-TIME TO THE OTHER, AND WOE TO ANY WHO WOULD STAND BEFORE ME.

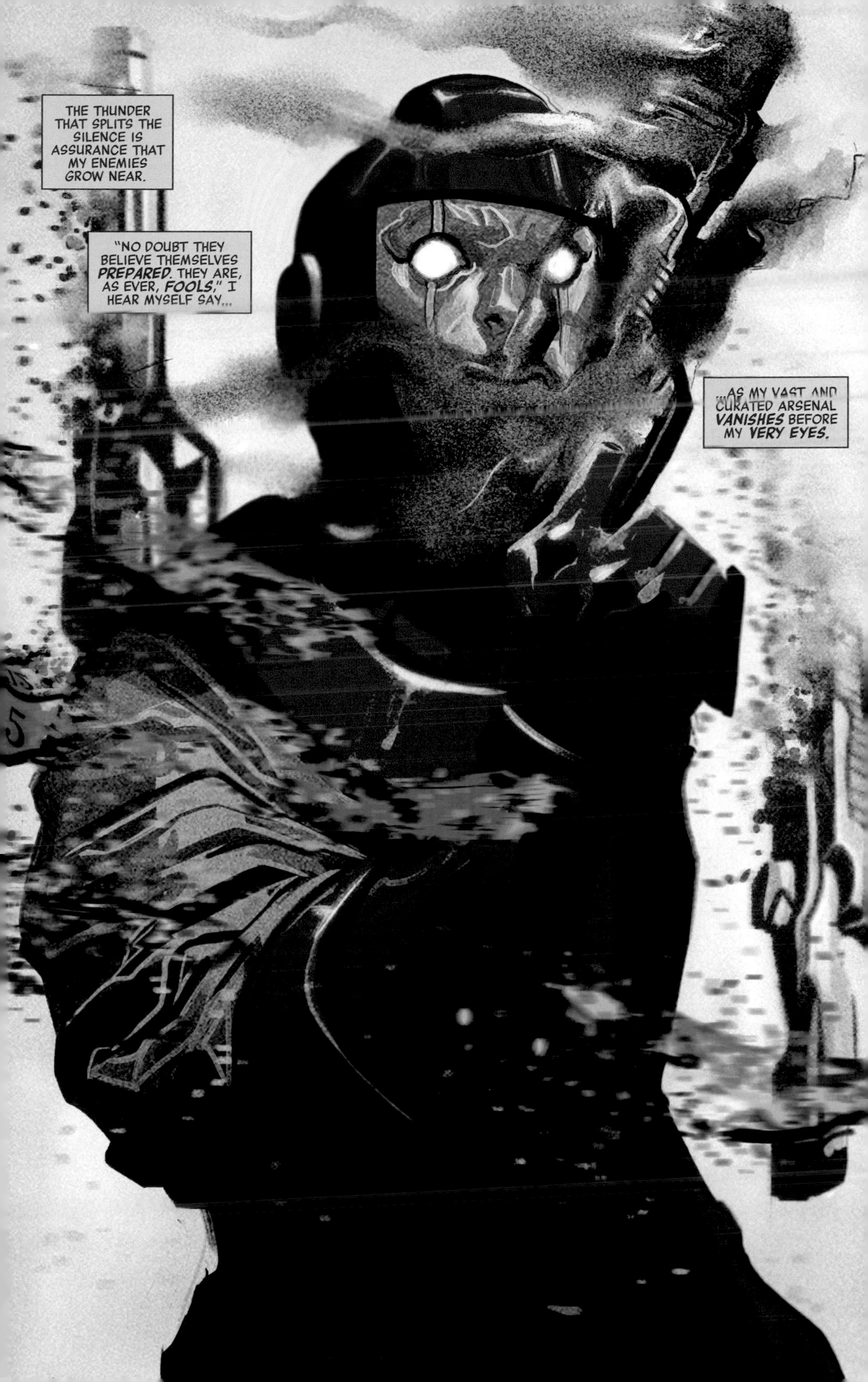
THE THUNDER THAT SPLITS THE SILENCE IS ASSURANCE THAT MY ENEMIES GROW NEAR.
"NO DOUBT THEY BELIEVE THEMSELVES **PREPARED**. THEY ARE, AS EVER, **FOOLS**," I HEAR MYSELF SAY...
...AS MY VAST AND CURATED ARSENAL **VANISHES** BEFORE MY **VERY EYES.**

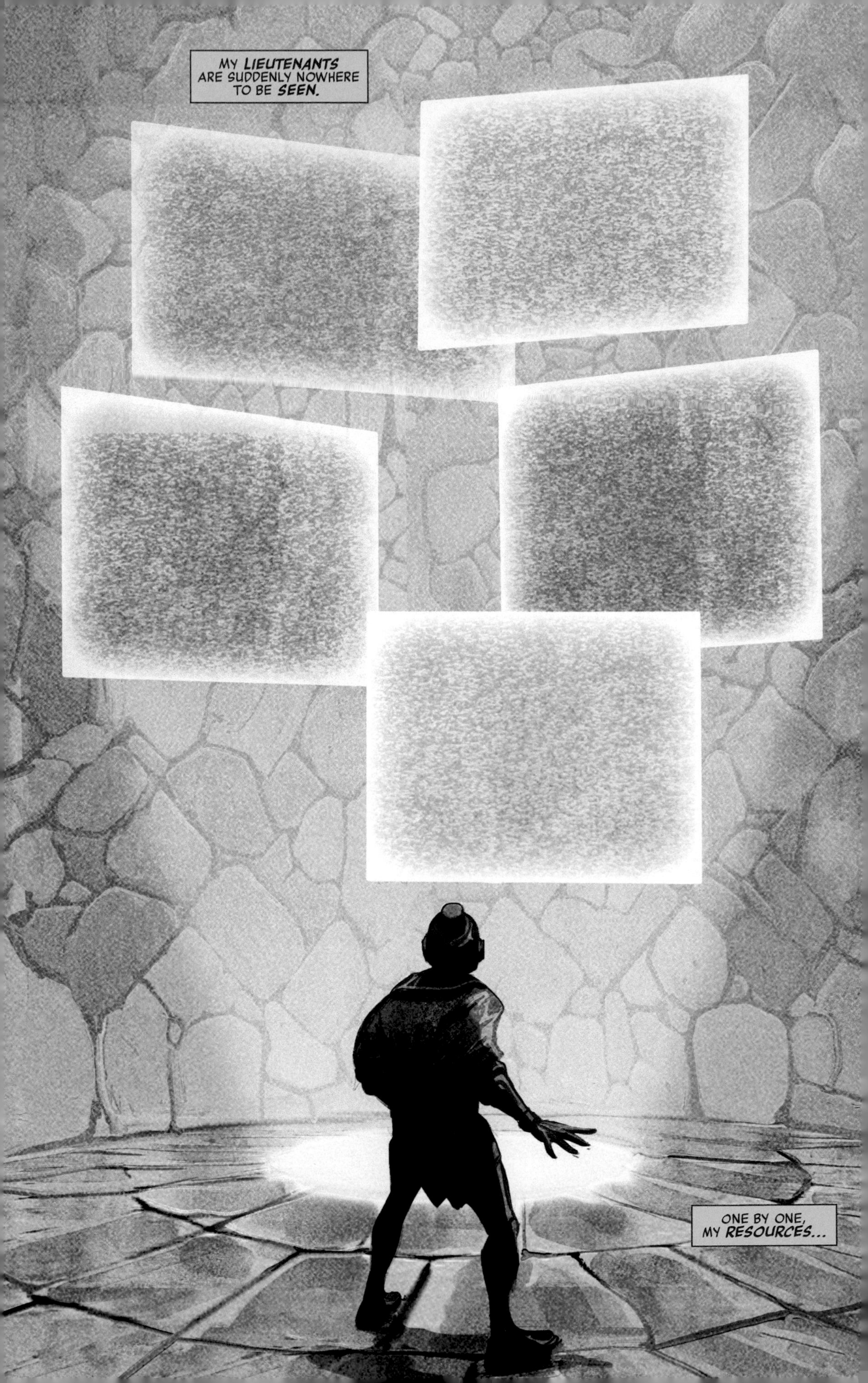
MY LIEUTENANTS ARE SUDDENLY NOWHERE TO BE SEEN.
ONE BY ONE, MY RESOURCES...

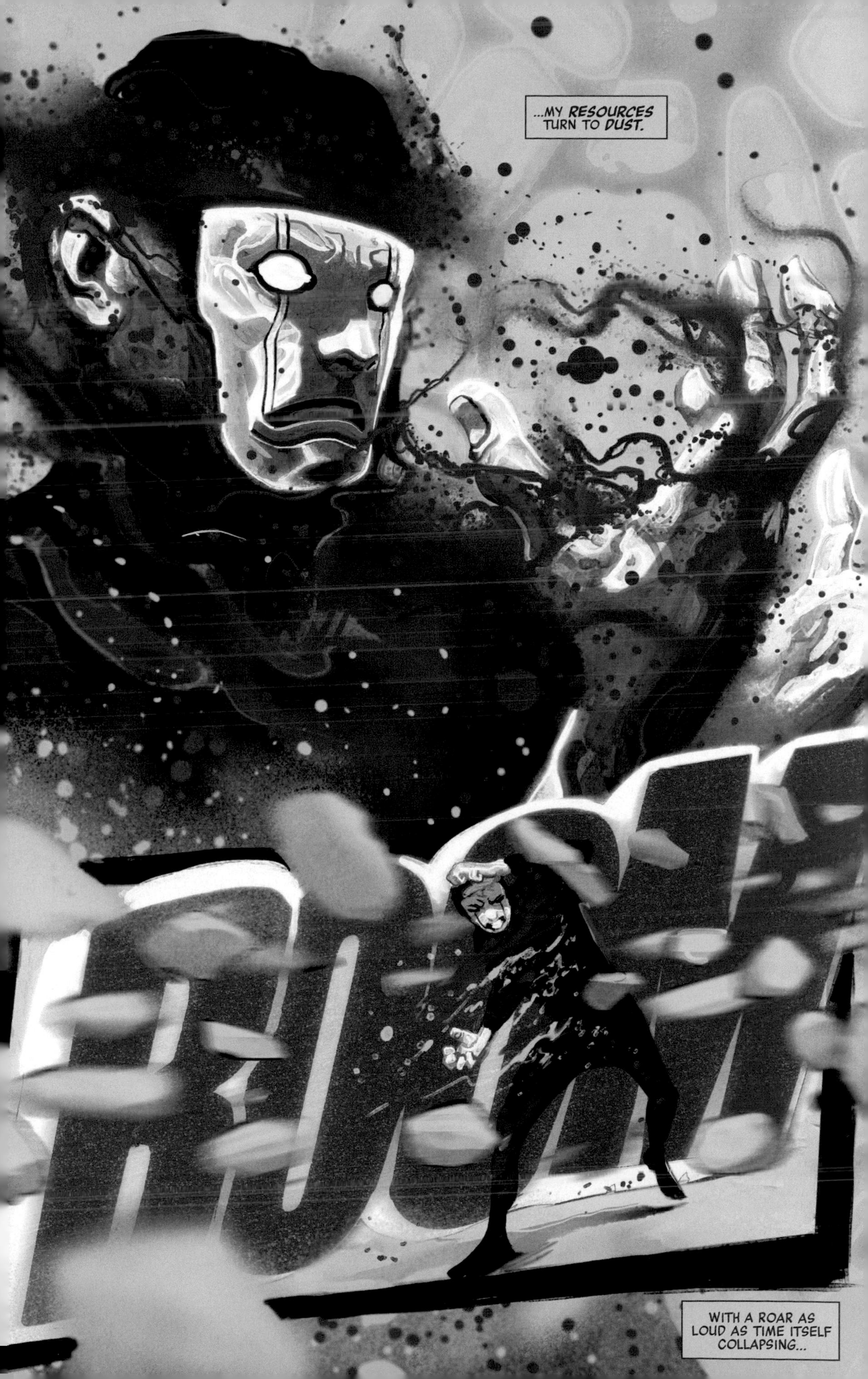
...MY RESOURCES TURN TO DUST.
WITH A ROAR AS LOUD AS TIME ITSELF COLLAPSING...

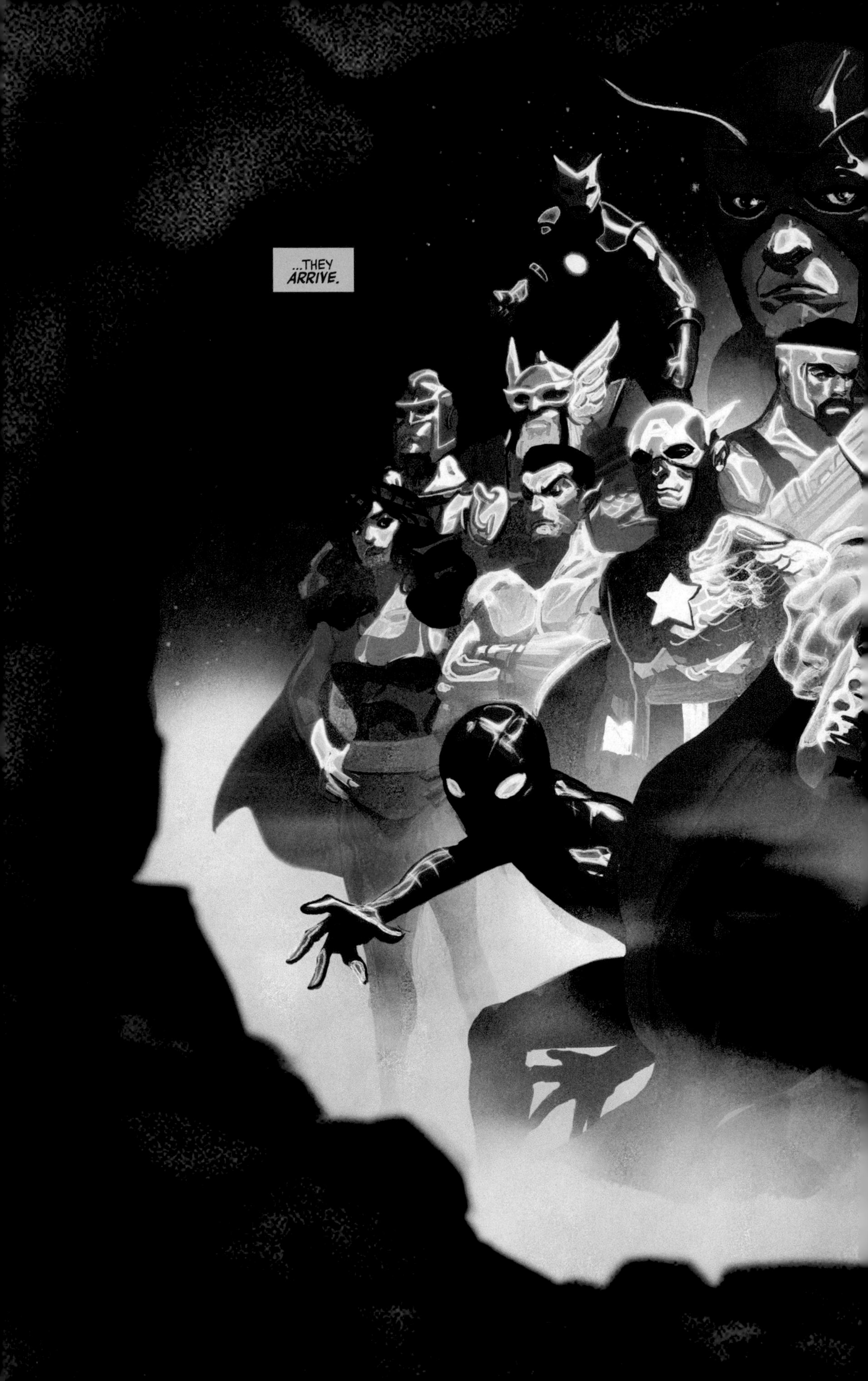
...THEY ARRIVE.

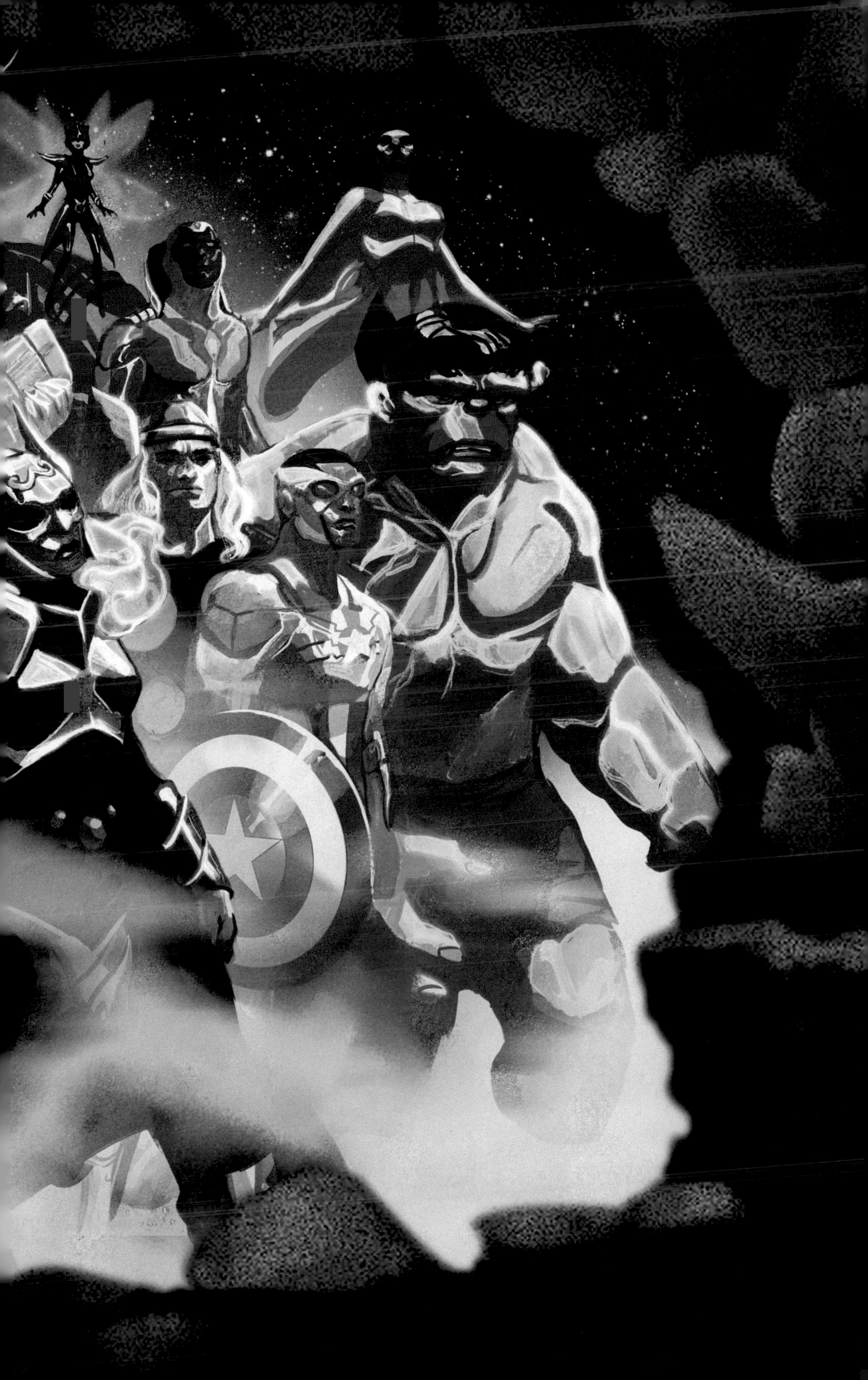

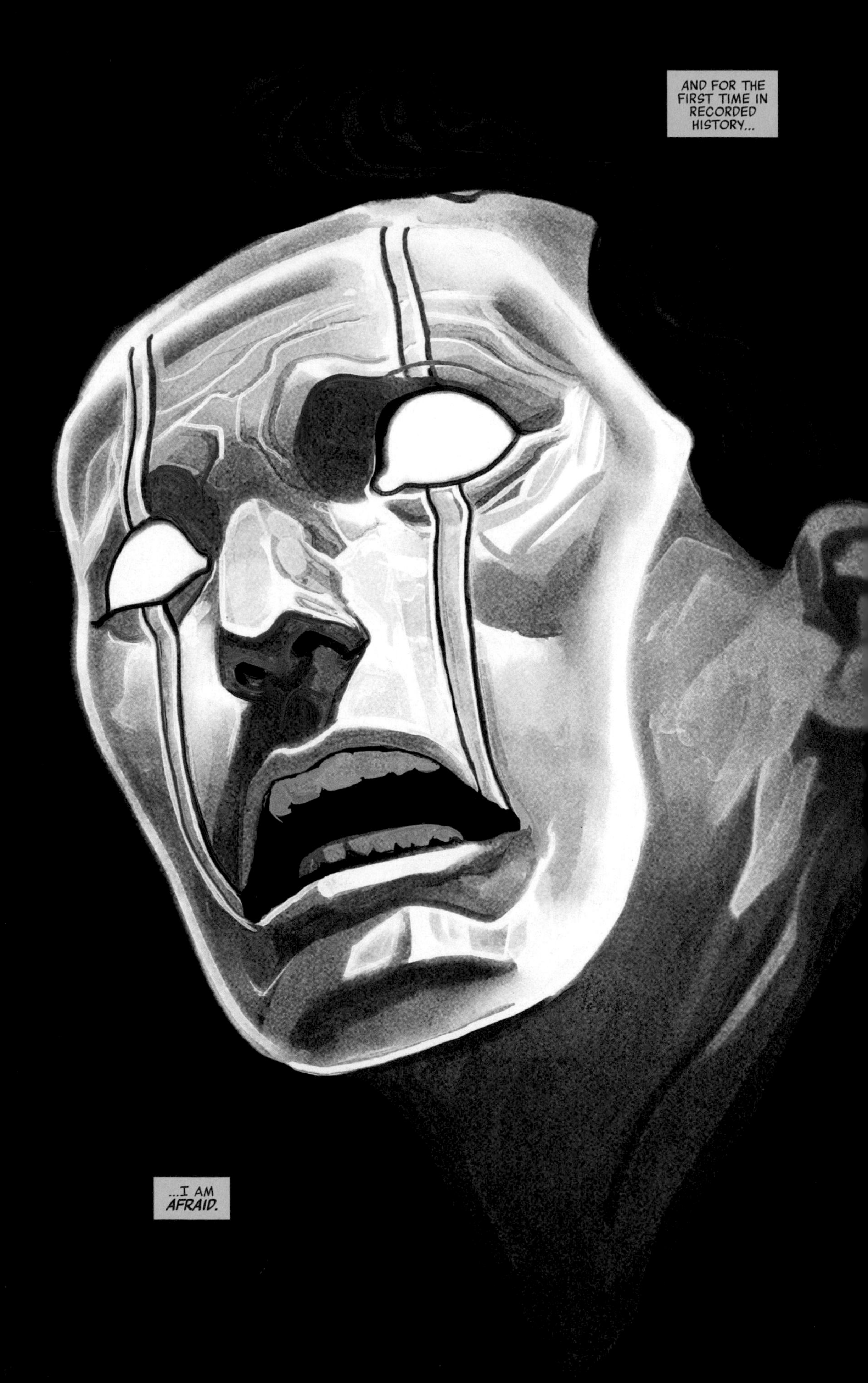
AND FOR THE FIRST TIME IN RECORDED HISTORY...
...I AM *AFRAID*.

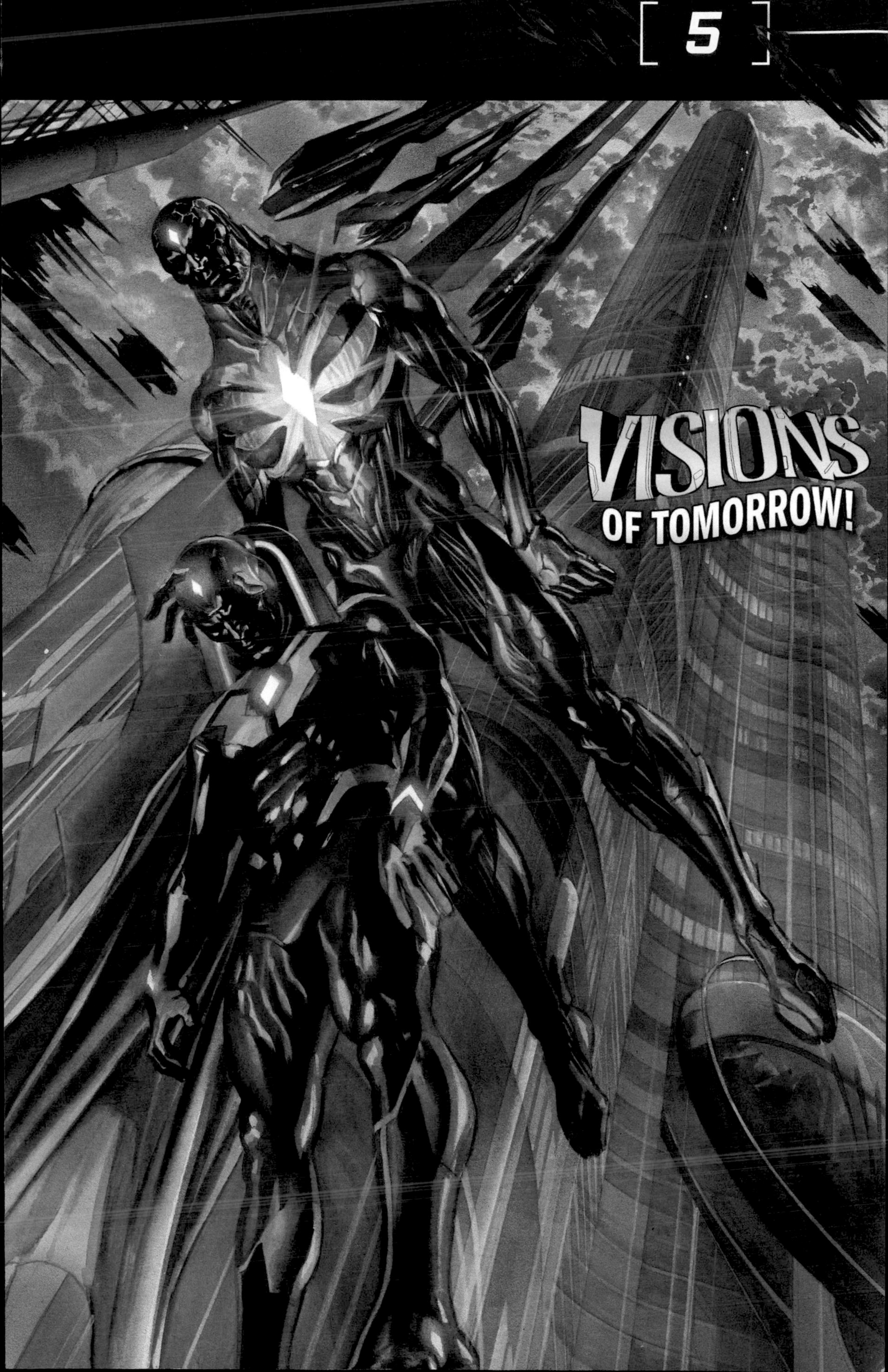
5
VISIONS
OF TOMORROW!

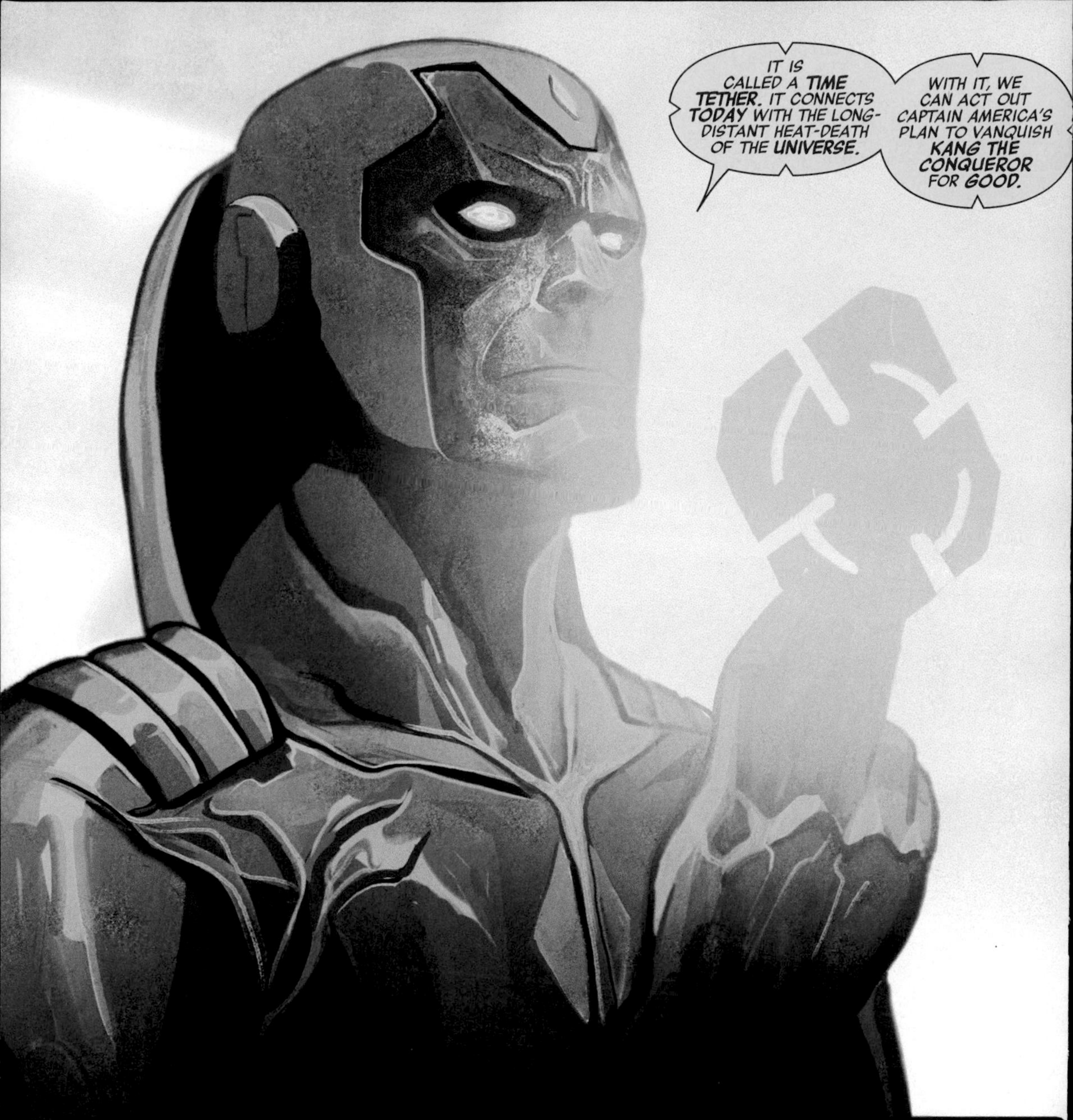
IT IS CALLED A TIME TETHER. IT CONNECTS TODAY WITH THE LONG-DISTANT HEAT-DEATH OF THE UNIVERSE.
WITH IT, WE CAN ACT OUT CAPTAIN AMERICA'S PLAN TO VANQUISH KANG THE CONQUEROR FOR GOOD.
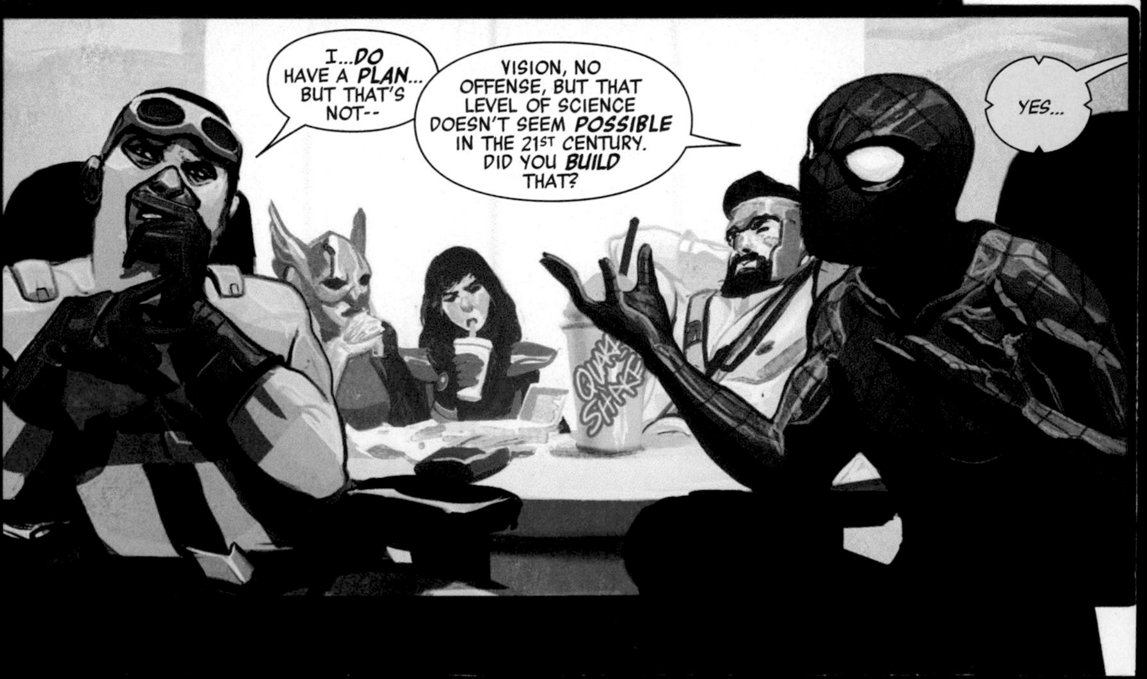
VISION, NO OFFENSE, BUT THAT LEVEL OF SCIENCE DOESN'T SEEM POSSIBLE IN THE 21ST CENTURY. DID YOU BUILD THAT?
YES...
I...DO HAVE A PLAN... BUT THAT'S NOT--

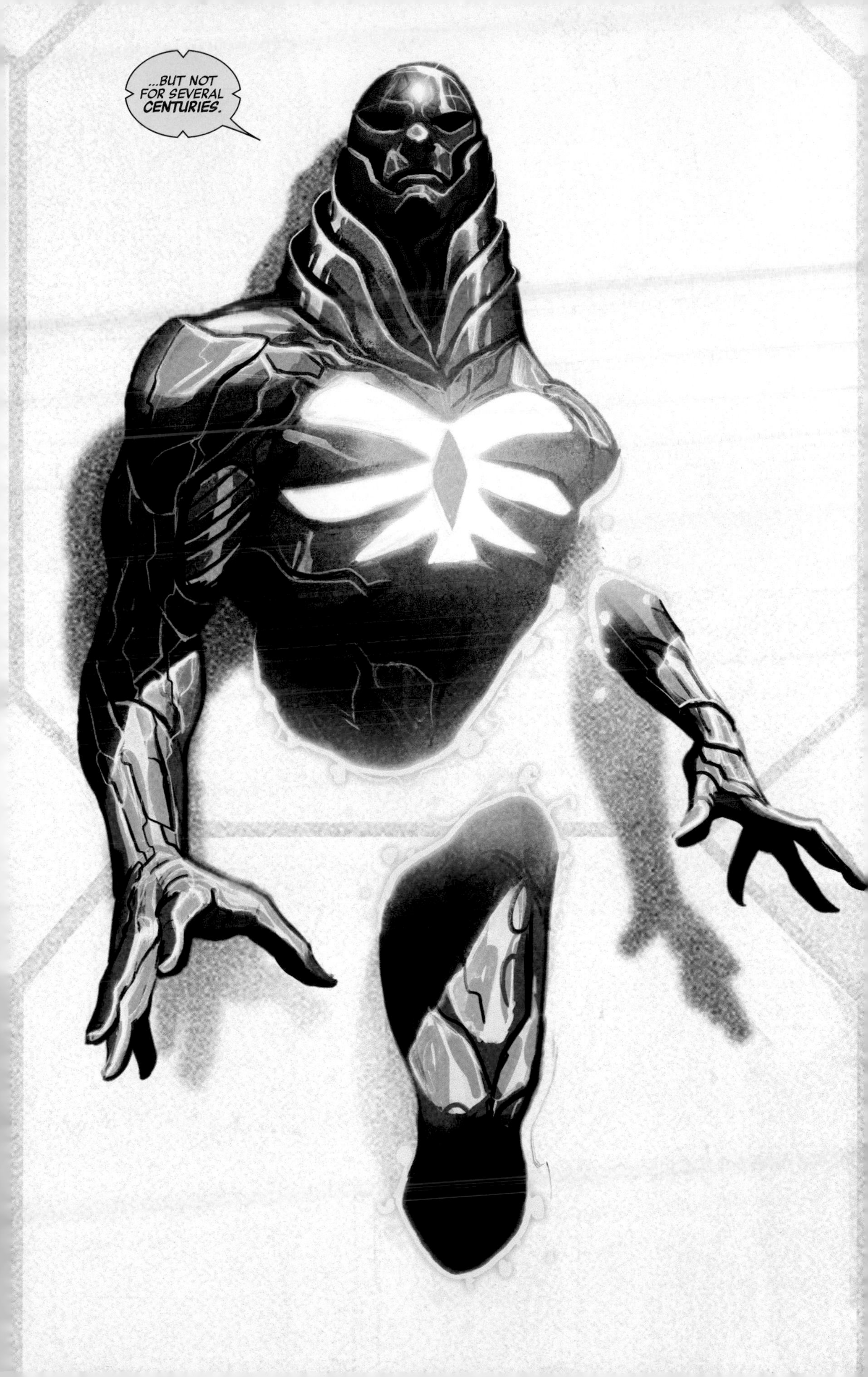
...BUT NOT FOR SEVERAL CENTURIES.

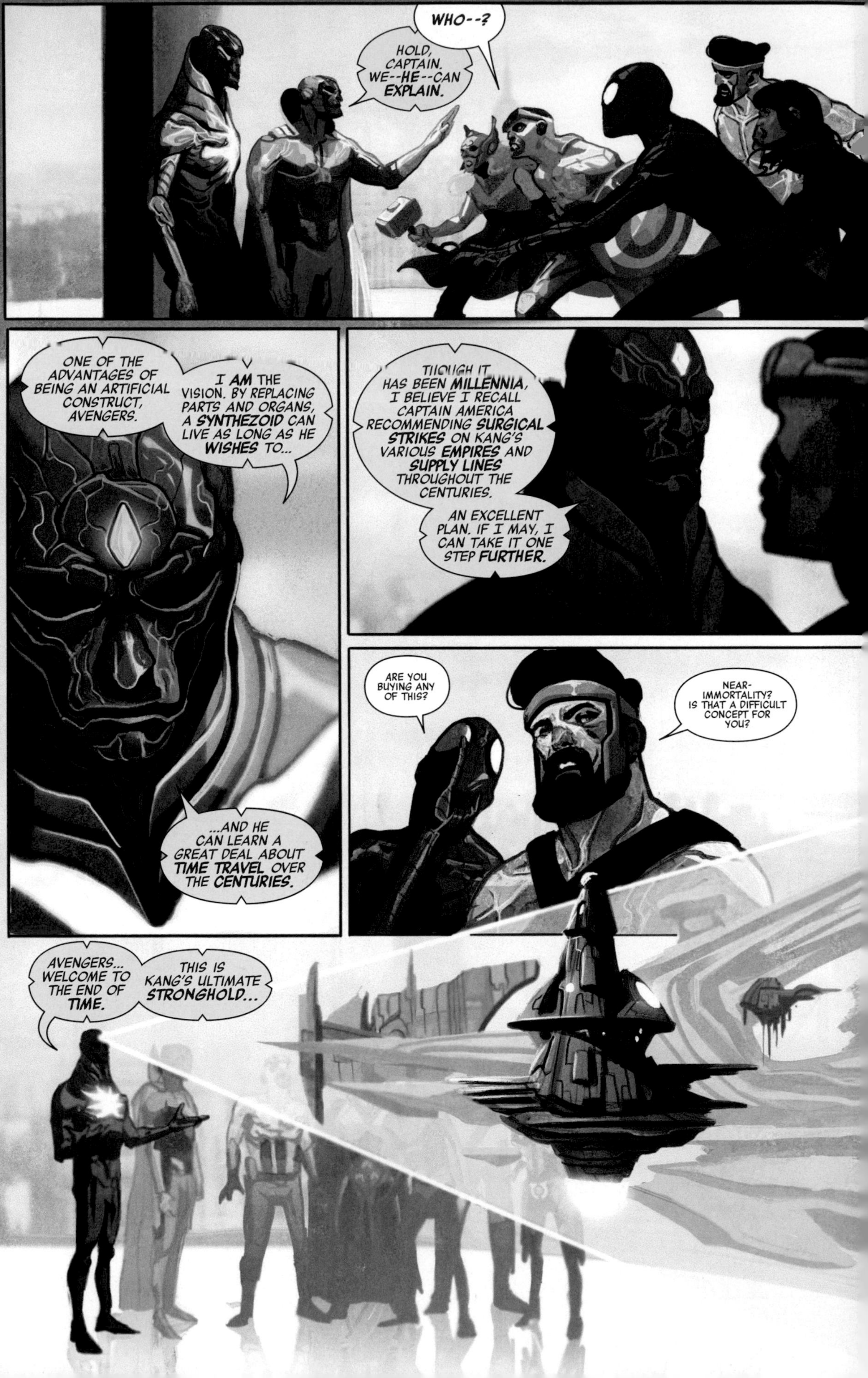
WHO--?
HOLD, CAPTAIN. WE--HE--CAN EXPLAIN.
ONE OF THE ADVANTAGES OF BEING AN ARTIFICIAL CONSTRUCT, AVENGERS.
I AM THE VISION. BY REPLACING PARTS AND ORGANS, A SYNTHEZOID CAN LIVE AS LONG AS HE WISHES TO...
...AND HE CAN LEARN A GREAT DEAL ABOUT TIME TRAVEL OVER THE CENTURIES.
THOUGH IT HAS BEEN MILLENNIA, I BELIEVE I RECALL CAPTAIN AMERICA RECOMMENDING SURGICAL STRIKES ON KANG'S VARIOUS EMPIRES AND SUPPLY LINES THROUGHOUT THE CENTURIES.
AN EXCELLENT PLAN. IF I MAY, I CAN TAKE IT ONE STEP FURTHER.
ARE YOU BUYING ANY OF THIS?
NEAR-IMMORTALITY? IS THAT A DIFFICULT CONCEPT FOR YOU?
AVENGERS... WELCOME TO THE END OF TIME.
THIS IS KANG'S ULTIMATE STRONGHOLD...

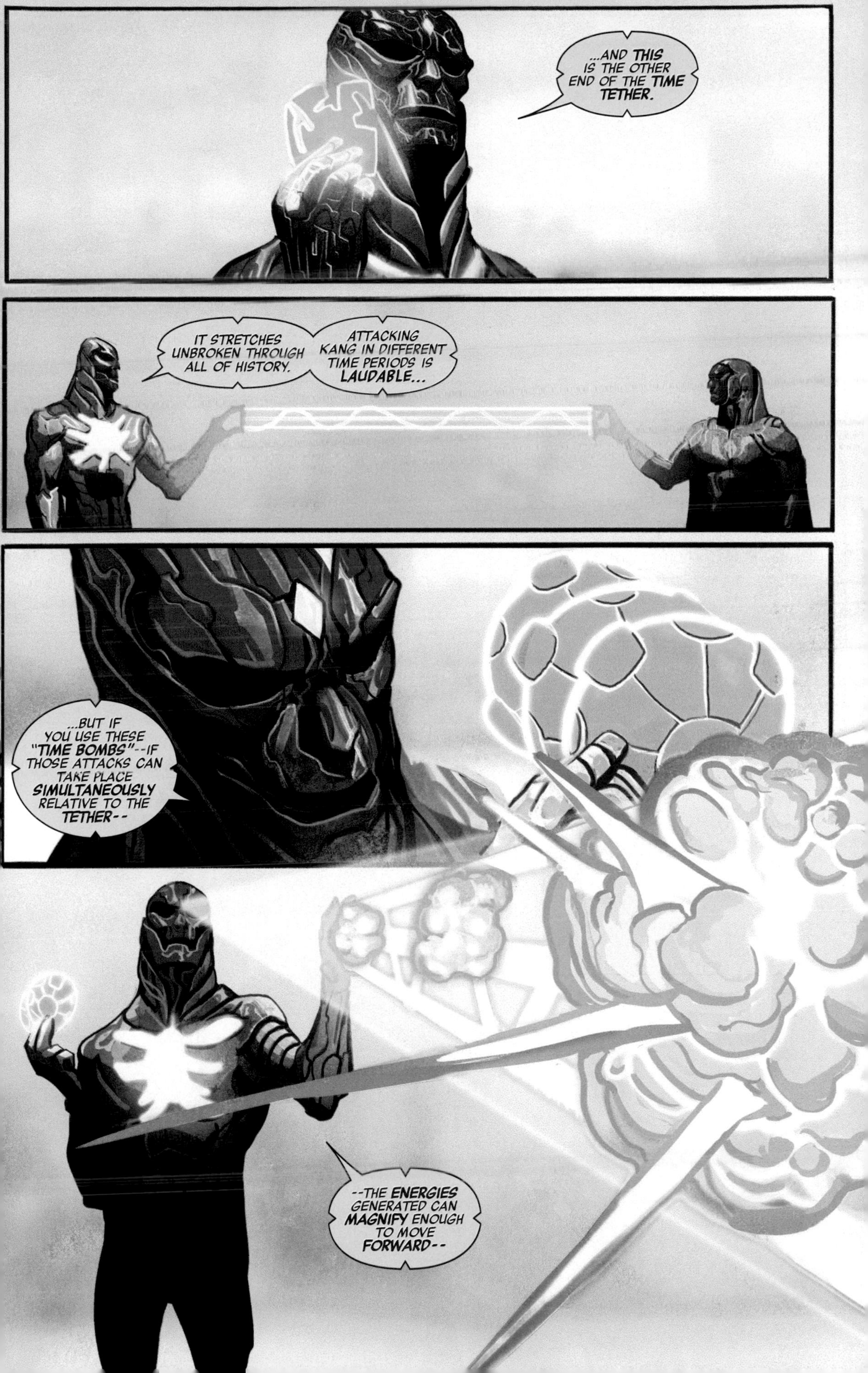
...AND THIS IS THE OTHER END OF THE TIME TETHER.
IT STRETCHES UNBROKEN THROUGH ALL OF HISTORY.
ATTACKING KANG IN DIFFERENT TIME PERIODS IS LAUDABLE...
...BUT IF YOU USE THESE "TIME BOMBS"--IF THOSE ATTACKS CAN TAKE PLACE SIMULTANEOUSLY RELATIVE TO THE TETHER--
--THE ENERGIES GENERATED CAN MAGNIFY ENOUGH TO MOVE FORWARD--

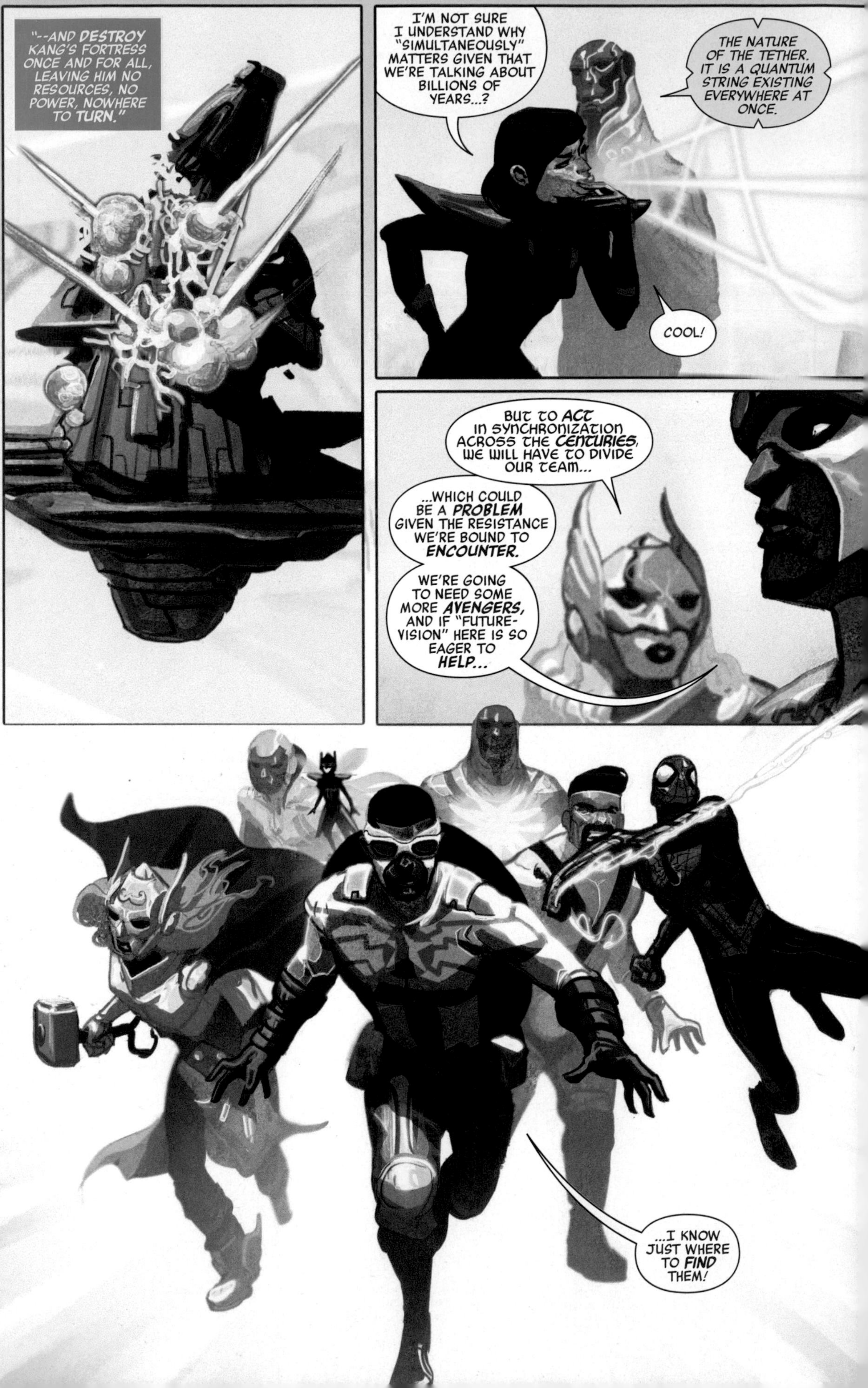
"--AND DESTROY KANG'S FORTRESS ONCE AND FOR ALL, LEAVING HIM NO RESOURCES, NO POWER, NOWHERE TO TURN."
I'M NOT SURE I UNDERSTAND WHY "SIMULTANEOUSLY" MATTERS GIVEN THAT WE'RE TALKING ABOUT BILLIONS OF YEARS...?
THE NATURE OF THE TETHER. IT IS A QUANTUM STRING EXISTING EVERYWHERE AT ONCE.
COOL!
BUT TO ACT IN SYNCHRONIZATION ACROSS THE CENTURIES, WE WILL HAVE TO DIVIDE OUR TEAM...
...WHICH COULD BE A PROBLEM GIVEN THE RESISTANCE WE'RE BOUND TO ENCOUNTER.
WE'RE GOING TO NEED SOME MORE AVENGERS, AND IF "FUTURE-VISION" HERE IS SO EAGER TO HELP...
...I KNOW JUST WHERE TO FIND THEM!

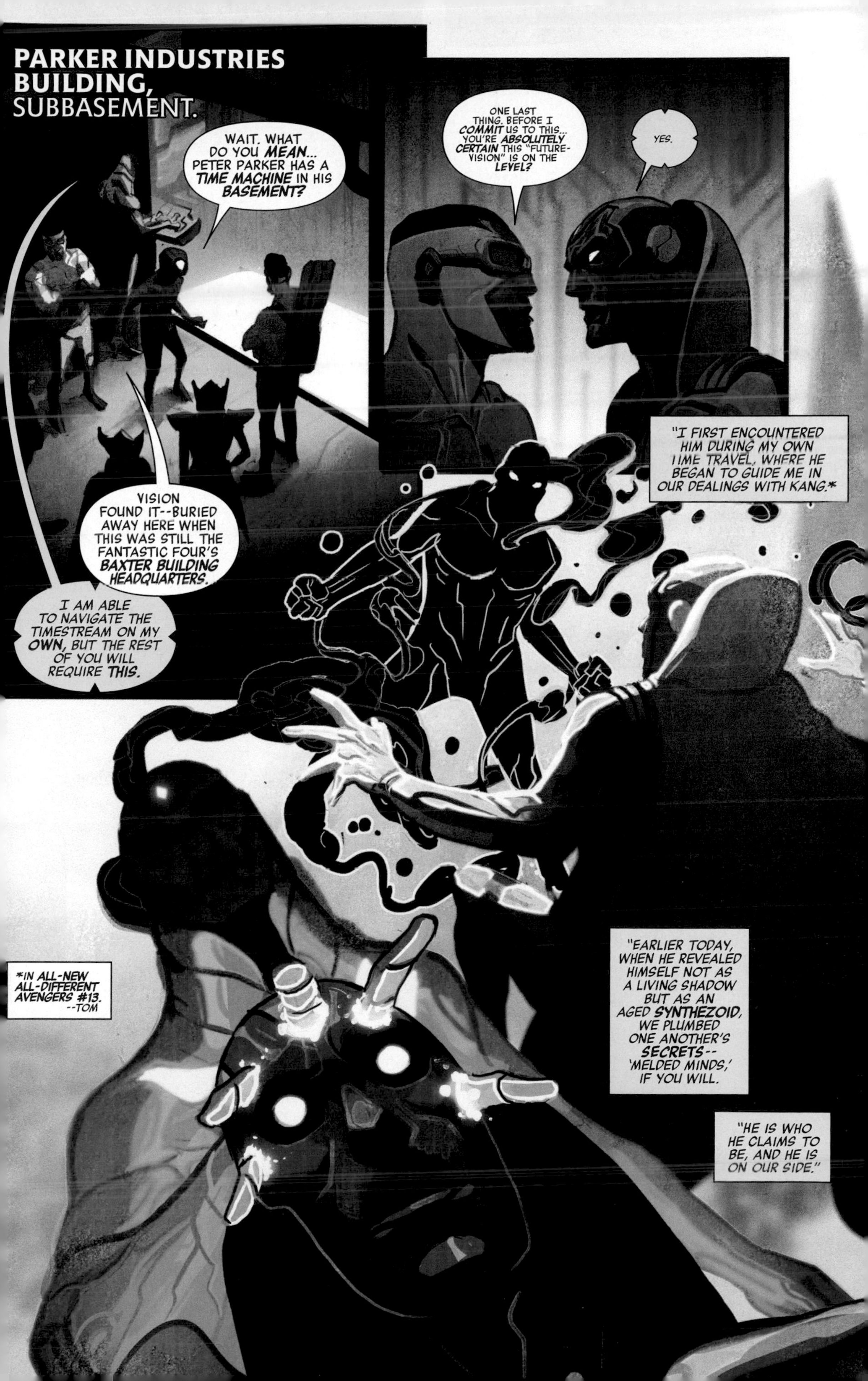
PARKER INDUSTRIES BUILDING, SUBBASEMENT.
WAIT. WHAT DO YOU MEAN... PETER PARKER HAS A TIME MACHINE IN HIS BASEMENT?
VISION FOUND IT--BURIED AWAY HERE WHEN THIS WAS STILL THE FANTASTIC FOUR'S BAXTER BUILDING HEADQUARTERS.
I AM ABLE TO NAVIGATE THE TIMESTREAM ON MY OWN, BUT THE REST OF YOU WILL REQUIRE THIS.
ONE LAST THING. BEFORE I COMMIT US TO THIS... YOU'RE ABSOLUTELY CERTAIN THIS "FUTURE-VISION" IS ON THE LEVEL?
YES.
"I FIRST ENCOUNTERED HIM DURING MY OWN TIME TRAVEL, WHERE HE BEGAN TO GUIDE ME IN OUR DEALINGS WITH KANG.*
*IN ALL-NEW ALL-DIFFERENT AVENGERS #13. --TOM
"EARLIER TODAY, WHEN HE REVEALED HIMSELF NOT AS A LIVING SHADOW BUT AS AN AGED SYNTHEZOID, WE PLUMBED ONE ANOTHER'S SECRETS--'MELDED MINDS,' IF YOU WILL.
"HE IS WHO HE CLAIMS TO BE, AND HE IS ON OUR SIDE."

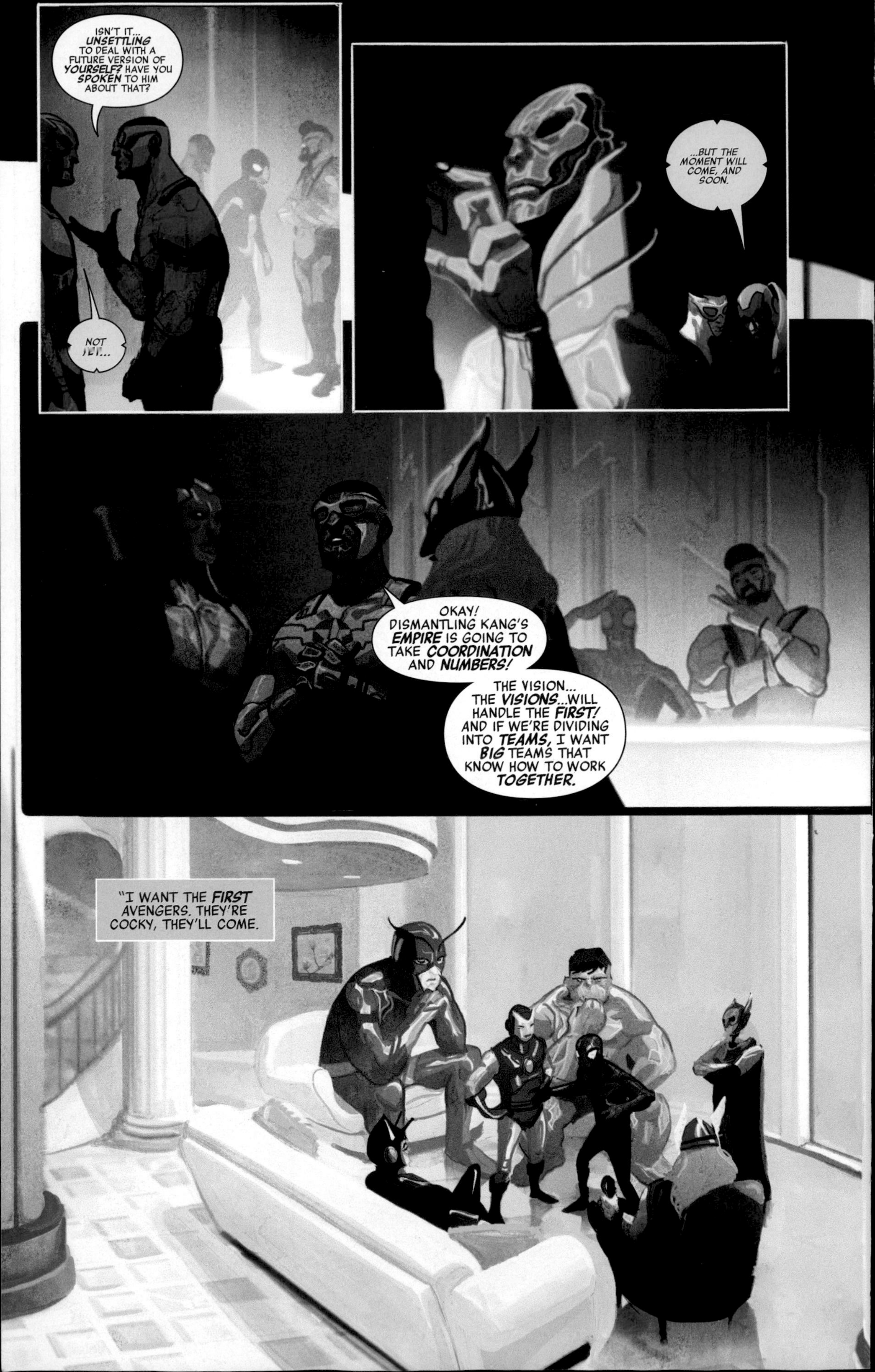
ISN'T IT... UNSETTLING TO DEAL WITH A FUTURE VERSION OF YOURSELF? HAVE YOU SPOKEN TO HIM ABOUT THAT?
NOT YET...
...BUT THE MOMENT WILL COME, AND SOON.
OKAY! DISMANTLING KANG'S EMPIRE IS GOING TO TAKE COORDINATION AND NUMBERS!
THE VISION... THE VISIONS...WILL HANDLE THE FIRST! AND IF WE'RE DIVIDING INTO TEAMS, I WANT BIG TEAMS THAT KNOW HOW TO WORK TOGETHER.
"I WANT THE FIRST AVENGERS. THEY'RE COCKY, THEY'LL COME.

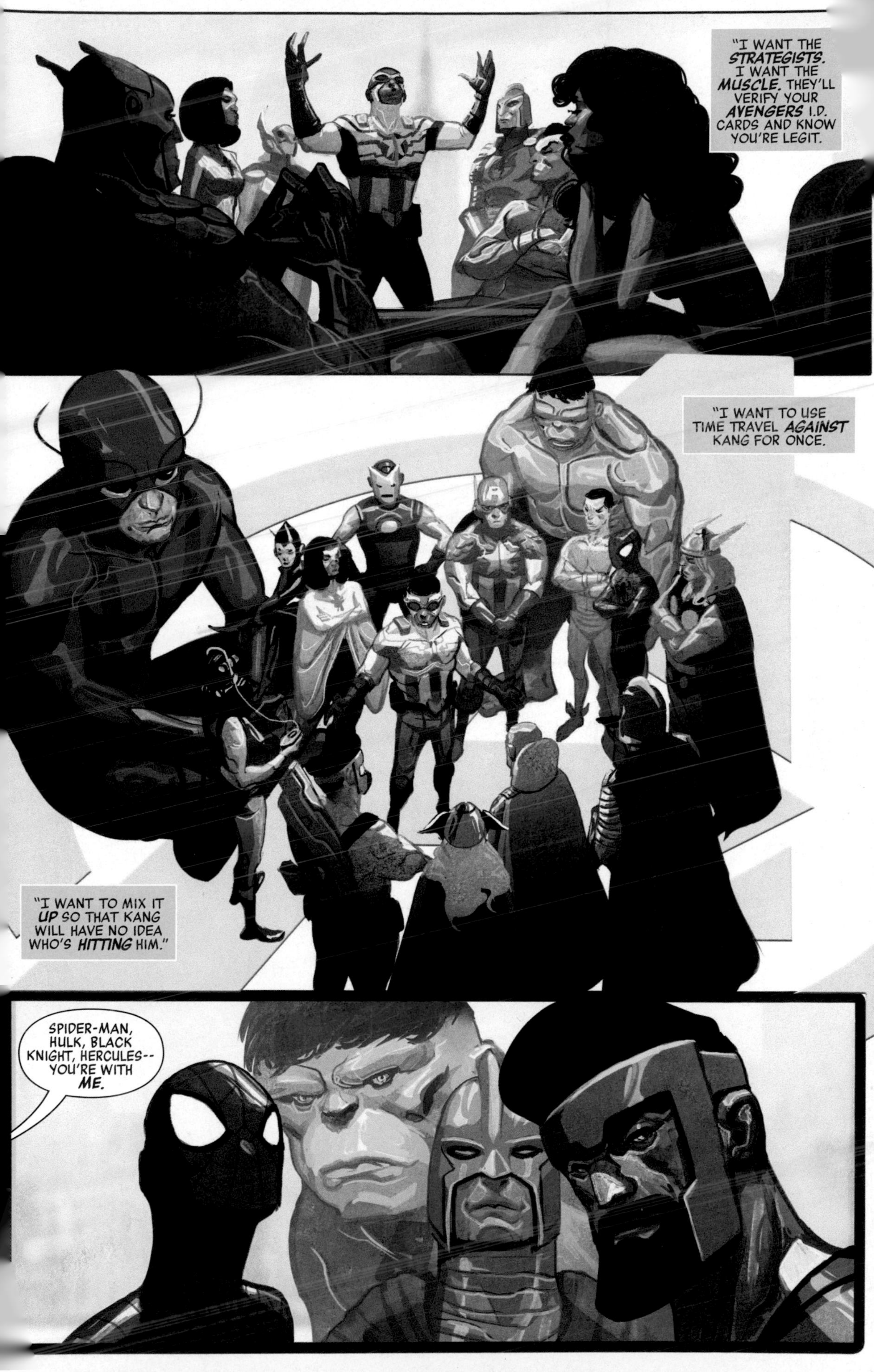
"I WANT THE STRATEGISTS. I WANT THE MUSCLE. THEY'LL VERIFY YOUR AVENGERS I.D. CARDS AND KNOW YOU'RE LEGIT.
"I WANT TO USE TIME TRAVEL AGAINST KANG FOR ONCE.
"I WANT TO MIX IT UP SO THAT KANG WILL HAVE NO IDEA WHO'S HITTING HIM."
SPIDER-MAN, HULK, BLACK KNIGHT, HERCULES-- YOU'RE WITH ME.

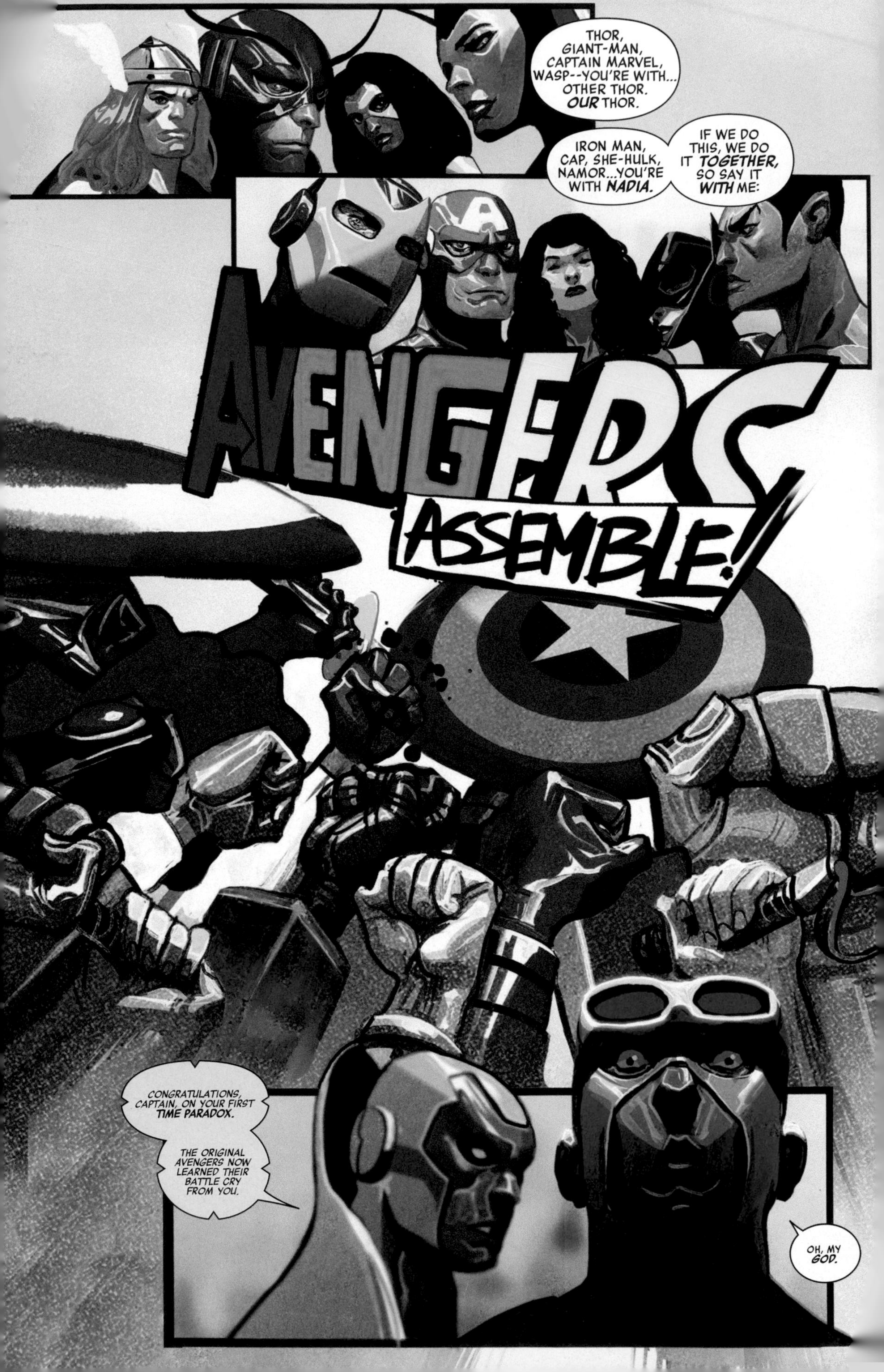
THOR, GIANT-MAN, CAPTAIN MARVEL, WASP--YOU'RE WITH... OTHER THOR. OUR THOR.
IRON MAN, CAP, SHE-HULK, NAMOR...YOU'RE WITH NADIA.
IF WE DO THIS, WE DO IT TOGETHER, SO SAY IT WITH ME:
AVENGERS
ASSEMBLE!
CONGRATULATIONS, CAPTAIN, ON YOUR FIRST TIME PARADOX.
THE ORIGINAL AVENGERS NOW LEARNED THEIR BATTLE CRY FROM YOU.
OH, MY GOD.

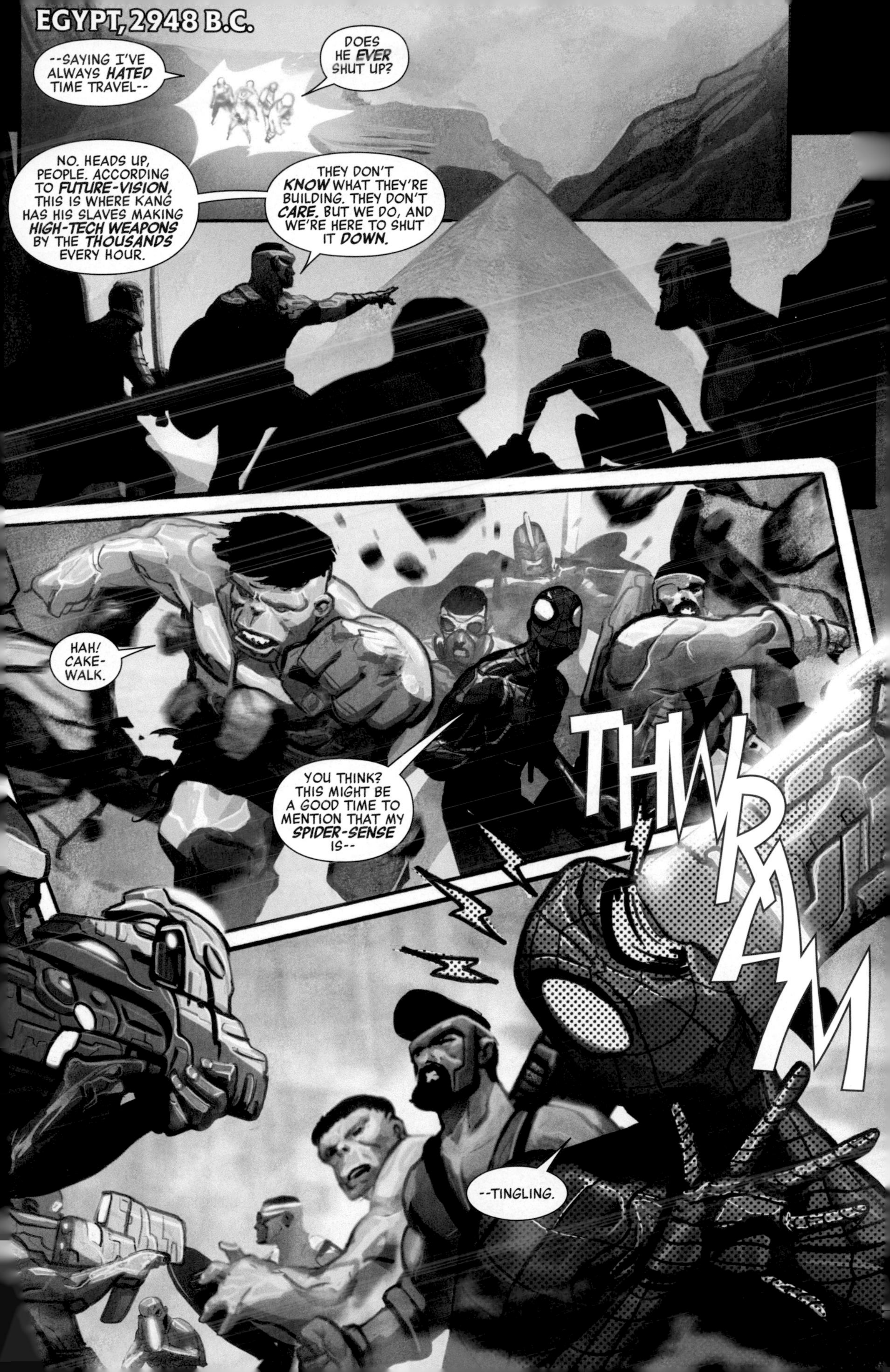
EGYPT, 2948 B.C.
--SAYING I'VE ALWAYS HATED TIME TRAVEL--
DOES HE EVER SHUT UP?
NO. HEADS UP, PEOPLE. ACCORDING TO FUTURE-VISION, THIS IS WHERE KANG HAS HIS SLAVES MAKING HIGH-TECH WEAPONS BY THE THOUSANDS EVERY HOUR.
THEY DON'T KNOW WHAT THEY'RE BUILDING. THEY DON'T CARE. BUT WE DO, AND WE'RE HERE TO SHUT IT DOWN.
HAH! CAKE-WALK.
YOU THINK? THIS MIGHT BE A GOOD TIME TO MENTION THAT MY SPIDER-SENSE IS--
THWRAM
--TINGLING.

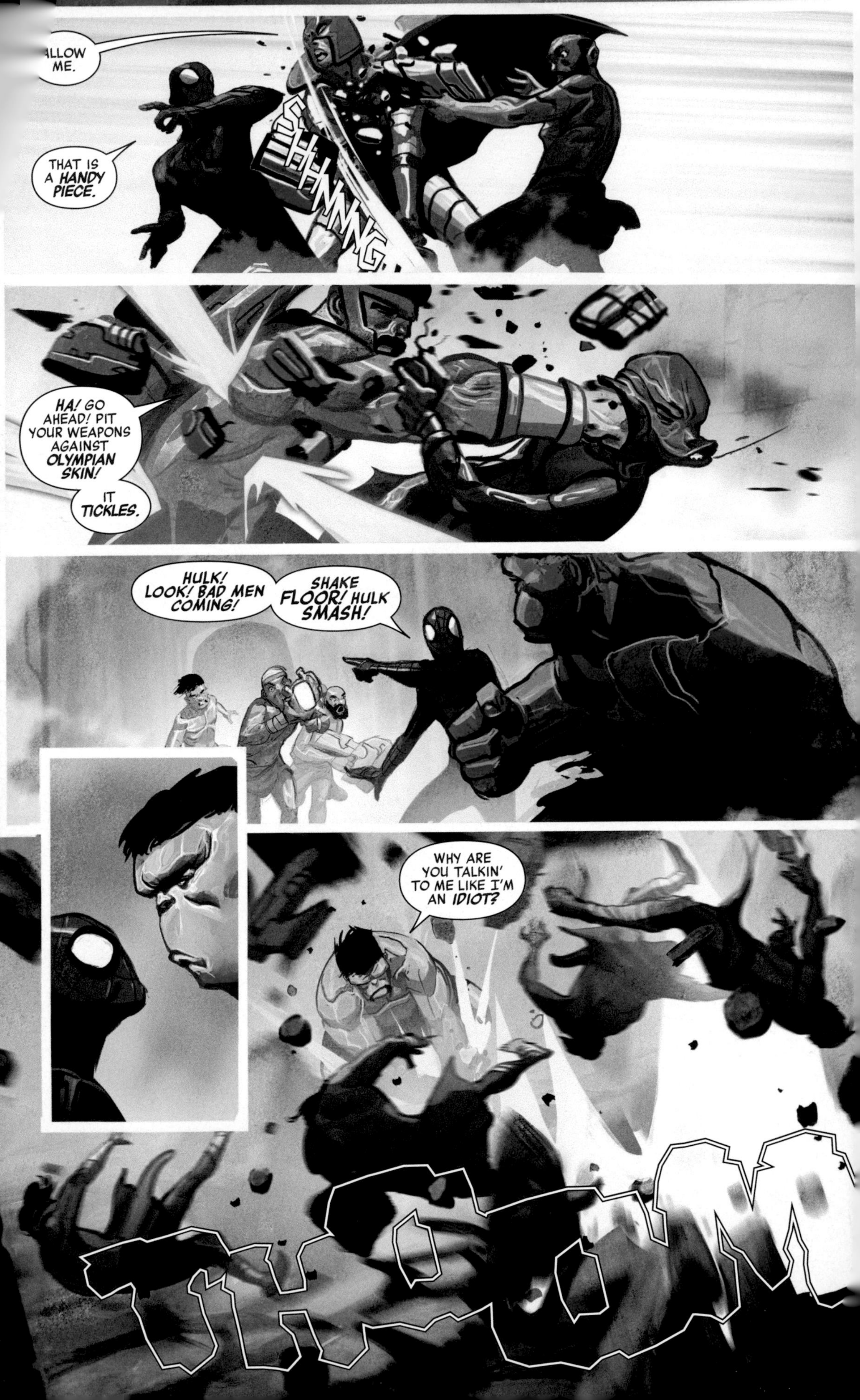
ALLOW ME.
THAT IS A HANDY PIECE.
SHHNNNG
HA! GO AHEAD! PIT YOUR WEAPONS AGAINST OLYMPIAN SKIN!
IT TICKLES.
HULK! LOOK! BAD MEN COMING!
SHAKE FLOOR! HULK SMASH!
WHY ARE YOU TALKIN' TO ME LIKE I'M AN IDIOT?
THOOM

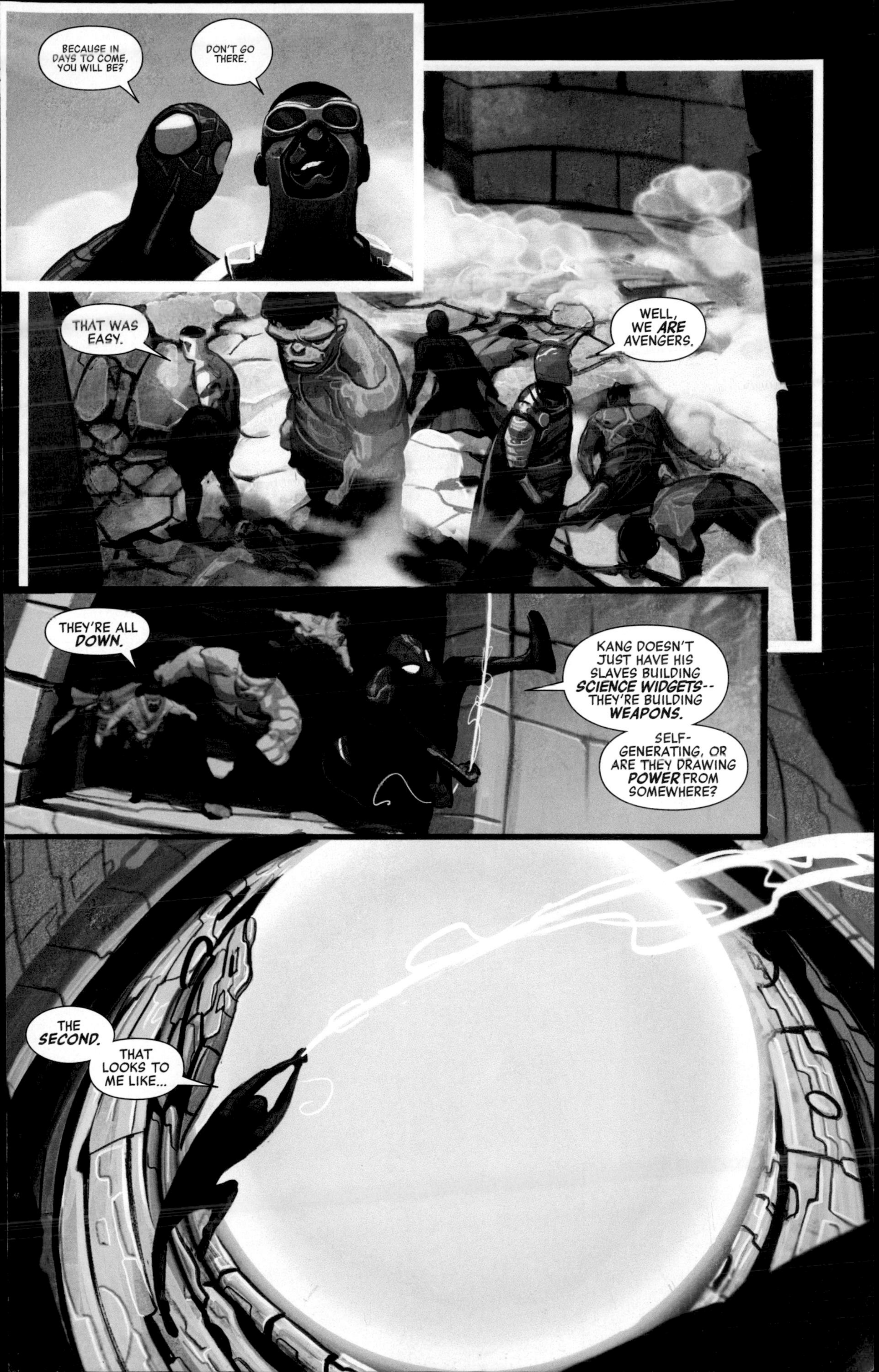
BECAUSE IN DAYS TO COME, YOU WILL BE?
DON'T GO THERE.
THAT WAS EASY.
WELL, WE ARE AVENGERS.
THEY'RE ALL DOWN.
KANG DOESN'T JUST HAVE HIS SLAVES BUILDING SCIENCE WIDGETS-- THEY'RE BUILDING WEAPONS.
SELF-GENERATING, OR ARE THEY DRAWING POWER FROM SOMEWHERE?
THE SECOND.
THAT LOOKS TO ME LIKE...

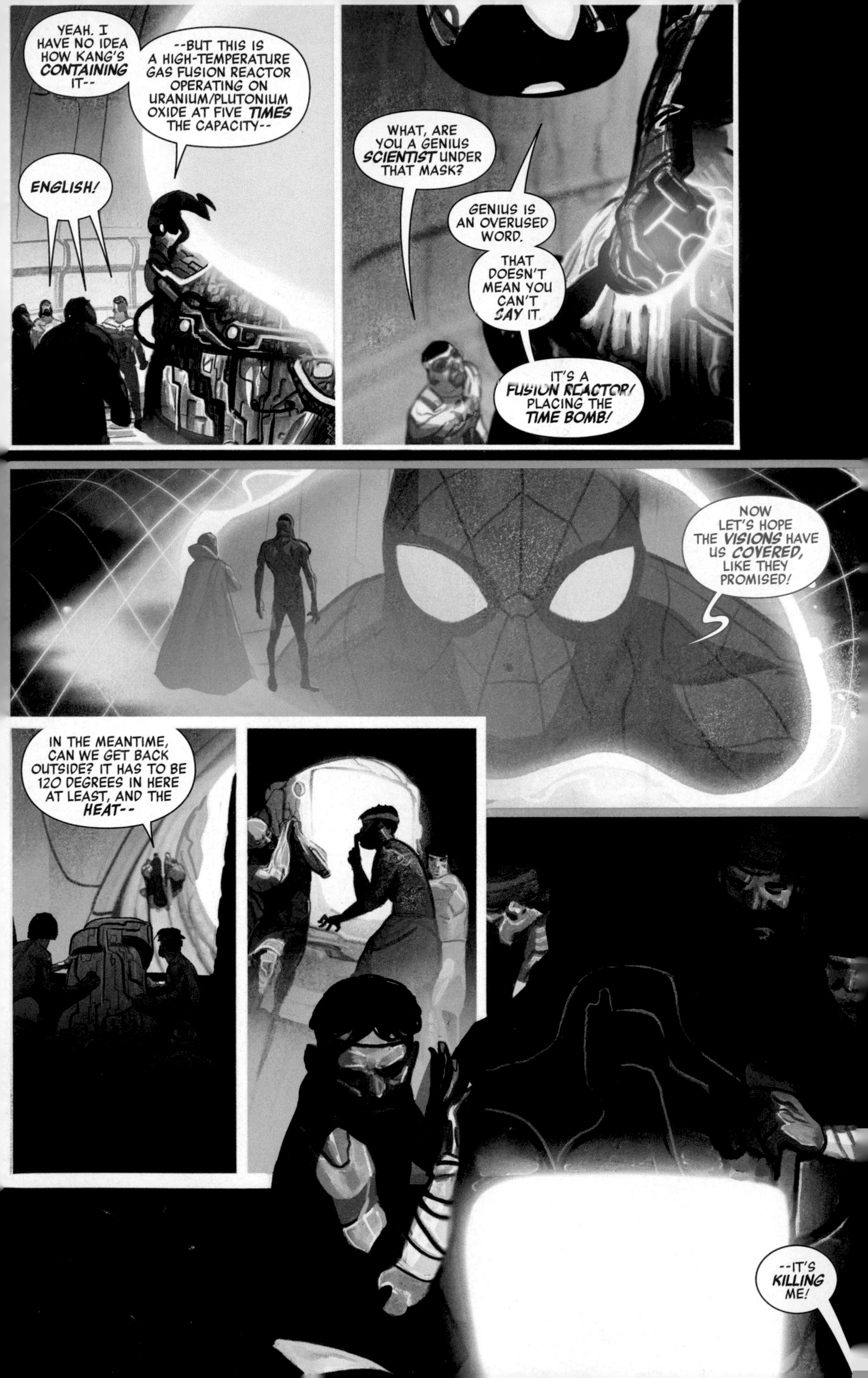

YEAH. I HAVE NO IDEA HOW KANG'S CONTAINING IT--
--BUT THIS IS A HIGH-TEMPERATURE GAS FUSION REACTOR OPERATING ON URANIUM/PLUTONIUM OXIDE AT FIVE TIMES THE CAPACITY--
ENGLISH!
WHAT, ARE YOU A GENIUS SCIENTIST UNDER THAT MASK?
GENIUS IS AN OVERUSED WORD.
THAT DOESN'T MEAN YOU CAN'T SAY IT.
IT'S A FUSION REACTOR! PLACING THE TIME BOMB!
NOW LET'S HOPE THE VISIONS HAVE US COVERED, LIKE THEY PROMISED!
IN THE MEANTIME, CAN WE GET BACK OUTSIDE? IT HAS TO BE 120 DEGREES IN HERE AT LEAST, AND THE HEAT--
--IT'S KILLING ME!

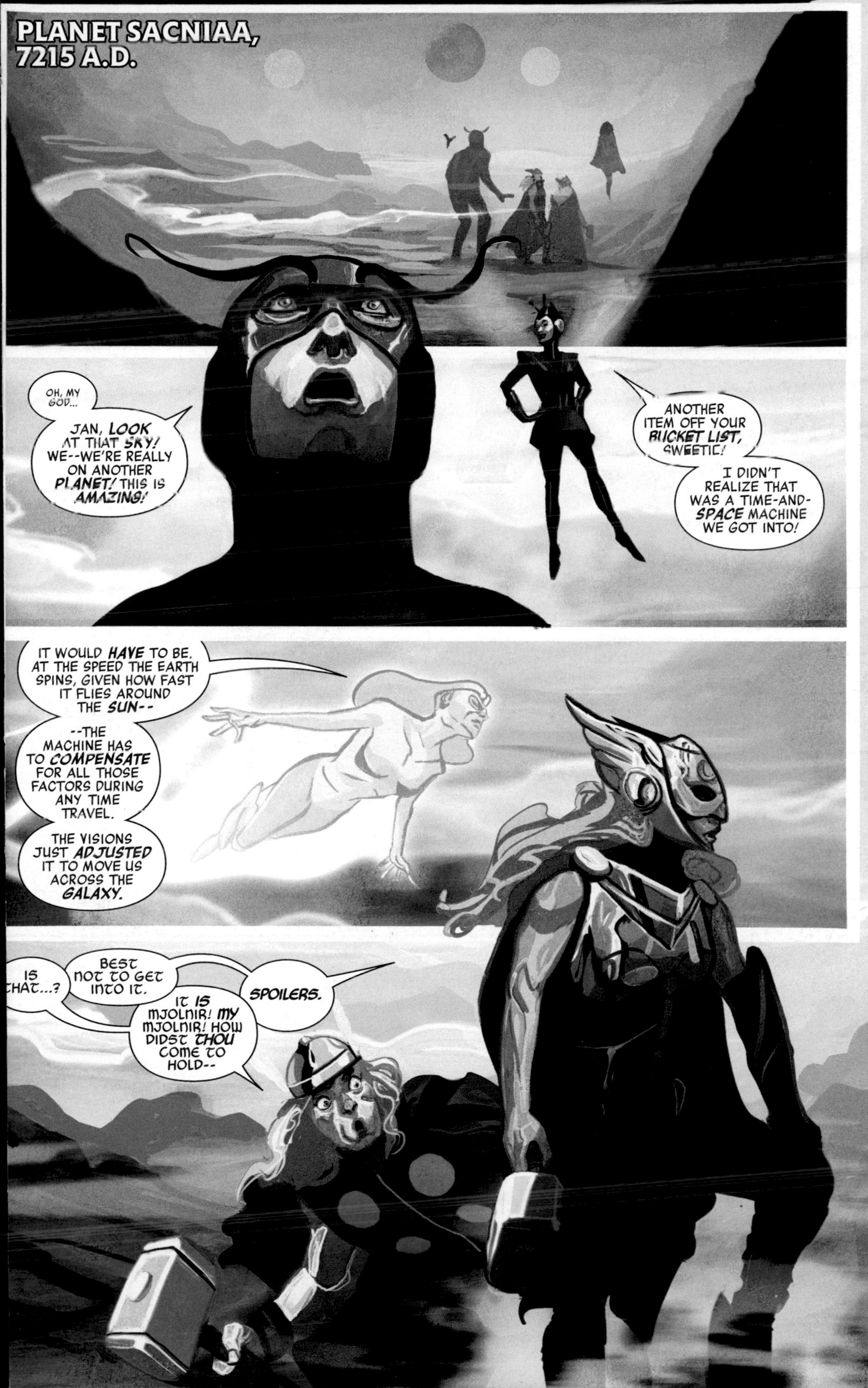
PLANET SACNIAA, 7215 A.D.
OH, MY GOD...
JAN, LOOK AT THAT SKY! WE--WE'RE REALLY ON ANOTHER PLANET! THIS IS AMAZING!
ANOTHER ITEM OFF YOUR BUCKET LIST, SWEETIE!
I DIDN'T REALIZE THAT WAS A TIME-AND-SPACE MACHINE WE GOT INTO!
IT WOULD HAVE TO BE. AT THE SPEED THE EARTH SPINS, GIVEN HOW FAST IT FLIES AROUND THE SUN--
--THE MACHINE HAS TO COMPENSATE FOR ALL THOSE FACTORS DURING ANY TIME TRAVEL.
THE VISIONS JUST ADJUSTED IT TO MOVE US ACROSS THE GALAXY.
IS THAT...?
BEST NOT TO GET INTO IT.
IT IS MJOLNIR! MY MJOLNIR! HOW DIDST THOU COME TO HOLD--
SPOILERS.

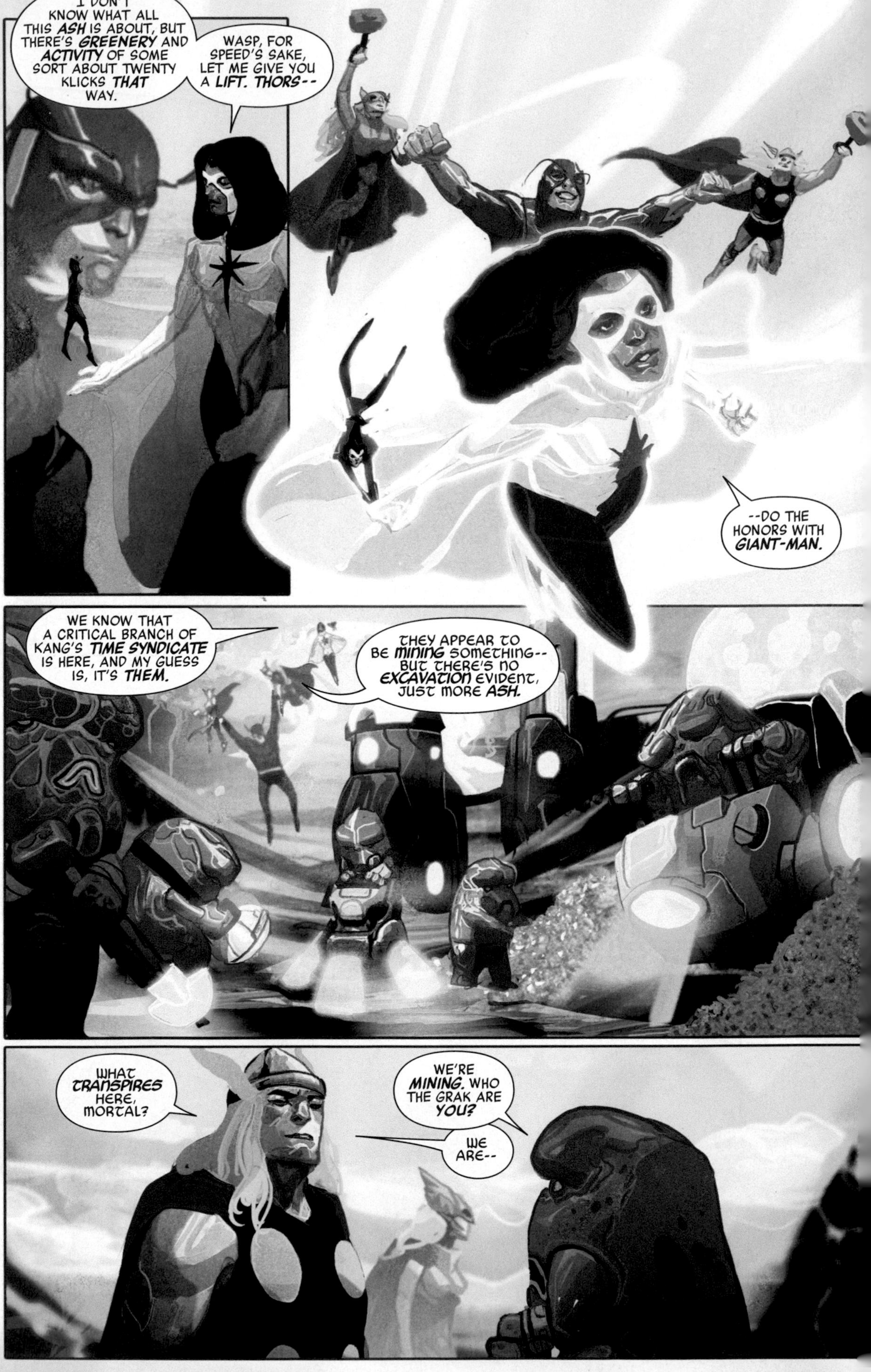
I DON'T KNOW WHAT ALL THIS ASH IS ABOUT, BUT THERE'S GREENERY AND ACTIVITY OF SOME SORT ABOUT TWENTY KLICKS THAT WAY.
WASP, FOR SPEED'S SAKE, LET ME GIVE YOU A LIFT. THORS--
--DO THE HONORS WITH GIANT-MAN.
WE KNOW THAT A CRITICAL BRANCH OF KANG'S TIME SYNDICATE IS HERE, AND MY GUESS IS, IT'S THEM.
THEY APPEAR TO BE MINING SOMETHING-- BUT THERE'S NO EXCAVATION EVIDENT, JUST MORE ASH.
WHAT TRANSPIRES HERE, MORTAL?
WE'RE MINING. WHO THE GRAK ARE YOU?
WE ARE--

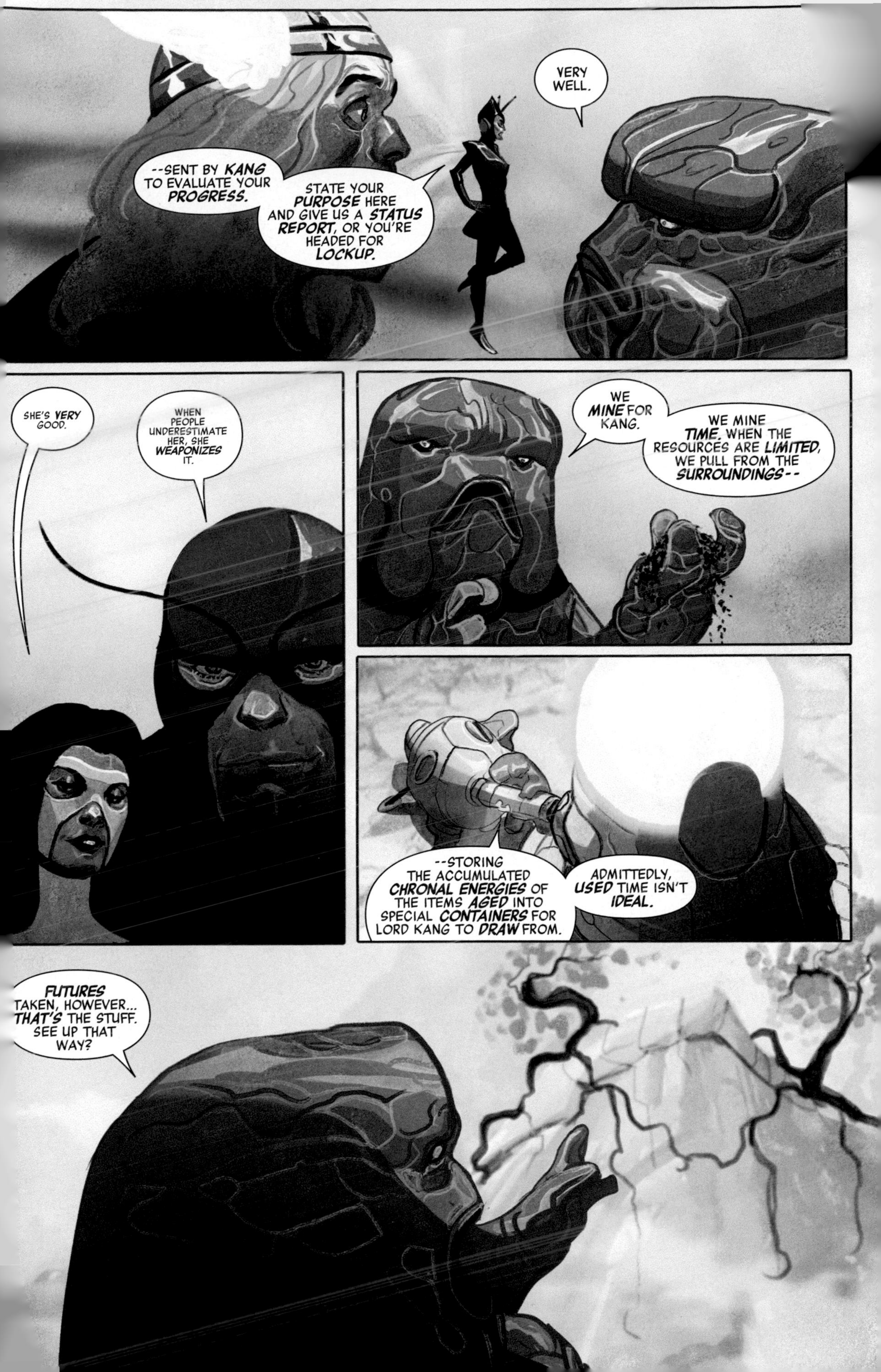
--SENT BY KANG TO EVALUATE YOUR PROGRESS.
STATE YOUR PURPOSE HERE AND GIVE US A STATUS REPORT, OR YOU'RE HEADED FOR LOCKUP.
VERY WELL.
SHE'S VERY GOOD.
WHEN PEOPLE UNDERESTIMATE HER, SHE WEAPONIZES IT.
WE MINE FOR KANG.
WE MINE TIME. WHEN THE RESOURCES ARE LIMITED, WE PULL FROM THE SURROUNDINGS--
--STORING THE ACCUMULATED CHRONAL ENERGIES OF THE ITEMS AGED INTO SPECIAL CONTAINERS FOR LORD KANG TO DRAW FROM.
ADMITTEDLY, USED TIME ISN'T IDEAL.
FUTURES TAKEN, HOWEVER... THAT'S THE STUFF. SEE UP THAT WAY?

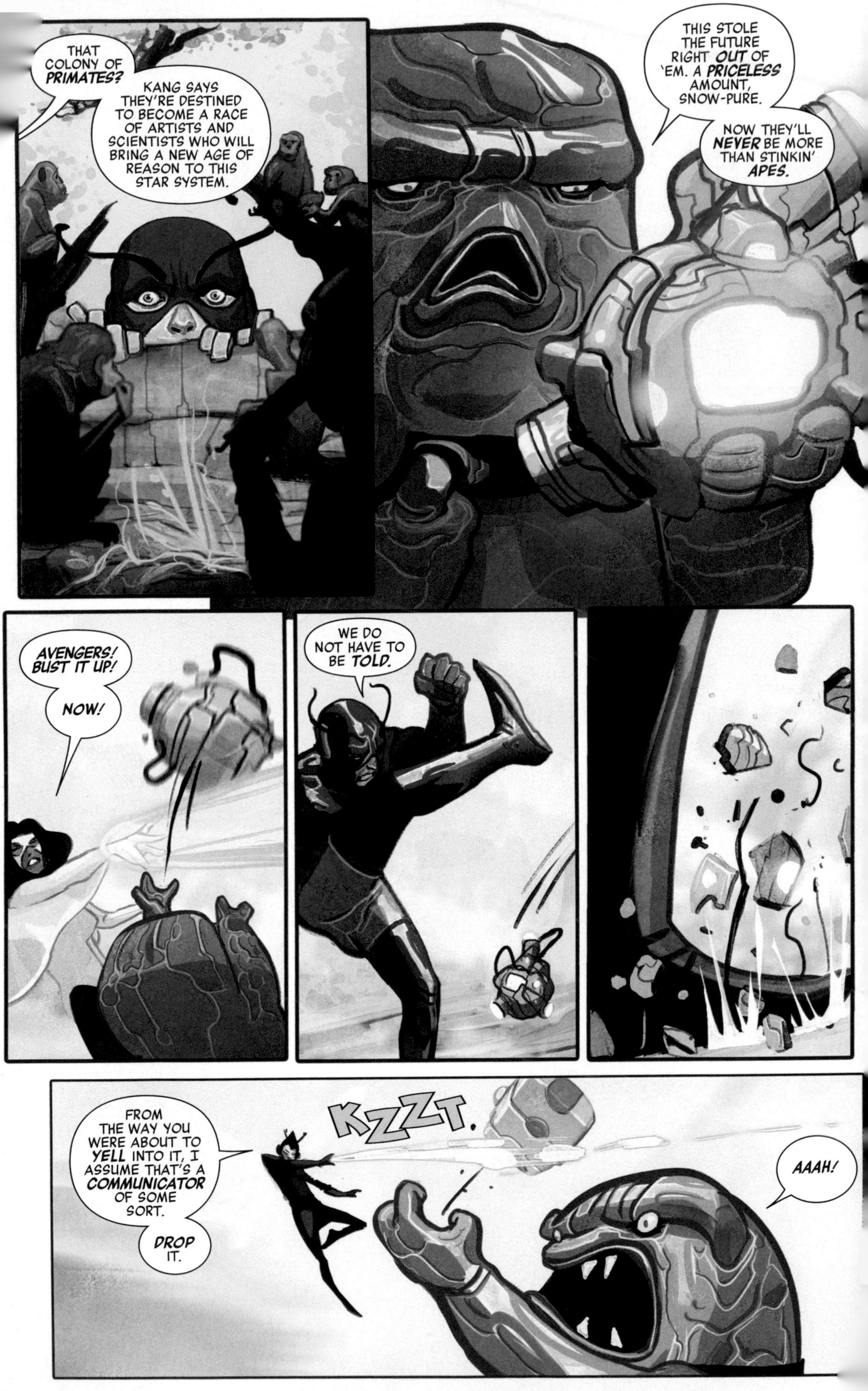
THAT COLONY OF PRIMATES?
KANG SAYS THEY'RE DESTINED TO BECOME A RACE OF ARTISTS AND SCIENTISTS WHO WILL BRING A NEW AGE OF REASON TO THIS STAR SYSTEM.
THIS STOLE THE FUTURE RIGHT OUT OF 'EM. A PRICELESS AMOUNT, SNOW-PURE.
NOW THEY'LL NEVER BE MORE THAN STINKIN' APES.
AVENGERS! BUST IT UP!
NOW!
WE DO NOT HAVE TO BE TOLD.
FROM THE WAY YOU WERE ABOUT TO YELL INTO IT, I ASSUME THAT'S A COMMUNICATOR OF SOME SORT.
DROP IT.
KZZZT.
AAAH!

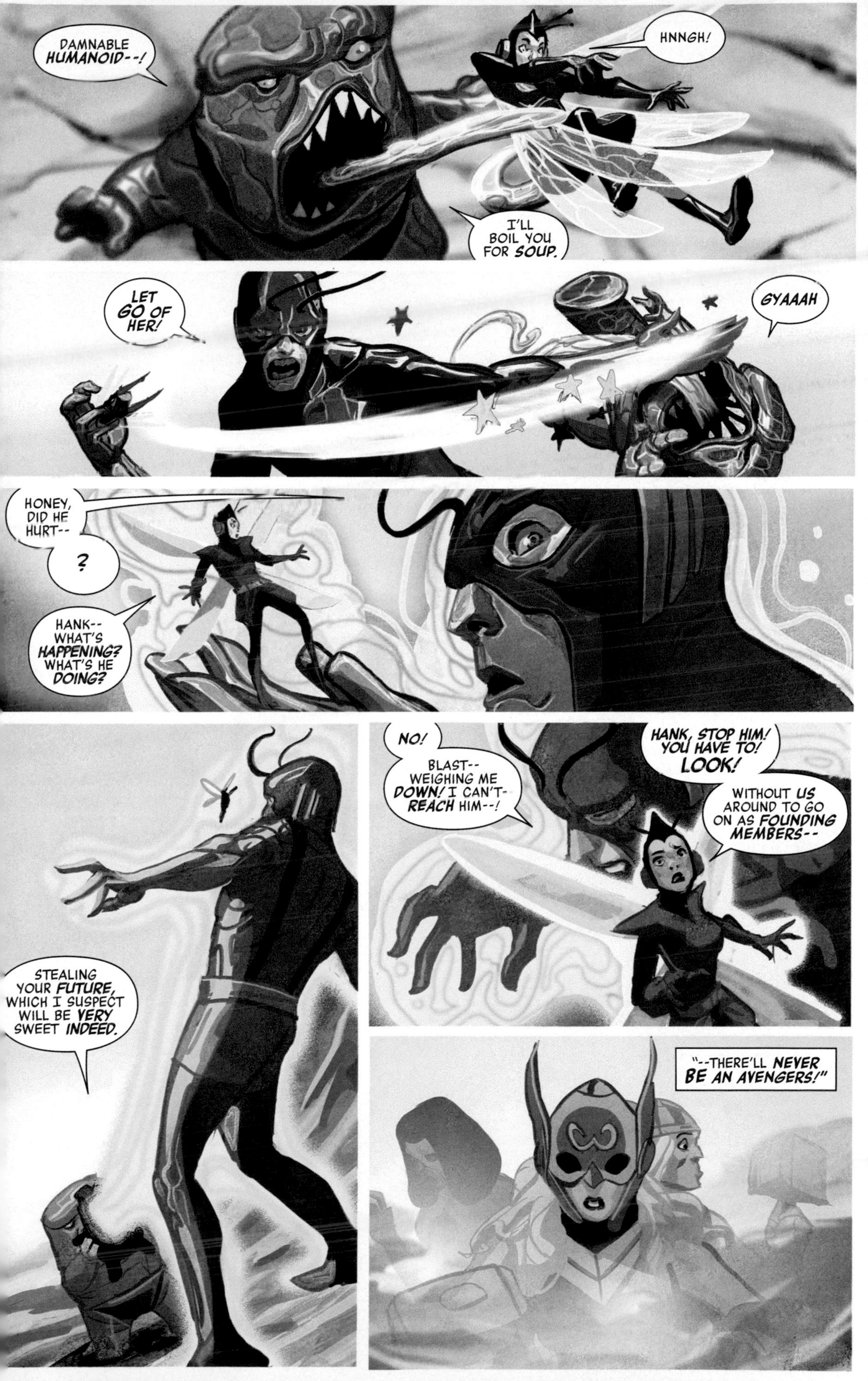
DAMNABLE HUMANOID--!
HNNGH!
I'LL BOIL YOU FOR SOUP.
LET GO OF HER!
GYAAAH
HONEY, DID HE HURT--
?
HANK-- WHAT'S HAPPENING? WHAT'S HE DOING?
STEALING YOUR FUTURE, WHICH I SUSPECT WILL BE VERY SWEET INDEED.
NO!
BLAST-- WEIGHING ME DOWN! I CAN'T-- REACH HIM--!
HANK, STOP HIM! YOU HAVE TO! LOOK!
WITHOUT US AROUND TO GO ON AS FOUNDING MEMBERS--
"--THERE'LL NEVER BE AN AVENGERS!"

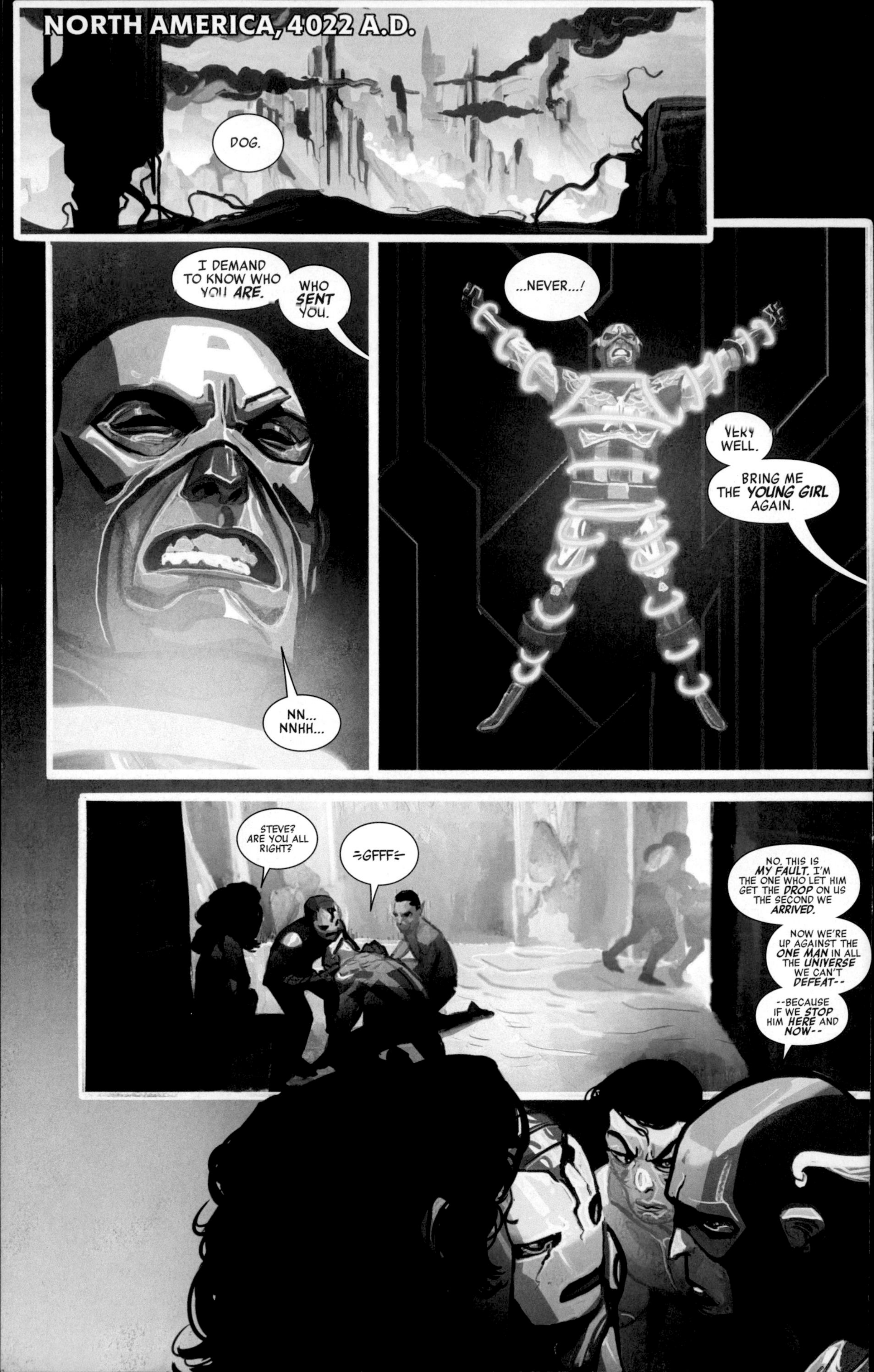
NORTH AMERICA, 4022 A.D.
DOG.
I DEMAND TO KNOW WHO YOU ARE.
WHO SENT YOU.
NN... NNHH...
...NEVER...!
VERY WELL.
BRING ME THE YOUNG GIRL AGAIN.
STEVE? ARE YOU ALL RIGHT?
GFFF
NO. THIS IS MY FAULT. I'M THE ONE WHO LET HIM GET THE DROP ON US THE SECOND WE ARRIVED.
NOW WE'RE UP AGAINST THE ONE MAN IN ALL THE UNIVERSE WE CAN'T DEFEAT--
--BECAUSE IF WE STOP HIM HERE AND NOW--

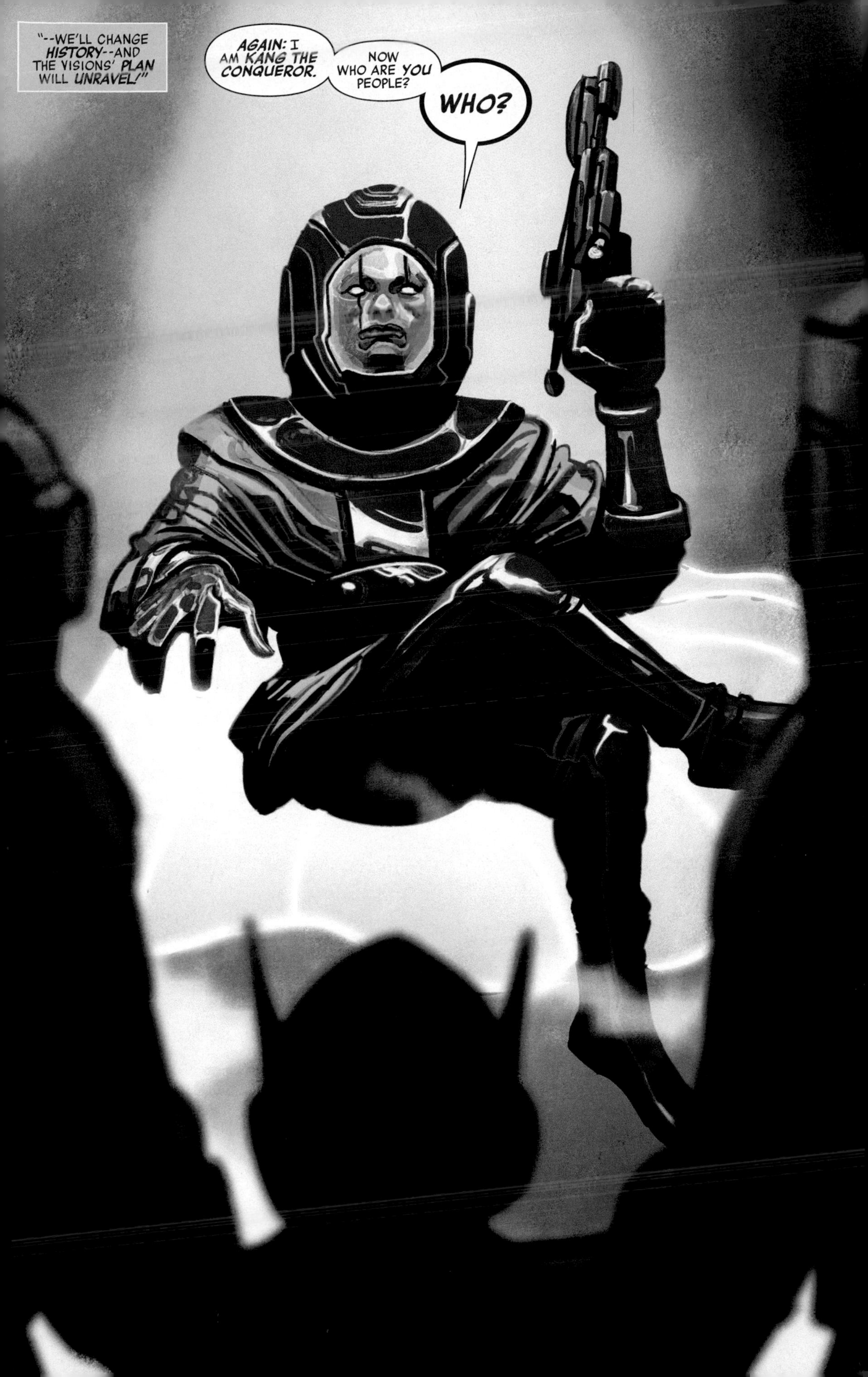
"--WE'LL CHANGE HISTORY--AND THE VISIONS' PLAN WILL UNRAVEL!"
AGAIN: I AM KANG THE CONQUEROR.
NOW WHO ARE YOU PEOPLE?
WHO?

6

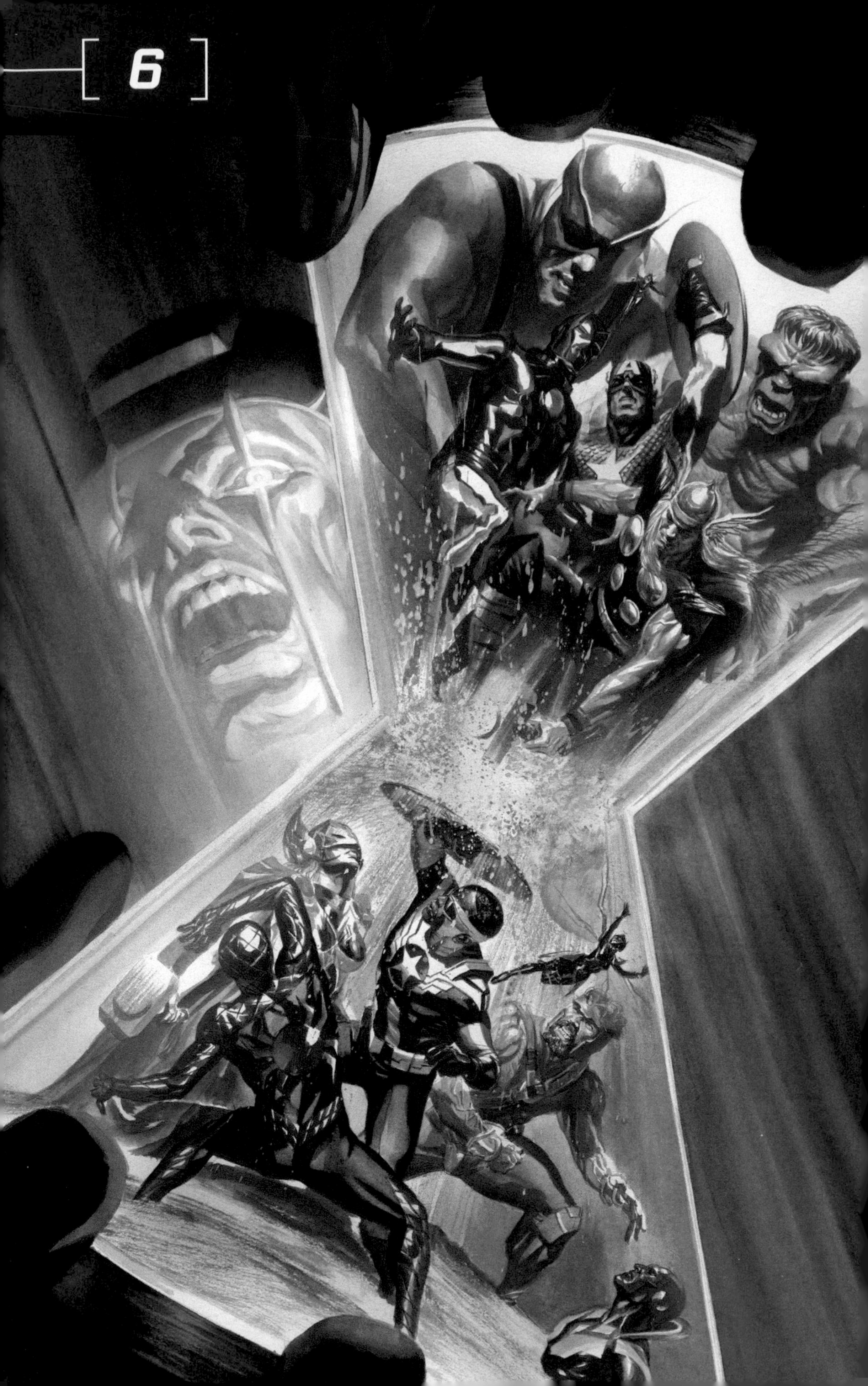

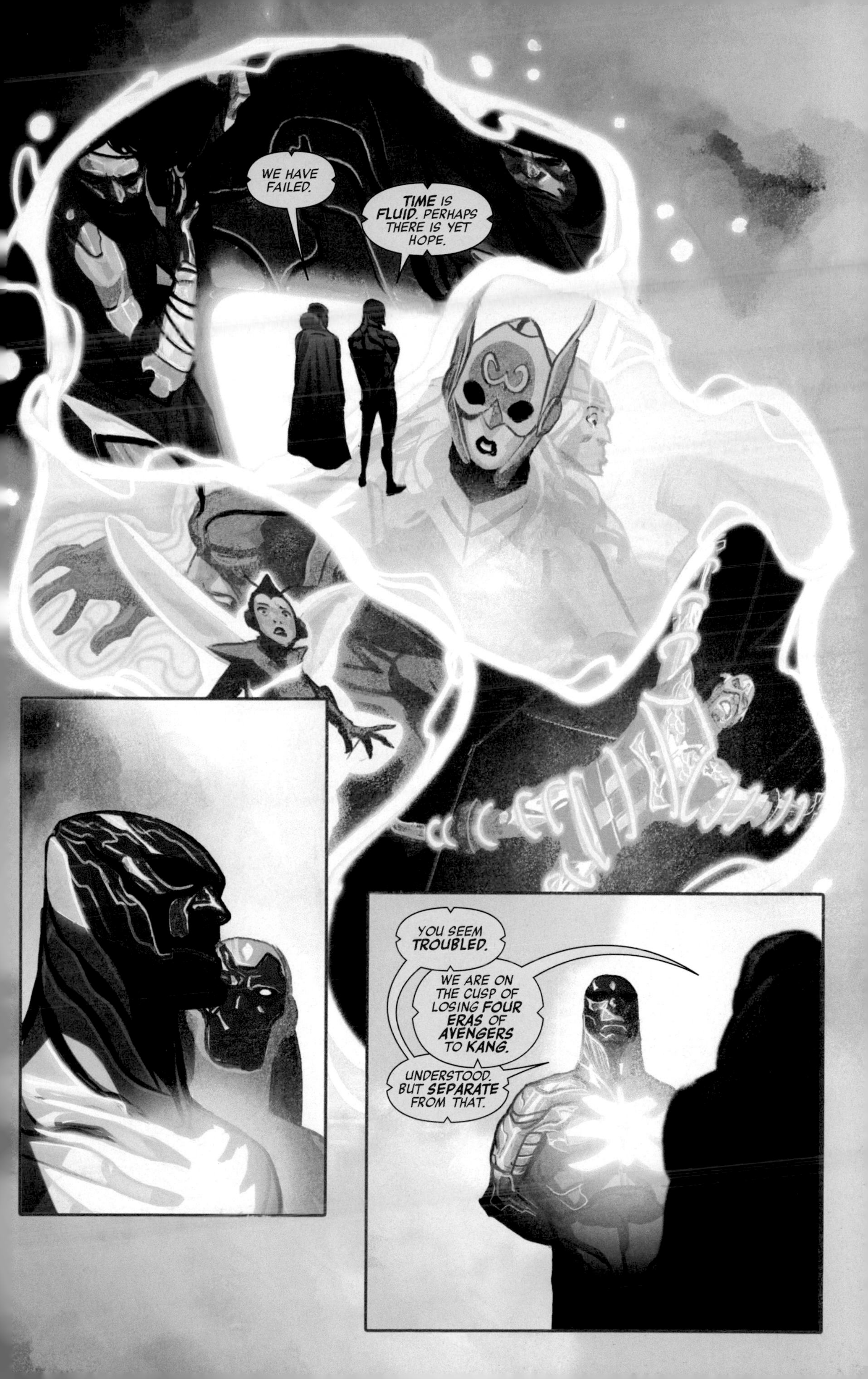
WE HAVE FAILED.
TIME IS FLUID. PERHAPS THERE IS YET HOPE.
YOU SEEM TROUBLED.
WE ARE ON THE CUSP OF LOSING FOUR ERAS OF AVENGERS TO KANG.
UNDERSTOOD. BUT SEPARATE FROM THAT.

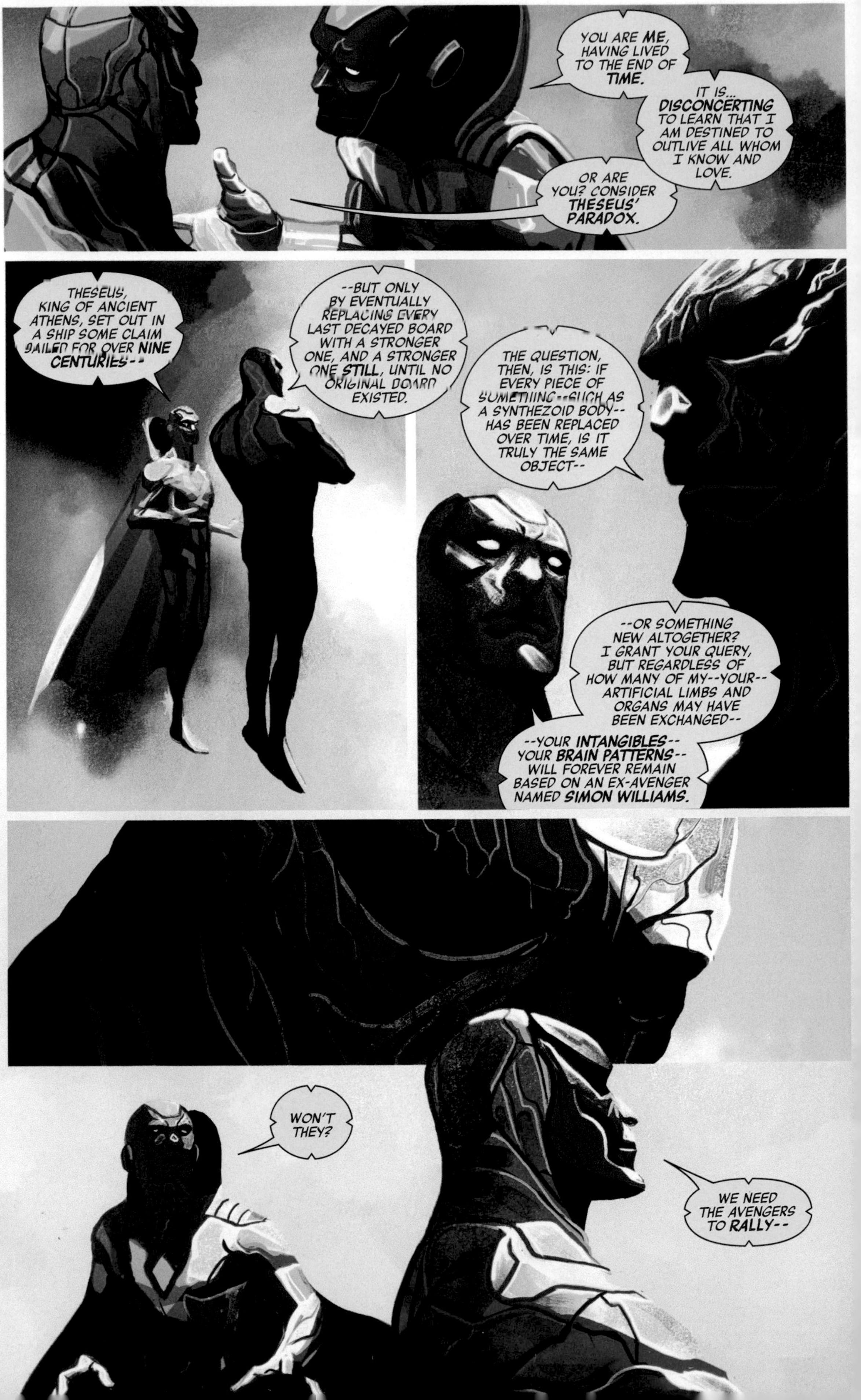
YOU ARE ME, HAVING LIVED TO THE END OF TIME.
IT IS... DISCONCERTING TO LEARN THAT I AM DESTINED TO OUTLIVE ALL WHOM I KNOW AND LOVE.
OR ARE YOU? CONSIDER THESEUS' PARADOX.
THESEUS, KING OF ANCIENT ATHENS, SET OUT IN A SHIP SOME CLAIM SAILED FOR OVER NINE CENTURIES--
--BUT ONLY BY EVENTUALLY REPLACING EVERY LAST DECAYED BOARD WITH A STRONGER ONE, AND A STRONGER ONE STILL, UNTIL NO ORIGINAL BOARD EXISTED.
THE QUESTION, THEN, IS THIS: IF EVERY PIECE OF SOMETHING--SUCH AS A SYNTHEZOID BODY--HAS BEEN REPLACED OVER TIME, IS IT TRULY THE SAME OBJECT--
--OR SOMETHING NEW ALTOGETHER? I GRANT YOUR QUERY, BUT REGARDLESS OF HOW MANY OF MY--YOUR--ARTIFICIAL LIMBS AND ORGANS MAY HAVE BEEN EXCHANGED--
--YOUR INTANGIBLES--YOUR BRAIN PATTERNS--WILL FOREVER REMAIN BASED ON AN EX-AVENGER NAMED SIMON WILLIAMS.
WON'T THEY?
WE NEED THE AVENGERS TO RALLY--

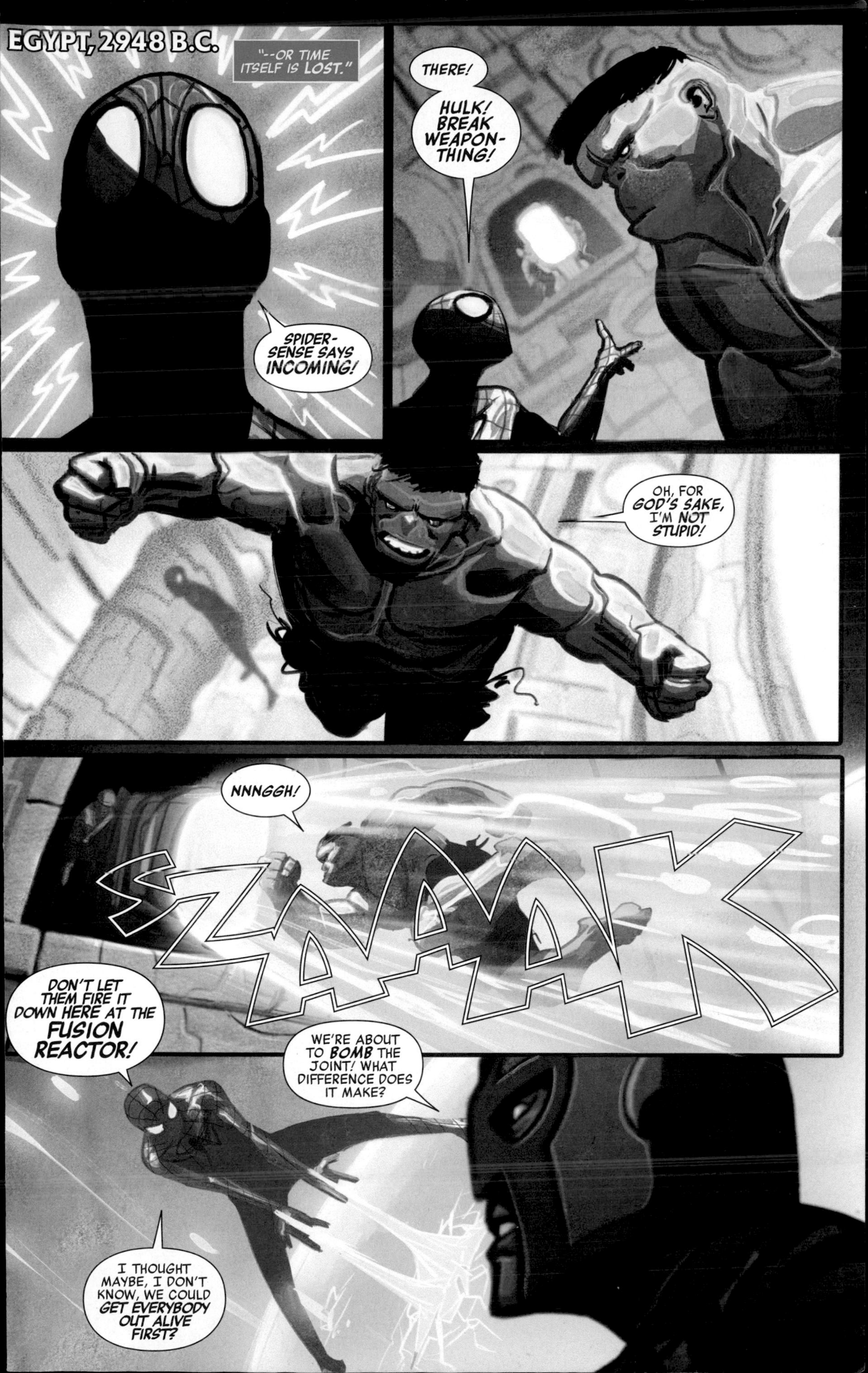
EGYPT, 2948 B.C.
"--OR TIME ITSELF IS LOST."
SPIDER-SENSE SAYS INCOMING!
THERE!
HULK! BREAK WEAPON-THING!
OH, FOR GOD'S SAKE, I'M NOT STUPID!
NNNGGH!
ZAAAK
DON'T LET THEM FIRE IT DOWN HERE AT THE FUSION REACTOR!
WE'RE ABOUT TO BOMB THE JOINT! WHAT DIFFERENCE DOES IT MAKE?
I THOUGHT MAYBE, I DON'T KNOW, WE COULD GET EVERYBODY OUT ALIVE FIRST?

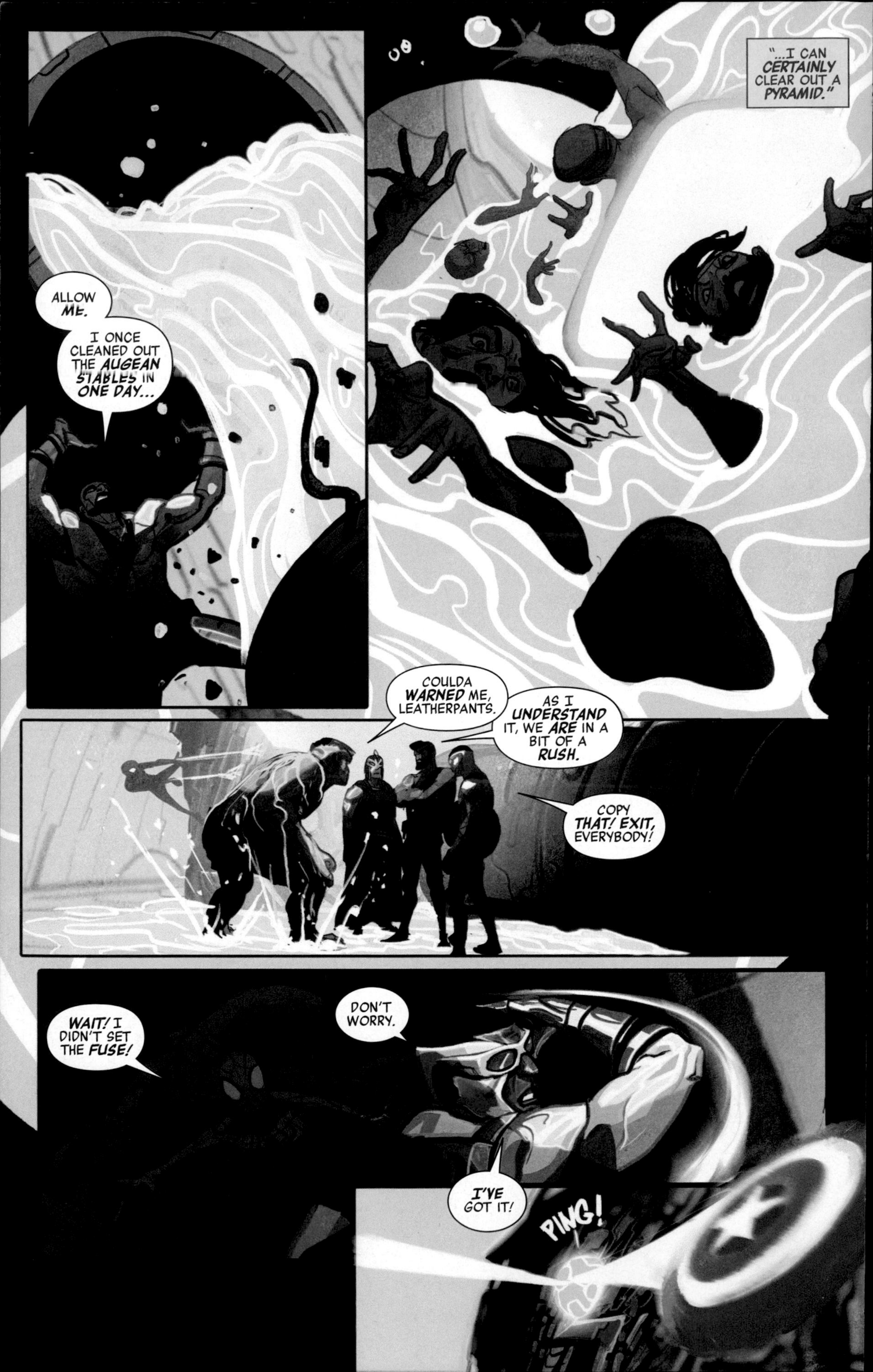

"...I CAN CERTAINLY CLEAR OUT A PYRAMID."
ALLOW ME.
I ONCE CLEANED OUT THE AUGEAN STABLES IN ONE DAY...
COULDA WARNED ME, LEATHERPANTS.
AS I UNDERSTAND IT, WE ARE IN A BIT OF A RUSH.
COPY THAT! EXIT, EVERYBODY!
WAIT! I DIDN'T SET THE FUSE!
DON'T WORRY.
I'VE GOT IT!
PING!

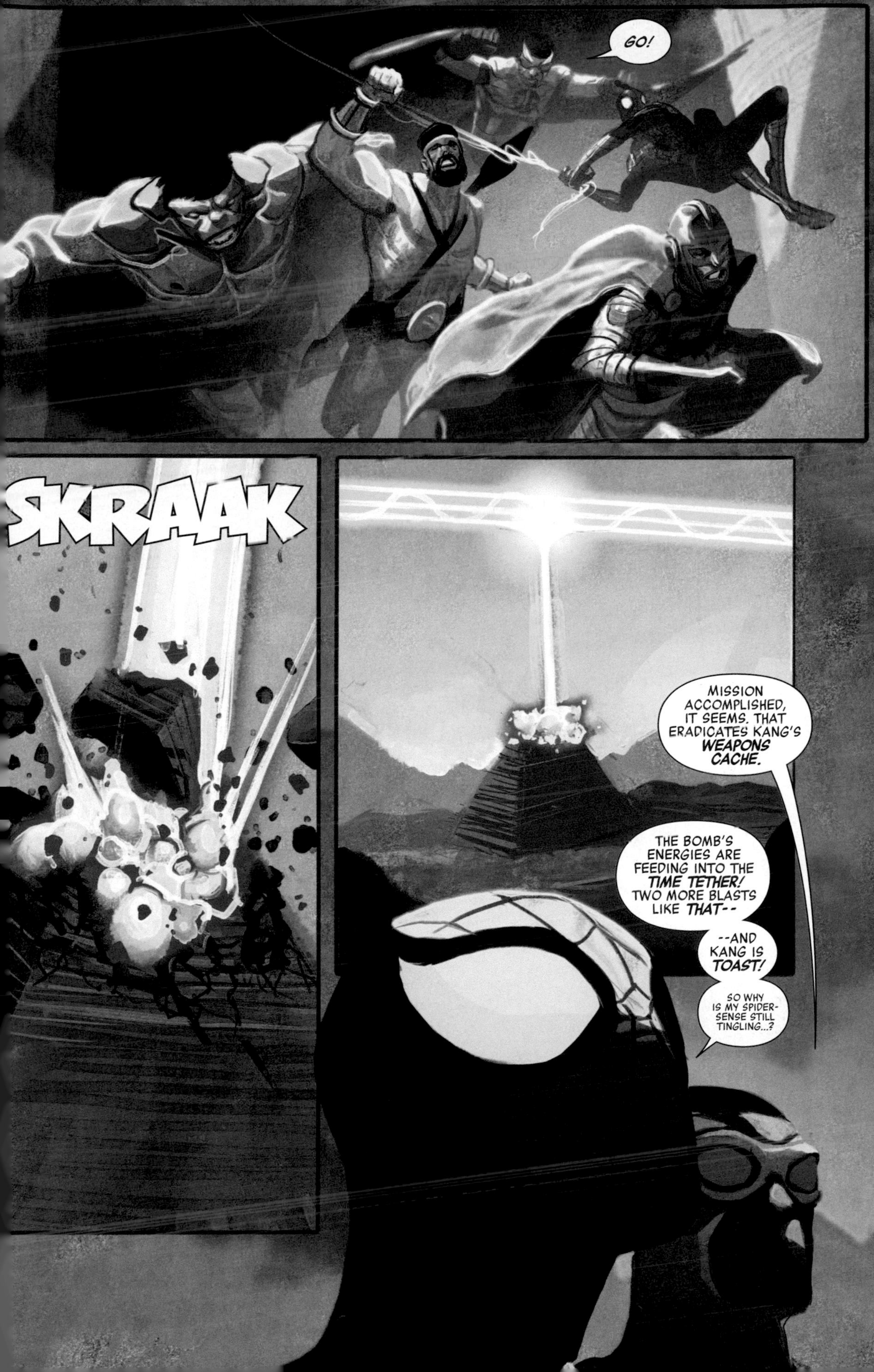
GO!
SKRAAK
MISSION ACCOMPLISHED, IT SEEMS. THAT ERADICATES KANG'S **WEAPONS CACHE.**
THE BOMB'S ENERGIES ARE FEEDING INTO THE ***TIME TETHER!*** TWO MORE BLASTS LIKE ***THAT*--**
--AND KANG IS ***TOAST!***
SO WHY IS MY SPIDER-SENSE STILL TINGLING...?

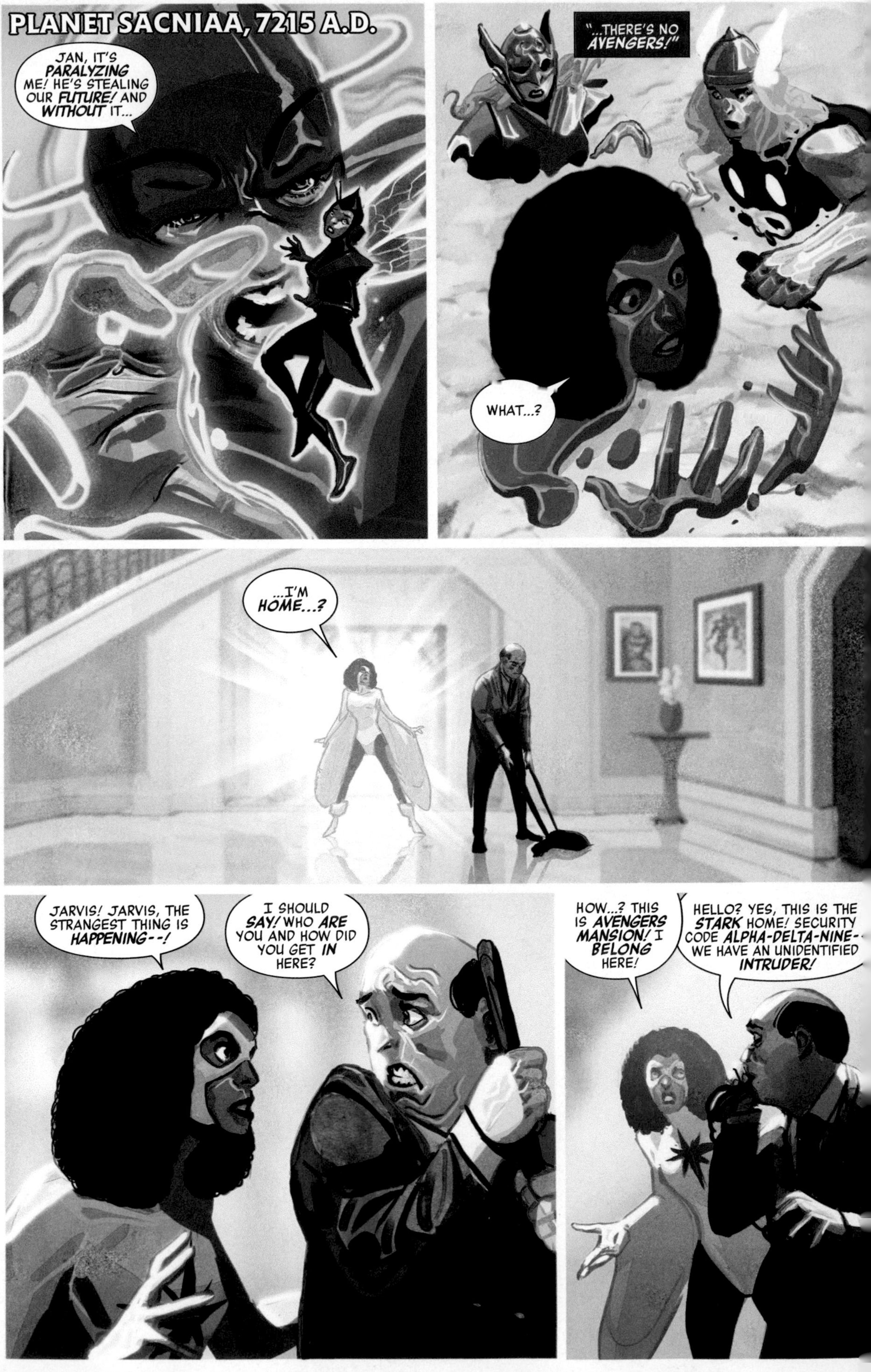
PLANET SACNIAA, 7215 A.D.
JAN, IT'S PARALYZING ME! HE'S STEALING OUR FUTURE! AND WITHOUT IT...
"...THERE'S NO AVENGERS!"
WHAT...?
...I'M HOME...?
JARVIS! JARVIS, THE STRANGEST THING IS HAPPENING--!
I SHOULD SAY! WHO ARE YOU AND HOW DID YOU GET IN HERE?
HOW...? THIS IS AVENGERS MANSION! I BELONG HERE!
HELLO? YES, THIS IS THE STARK HOME! SECURITY CODE ALPHA-DELTA-NINE--WE HAVE AN UNIDENTIFIED INTRUDER!

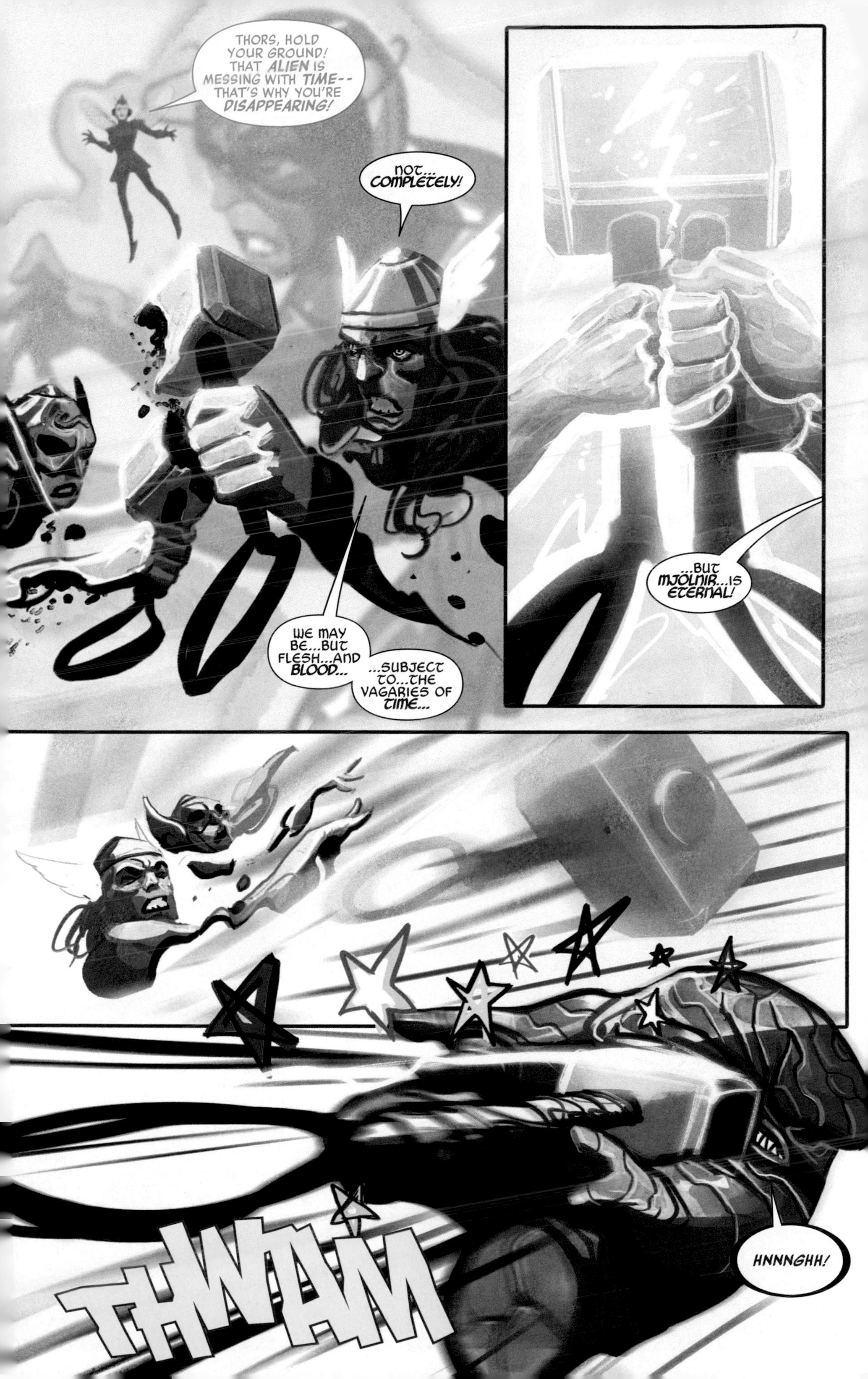
THORS, HOLD YOUR GROUND! THAT ALIEN IS MESSING WITH TIME-- THAT'S WHY YOU'RE DISAPPEARING!
NOT... COMPLETELY!
WE MAY BE...BUT FLESH...AND BLOOD...
...SUBJECT TO...THE VAGARIES OF TIME...
...BUT MJOLNIR...IS ETERNAL!
THWAM
HNNNGHH!

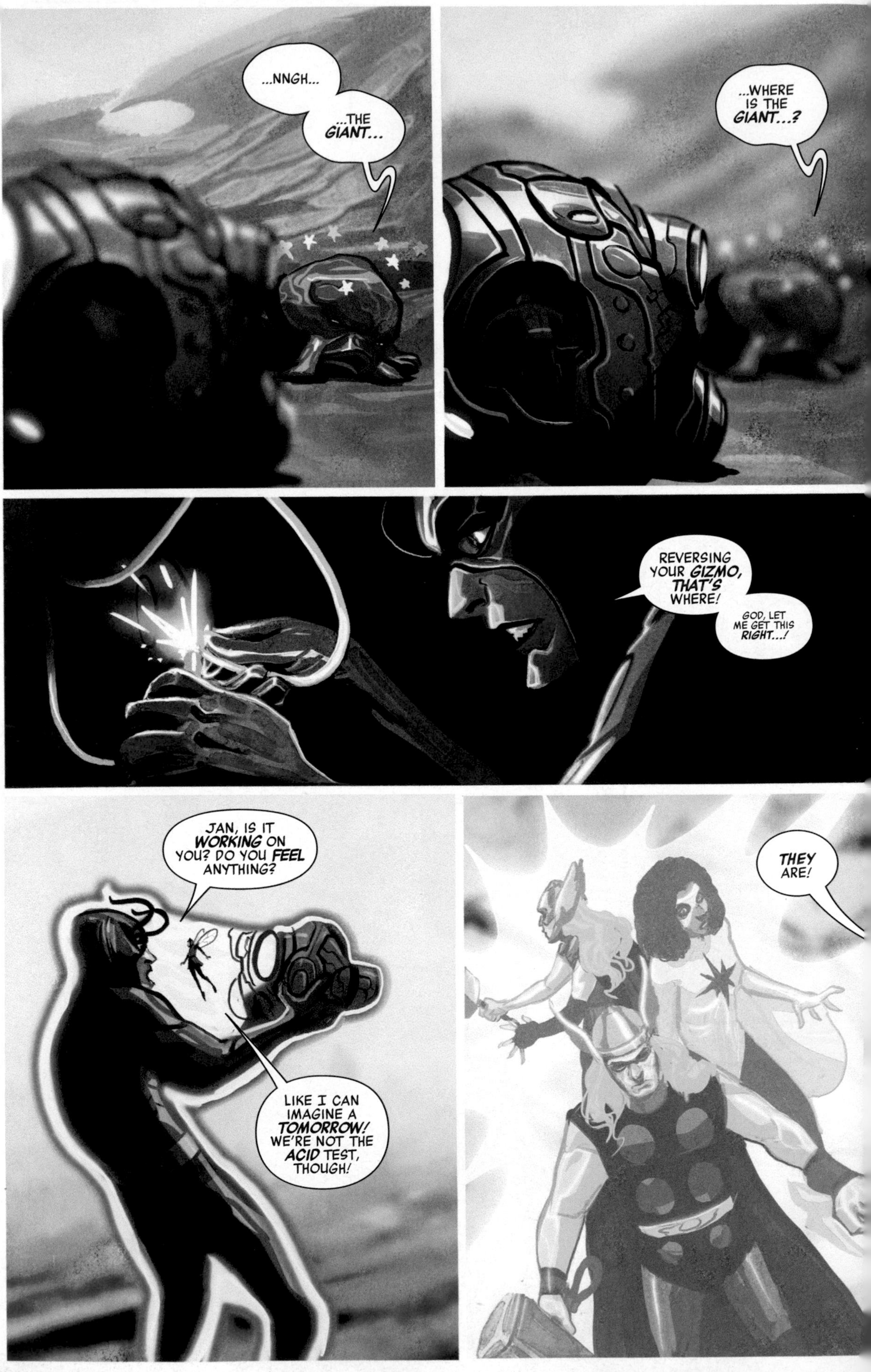
...NNGH...
...THE GIANT...
...WHERE IS THE GIANT...?
REVERSING YOUR GIZMO, THAT'S WHERE!
GOD, LET ME GET THIS RIGHT...!
JAN, IS IT WORKING ON YOU? DO YOU FEEL ANYTHING?
LIKE I CAN IMAGINE A TOMORROW! WE'RE NOT THE ACID TEST, THOUGH!
THEY ARE!

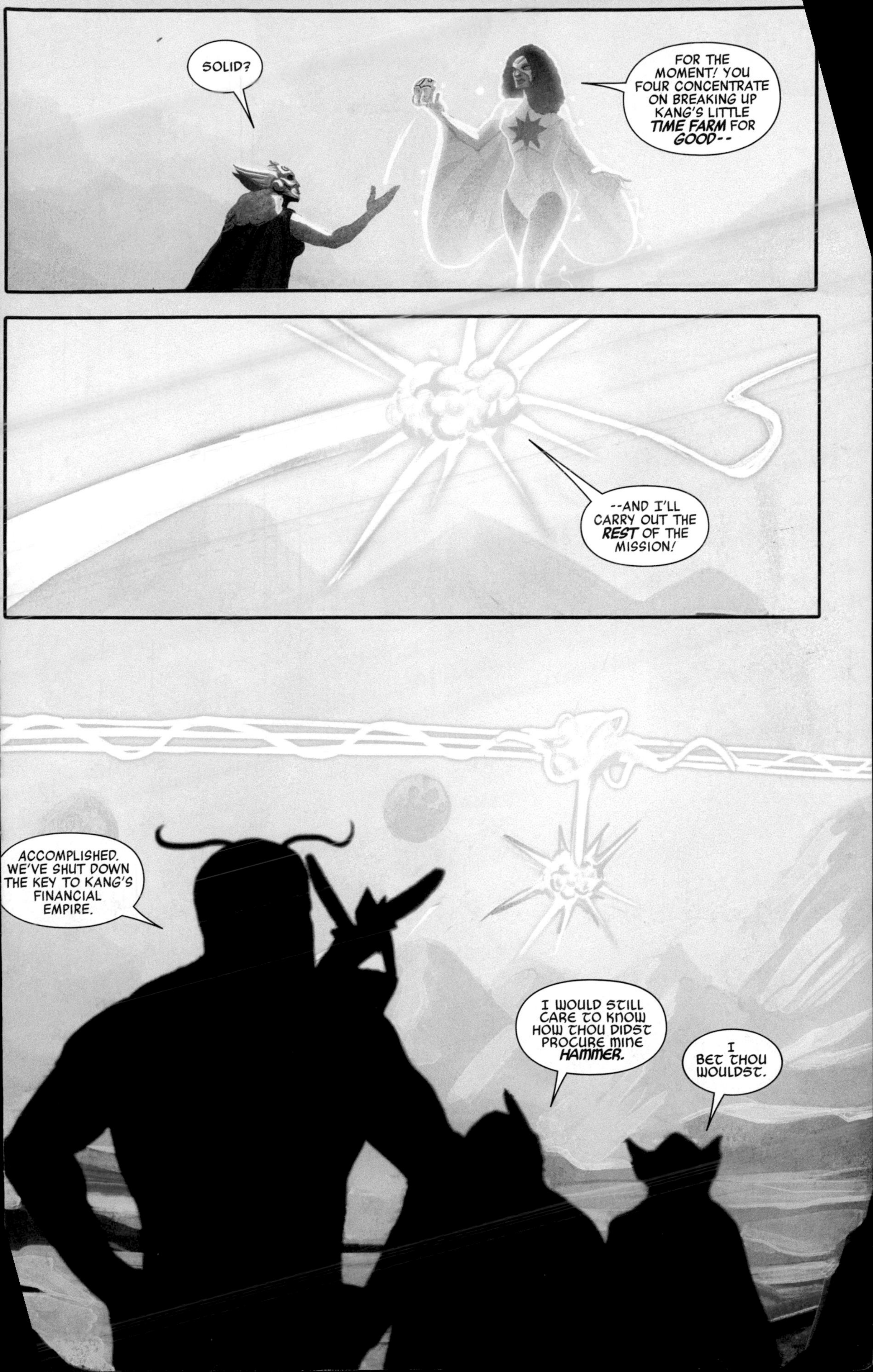
SOLID?
FOR THE MOMENT! YOU FOUR CONCENTRATE ON BREAKING UP KANG'S LITTLE TIME FARM FOR GOOD--
--AND I'LL CARRY OUT THE REST OF THE MISSION!
ACCOMPLISHED. WE'VE SHUT DOWN THE KEY TO KANG'S FINANCIAL EMPIRE.
I WOULD STILL CARE TO KNOW HOW THOU DIDST PROCURE MINE HAMMER.
I BET THOU WOULDST.

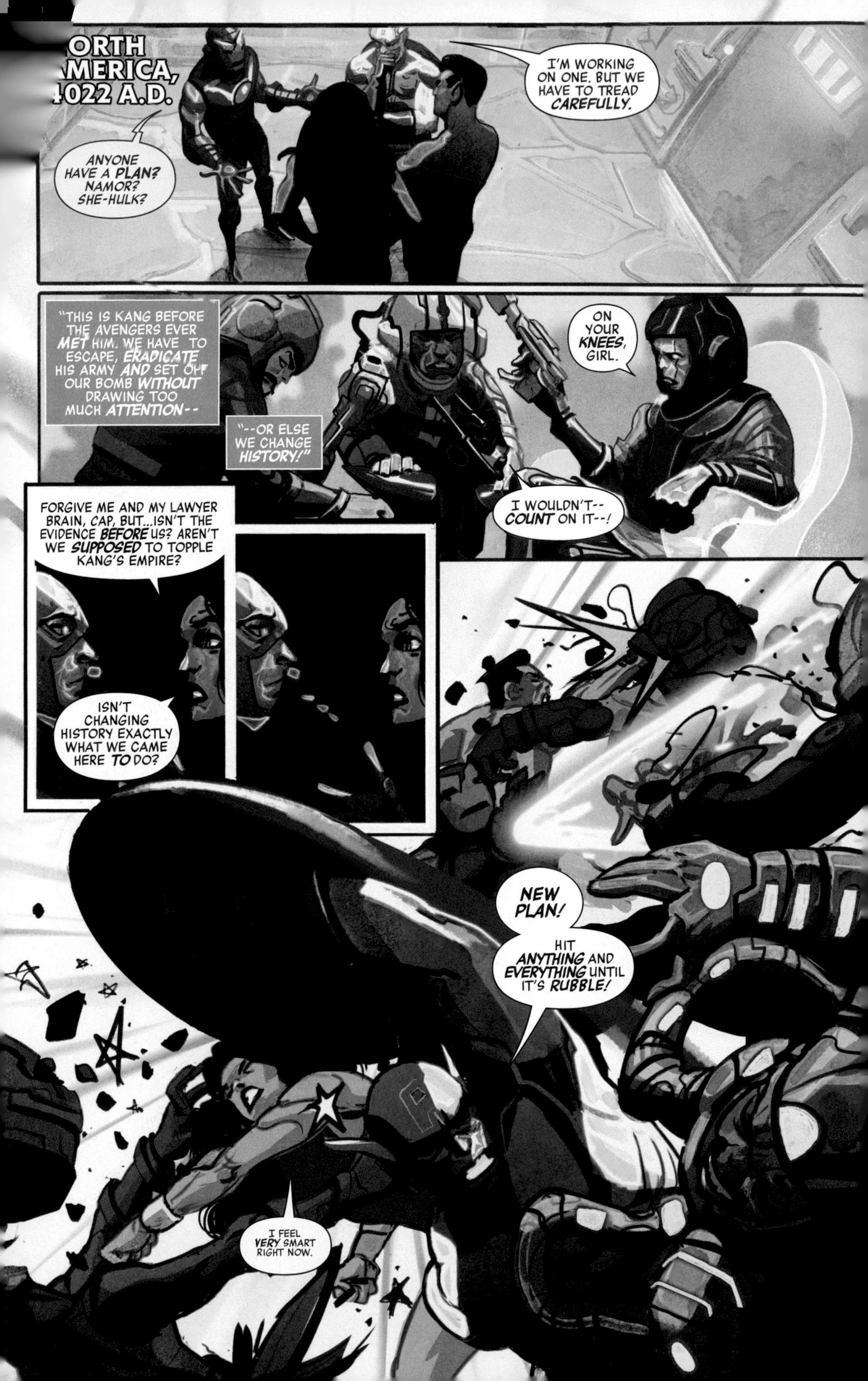
ORTH AMERICA, 4022 A.D.
I'M WORKING ON ONE. BUT WE HAVE TO TREAD CAREFULLY.
ANYONE HAVE A PLAN? NAMOR? SHE-HULK?
"THIS IS KANG BEFORE THE AVENGERS EVER MET HIM. WE HAVE TO ESCAPE, ERADICATE HIS ARMY AND SET OFF OUR BOMB WITHOUT DRAWING TOO MUCH ATTENTION--
"--OR ELSE WE CHANGE HISTORY!"
ON YOUR KNEES, GIRL.
I WOULDN'T--COUNT ON IT--!
FORGIVE ME AND MY LAWYER BRAIN, CAP, BUT...ISN'T THE EVIDENCE BEFORE US? AREN'T WE SUPPOSED TO TOPPLE KANG'S EMPIRE?
ISN'T CHANGING HISTORY EXACTLY WHAT WE CAME HERE TO DO?
NEW PLAN!
HIT ANYTHING AND EVERYTHING UNTIL IT'S RUBBLE!
I FEEL VERY SMART RIGHT NOW.

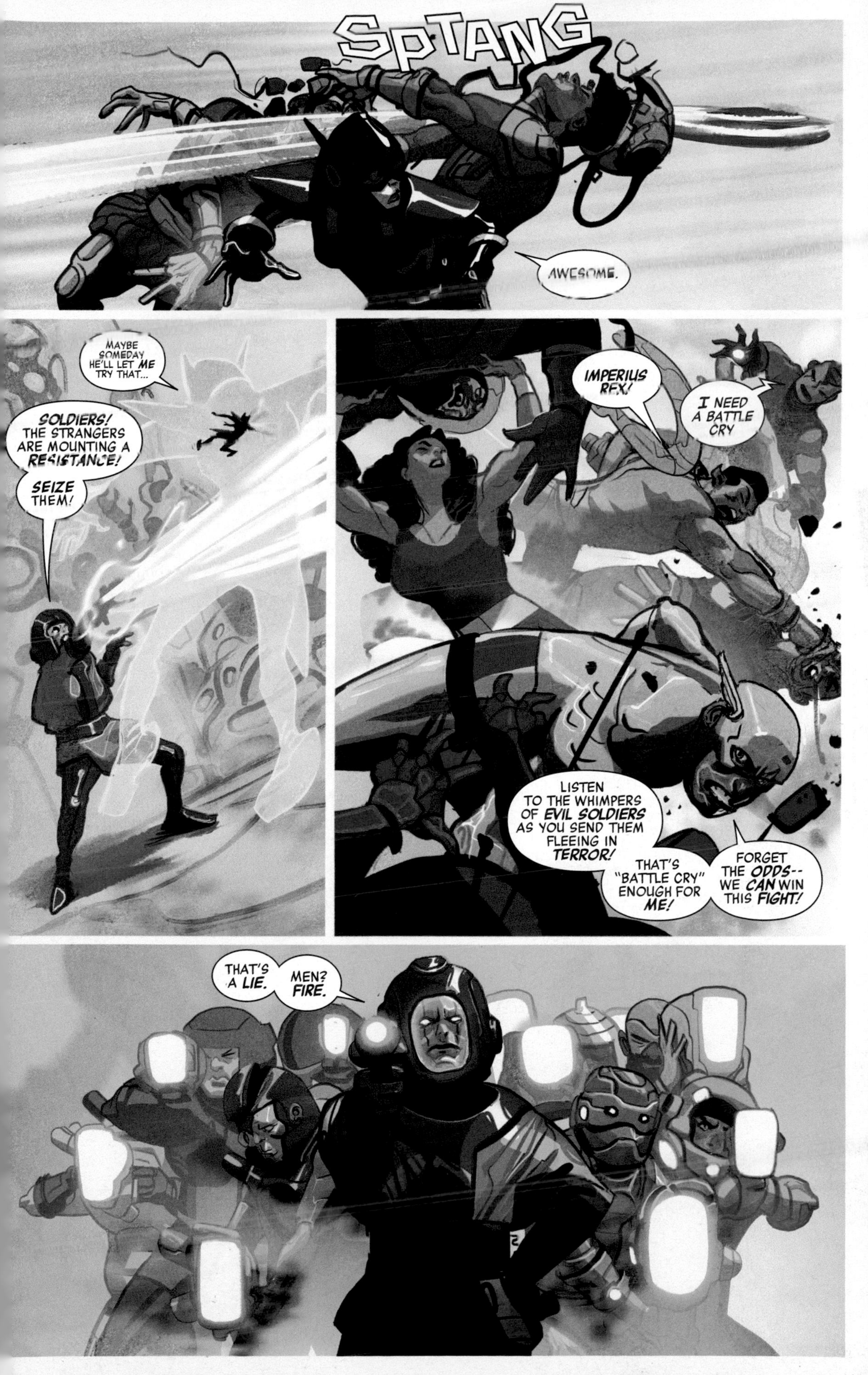
SPTANG
AWESOME.
MAYBE SOMEDAY HE'LL LET ME TRY THAT...
SOLDIERS! THE STRANGERS ARE MOUNTING A RESISTANCE!
SEIZE THEM!
IMPERIUS REX!
I NEED A BATTLE CRY
LISTEN TO THE WHIMPERS OF EVIL SOLDIERS AS YOU SEND THEM FLEEING IN TERROR!
THAT'S "BATTLE CRY" ENOUGH FOR ME!
FORGET THE ODDS-- WE CAN WIN THIS FIGHT!
THAT'S A LIE.
MEN? FIRE.

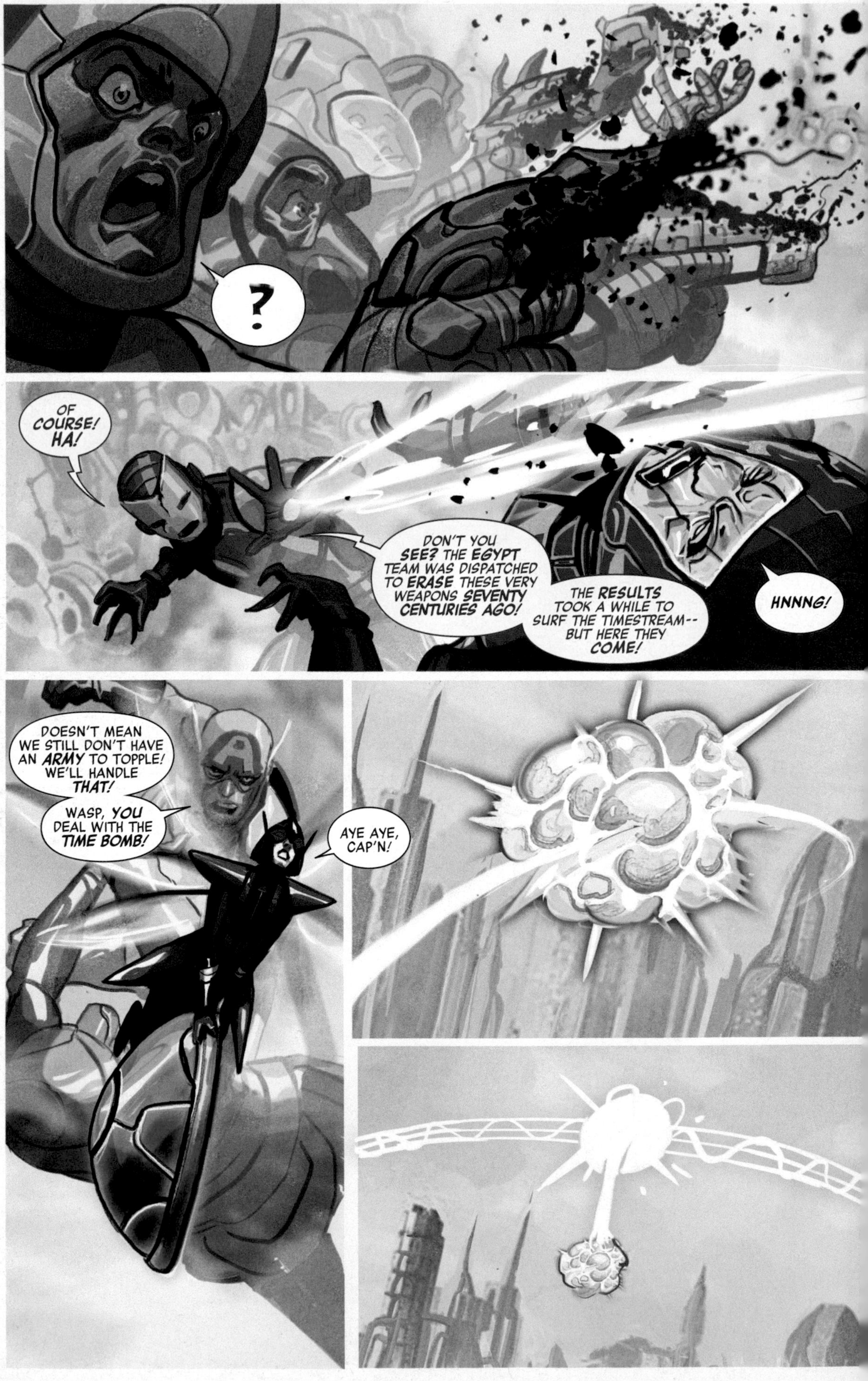
?
OF COURSE! HA!
DON'T YOU SEE? THE EGYPT TEAM WAS DISPATCHED TO ERASE THESE VERY WEAPONS SEVENTY CENTURIES AGO!
THE RESULTS TOOK A WHILE TO SURF THE TIMESTREAM-- BUT HERE THEY COME!
HNNNG!
DOESN'T MEAN WE STILL DON'T HAVE AN ARMY TO TOPPLE! WE'LL HANDLE THAT!
WASP, YOU DEAL WITH THE TIME BOMB!
AYE AYE, CAP'N!

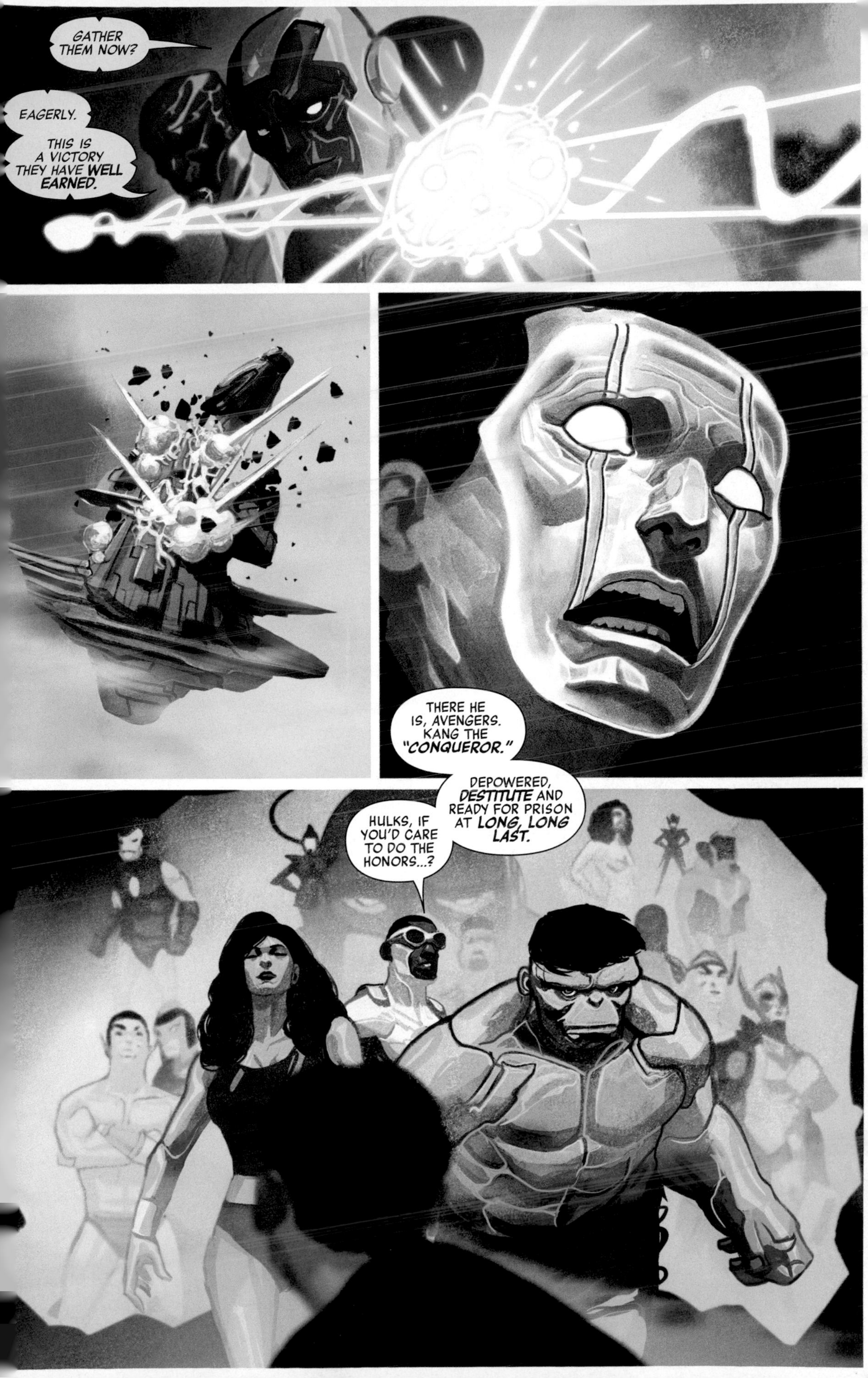
GATHER THEM NOW?
EAGERLY.
THIS IS A VICTORY THEY HAVE WELL EARNED.
THERE HE IS, AVENGERS. KANG THE "CONQUEROR."
DEPOWERED, DESTITUTE AND READY FOR PRISON AT LONG, LONG LAST.
HULKS, IF YOU'D CARE TO DO THE HONORS...?

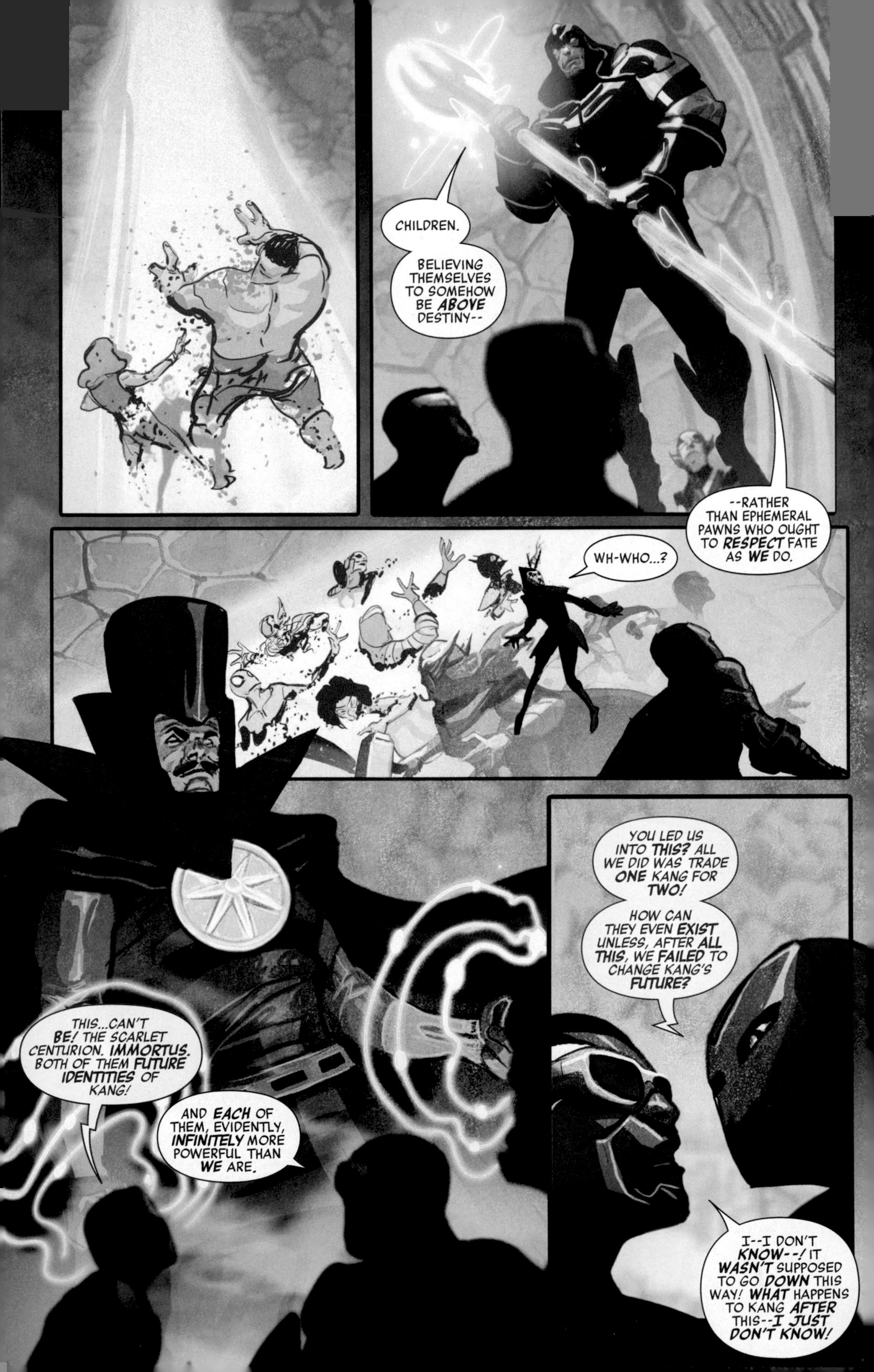
CHILDREN.
BELIEVING THEMSELVES TO SOMEHOW BE ABOVE DESTINY--
--RATHER THAN EPHEMERAL PAWNS WHO OUGHT TO RESPECT FATE AS WE DO.
WH-WHO...?
THIS...CAN'T BE! THE SCARLET CENTURION. IMMORTUS. BOTH OF THEM FUTURE IDENTITIES OF KANG!
AND EACH OF THEM, EVIDENTLY, INFINITELY MORE POWERFUL THAN WE ARE.
YOU LED US INTO THIS? ALL WE DID WAS TRADE ONE KANG FOR TWO!
HOW CAN THEY EVEN EXIST UNLESS, AFTER ALL THIS, WE FAILED TO CHANGE KANG'S FUTURE?
I--I DON'T KNOW--! IT WASN'T SUPPOSED TO GO DOWN THIS WAY! WHAT HAPPENS TO KANG AFTER THIS--I JUST DON'T KNOW!

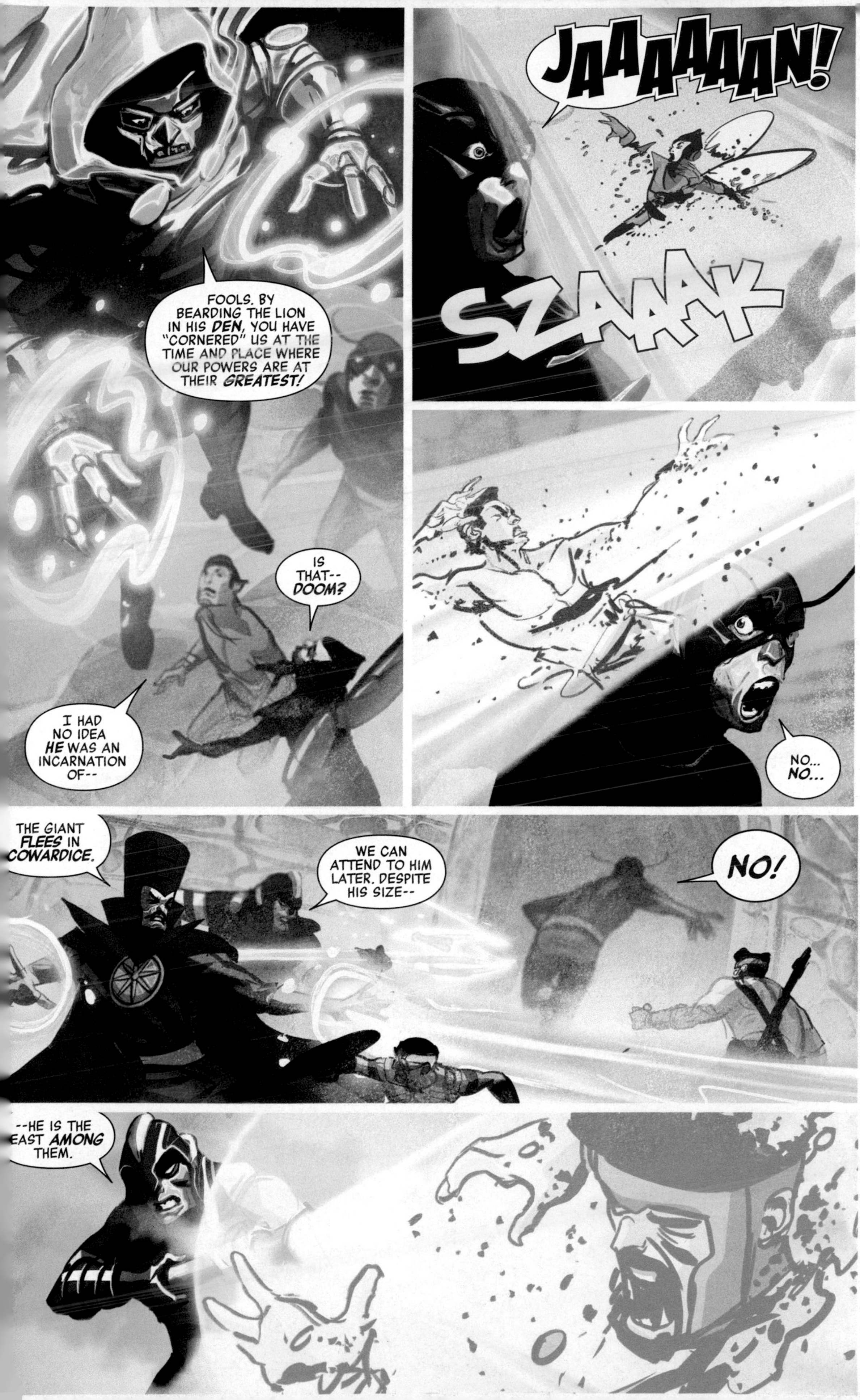
FOOLS. BY BEARDING THE LION IN HIS DEN, YOU HAVE "CORNERED" US AT THE TIME AND PLACE WHERE OUR POWERS ARE AT THEIR GREATEST!
IS THAT-- DOOM?
I HAD NO IDEA HE WAS AN INCARNATION OF--
JAAAAAAN!
SZAAAK
NO... NO...
THE GIANT FLEES IN COWARDICE.
WE CAN ATTEND TO HIM LATER. DESPITE HIS SIZE--
NO!
--HE IS THE EAST AMONG THEM.

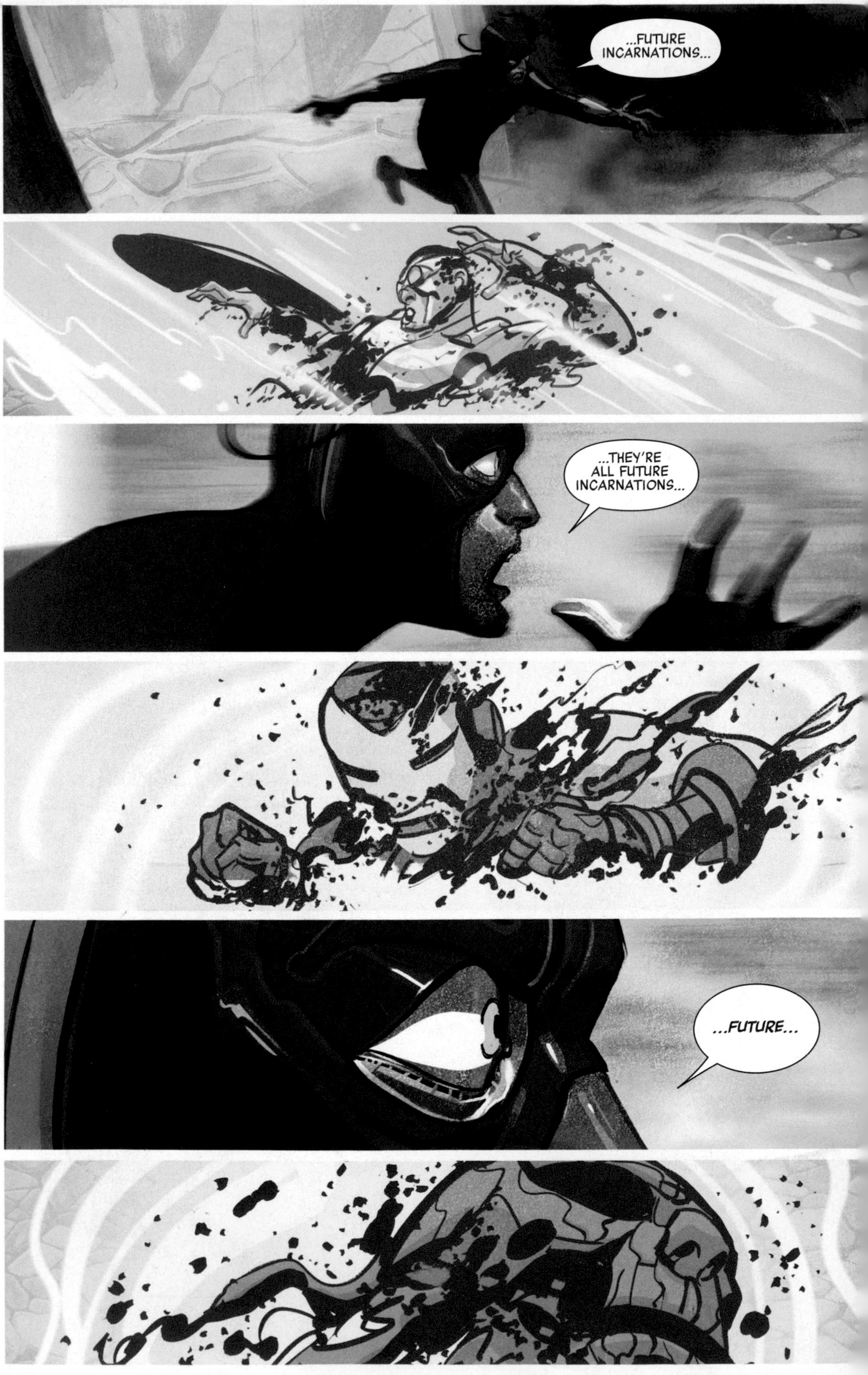
...FUTURE INCARNATIONS...
...THEY'RE ALL FUTURE INCARNATIONS...
...FUTURE...

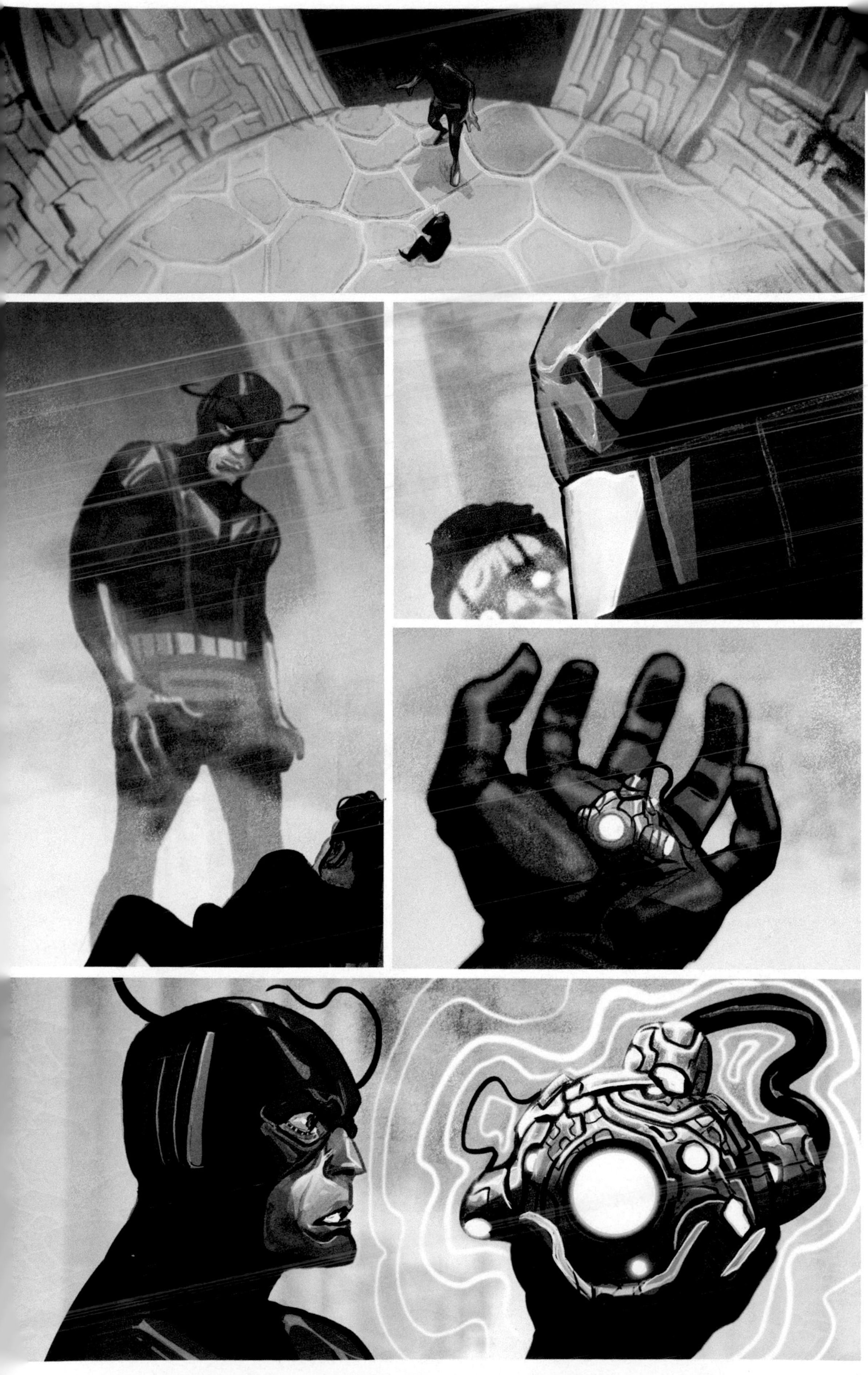

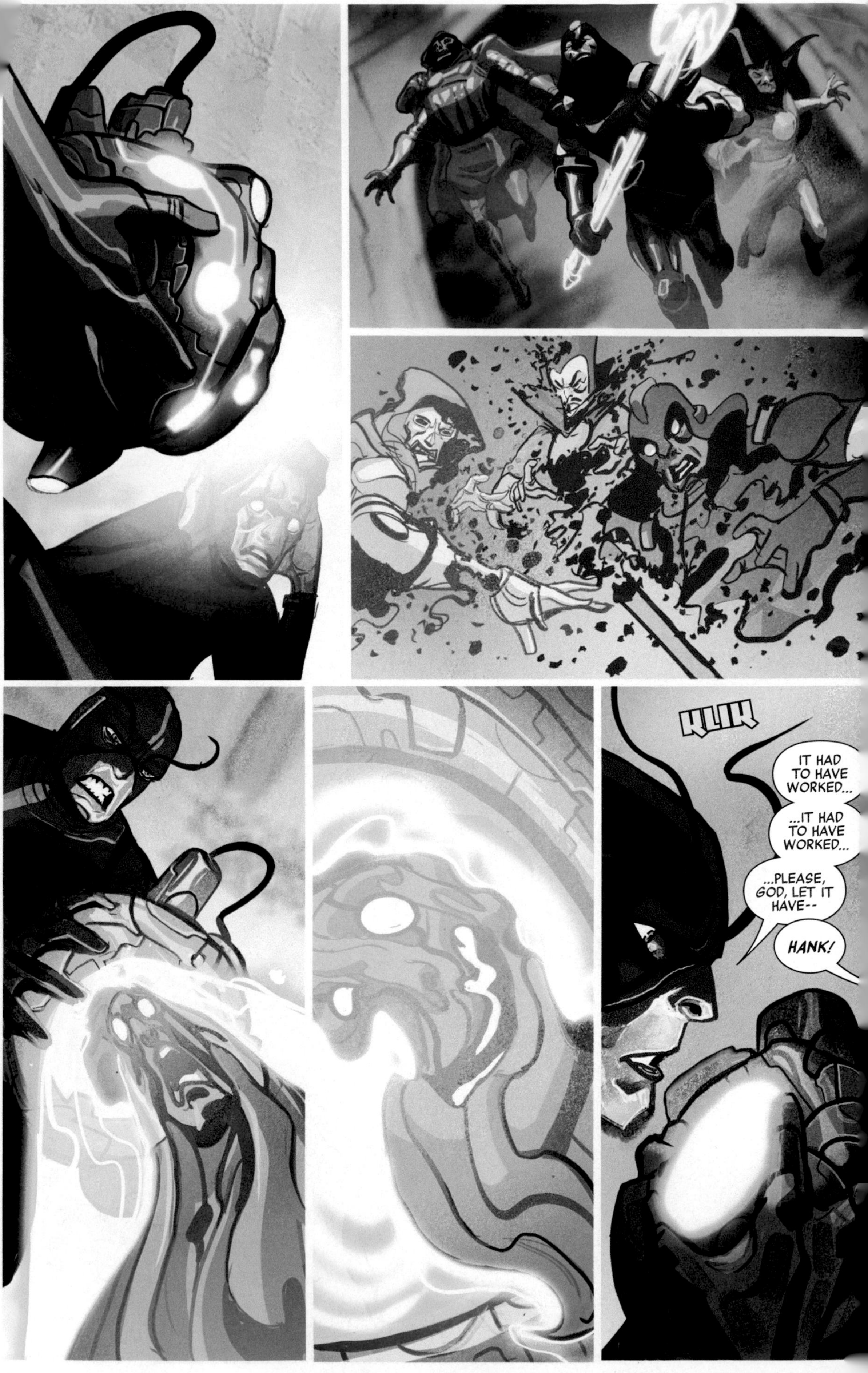
KLIK
IT HAD TO HAVE WORKED...
...IT HAD TO HAVE WORKED...
...PLEASE, GOD, LET IT HAVE--
HANK!

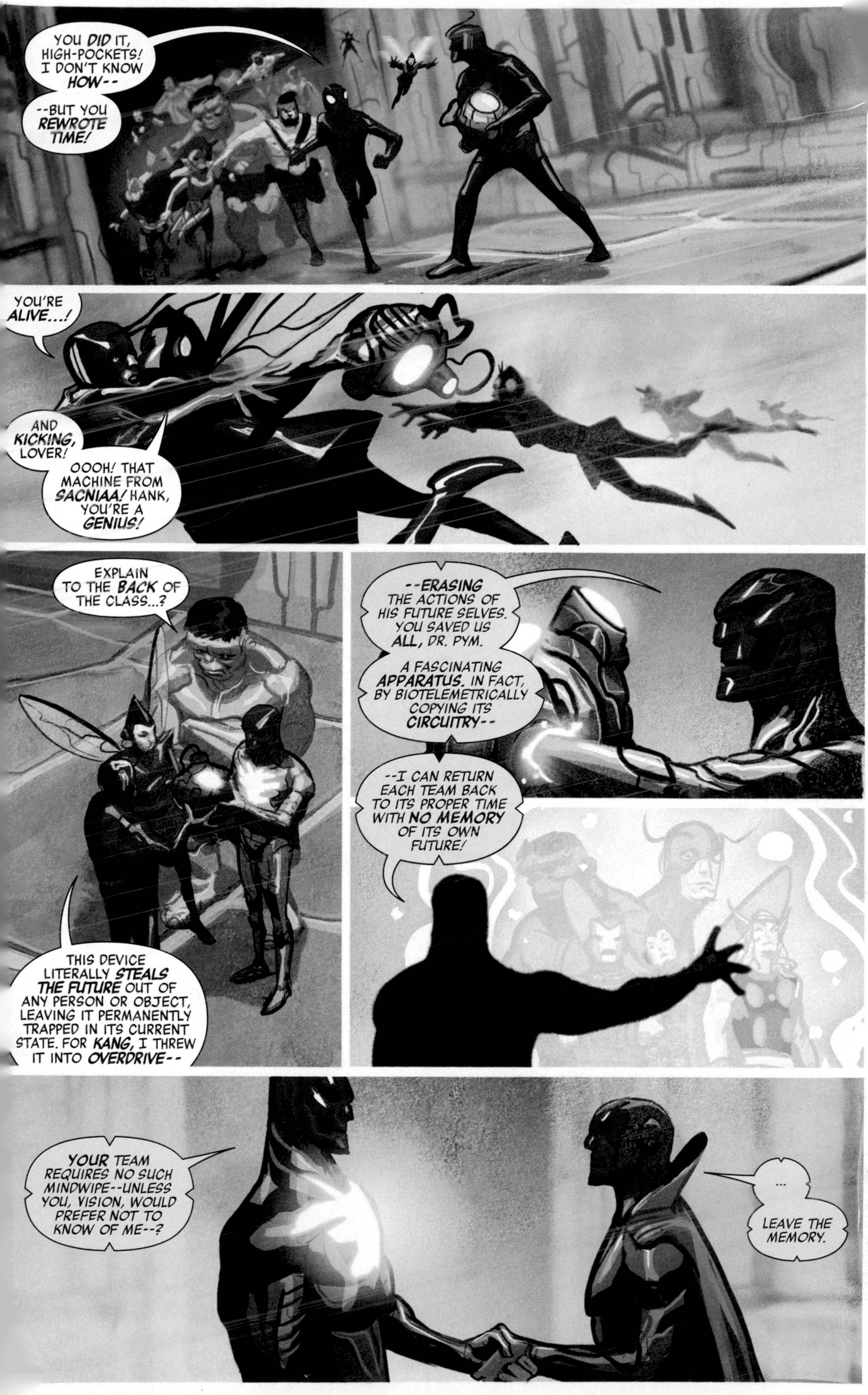
YOU DID IT, HIGH-POCKETS! I DON'T KNOW HOW--
--BUT YOU REWROTE TIME!
YOU'RE ALIVE...!
AND KICKING, LOVER!
OOOH! THAT MACHINE FROM SACNIAA! HANK, YOU'RE A GENIUS!
EXPLAIN TO THE BACK OF THE CLASS...?
THIS DEVICE LITERALLY STEALS THE FUTURE OUT OF ANY PERSON OR OBJECT, LEAVING IT PERMANENTLY TRAPPED IN ITS CURRENT STATE. FOR KANG, I THREW IT INTO OVERDRIVE--
--ERASING THE ACTIONS OF HIS FUTURE SELVES. YOU SAVED US ALL, DR. PYM.
A FASCINATING APPARATUS. IN FACT, BY BIOTELEMETRICALLY COPYING ITS CIRCUITRY--
--I CAN RETURN EACH TEAM BACK TO ITS PROPER TIME WITH NO MEMORY OF ITS OWN FUTURE!
YOUR TEAM REQUIRES NO SUCH MINDWIPE--UNLESS YOU, VISION, WOULD PREFER NOT TO KNOW OF ME--?
...
LEAVE THE MEMORY.

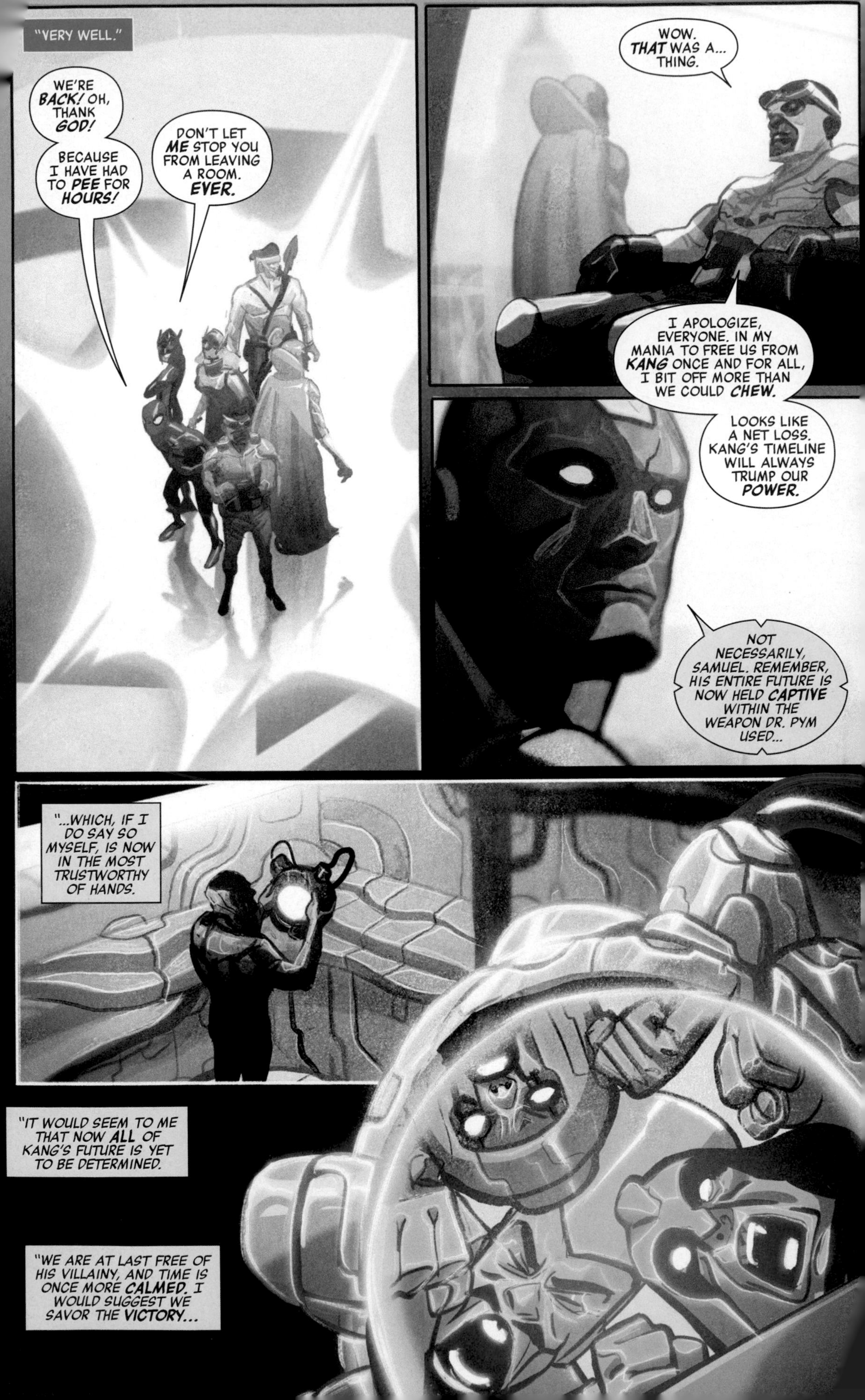
"VERY WELL."
WE'RE BACK! OH, THANK GOD!
BECAUSE I HAVE HAD TO PEE FOR HOURS!
DON'T LET ME STOP YOU FROM LEAVING A ROOM. EVER.
WOW. THAT WAS A... THING.
I APOLOGIZE, EVERYONE. IN MY MANIA TO FREE US FROM KANG ONCE AND FOR ALL, I BIT OFF MORE THAN WE COULD CHEW.
LOOKS LIKE A NET LOSS. KANG'S TIMELINE WILL ALWAYS TRUMP OUR POWER.
NOT NECESSARILY, SAMUEL. REMEMBER, HIS ENTIRE FUTURE IS NOW HELD CAPTIVE WITHIN THE WEAPON DR. PYM USED...
"...WHICH, IF I DO SAY SO MYSELF, IS NOW IN THE MOST TRUSTWORTHY OF HANDS.
"IT WOULD SEEM TO ME THAT NOW ALL OF KANG'S FUTURE IS YET TO BE DETERMINED.
"WE ARE AT LAST FREE OF HIS VILLAINY, AND TIME IS ONCE MORE CALMED. I WOULD SUGGEST WE SAVOR THE VICTORY...

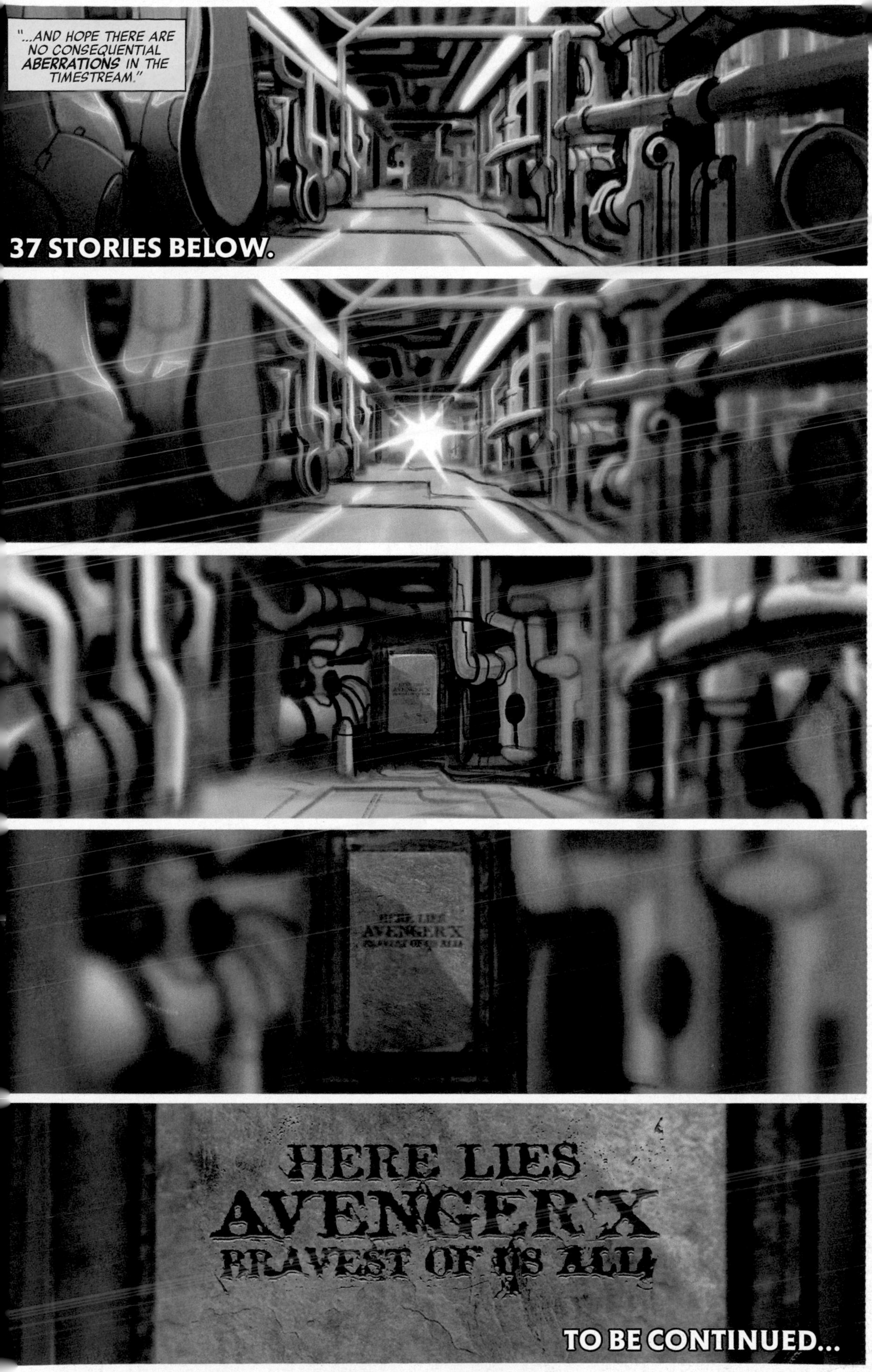
"...AND HOPE THERE ARE NO CONSEQUENTIAL ABERRATIONS IN THE TIMESTREAM."
37 STORIES BELOW.
HERE LIES AVENGER X BRAVEST OF US ALL
TO BE CONTINUED...

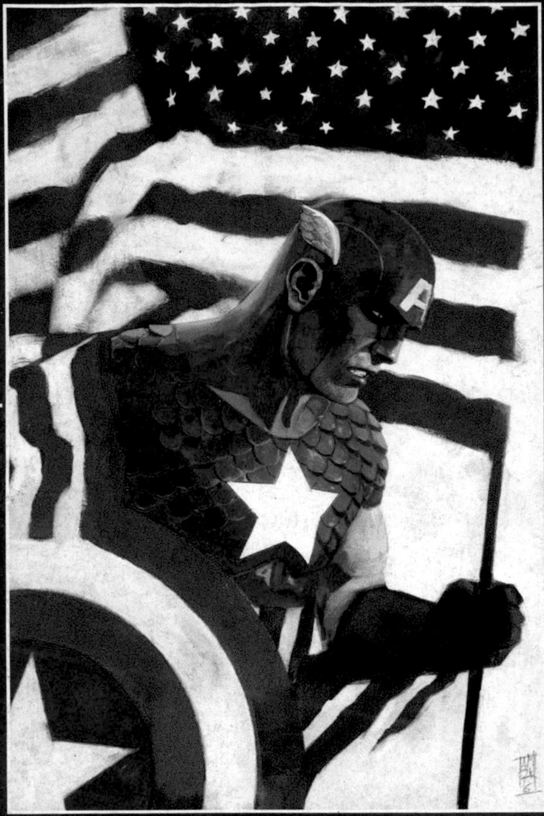

#1 CAPTAIN AMERICA 75TH ANNIVERSARY VARIANT BY

ALEX MALEEV

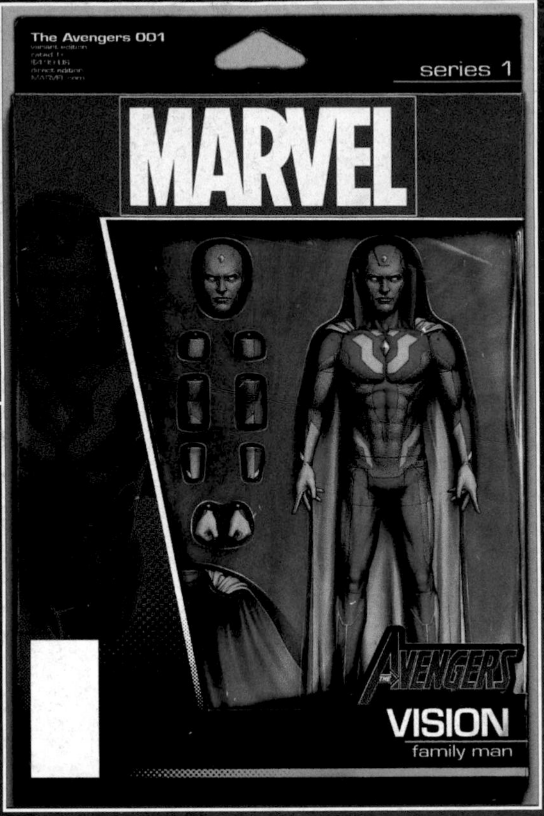
The Avengers 001
series 1
MARVEL
AVENGERS
VISION
family man

#1 ACTION FIGURE VARIANT BY

JOHN TYLER CHRISTOPHER

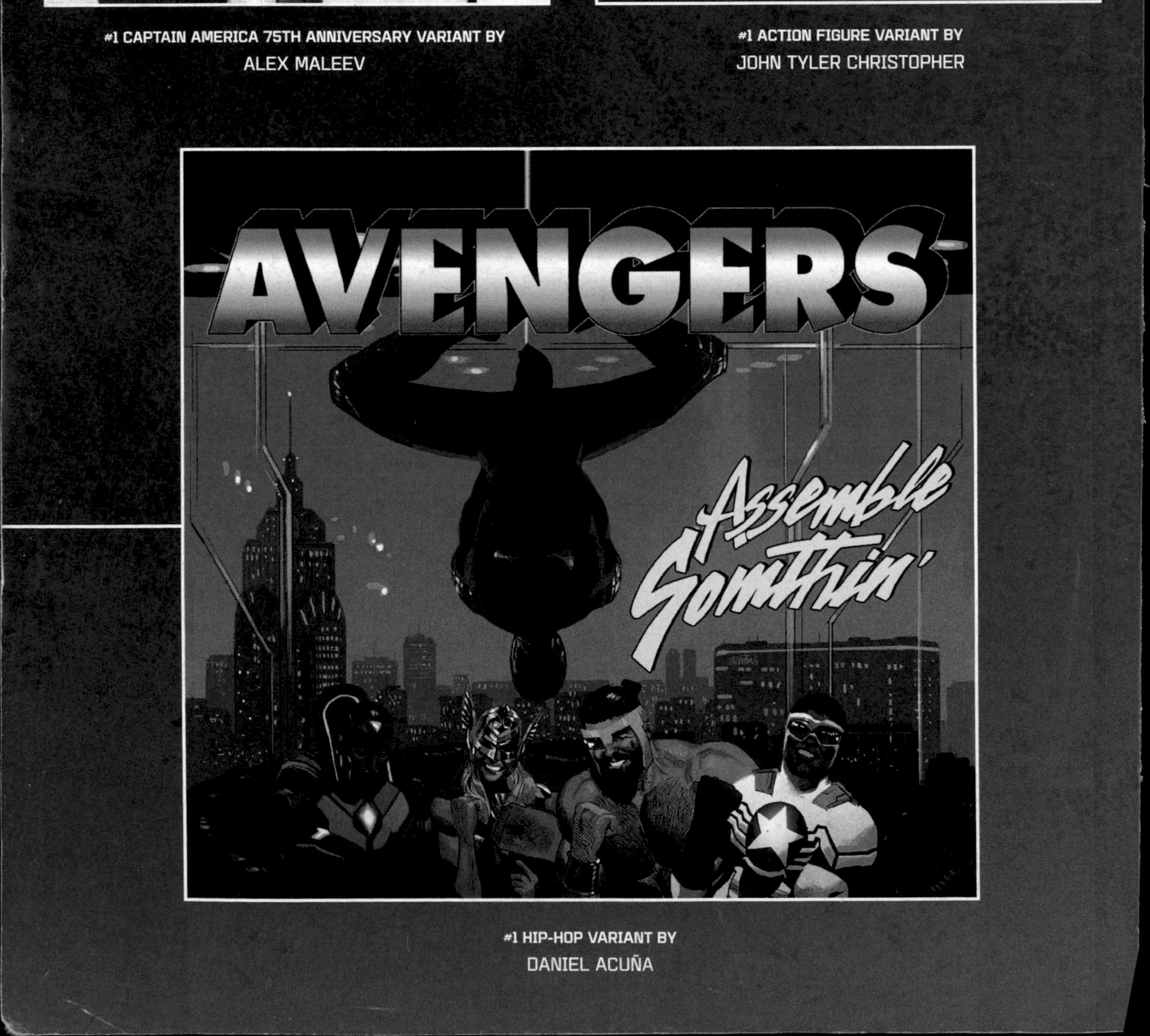
AVENGERS
Assemble Somthin'

#1 HIP-HOP VARIANT BY

DANIEL ACUÑA

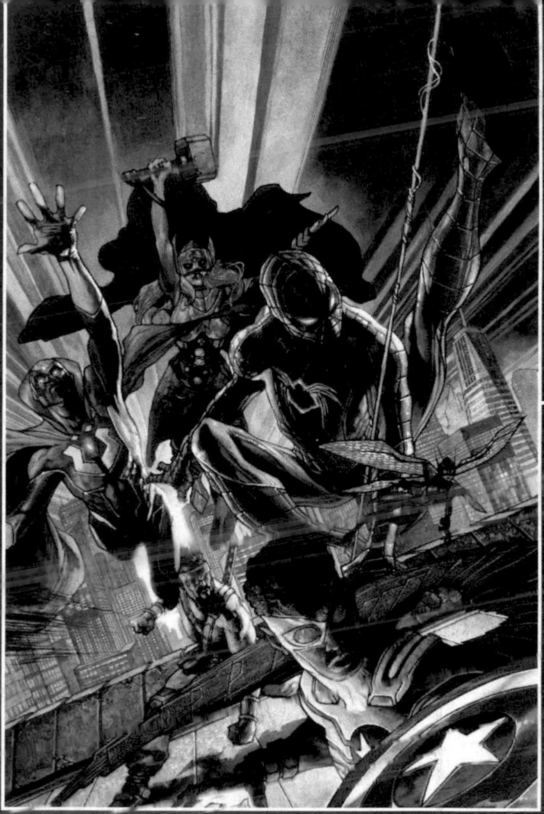

#2 VARIANT BY
SIMONE BIANCHI

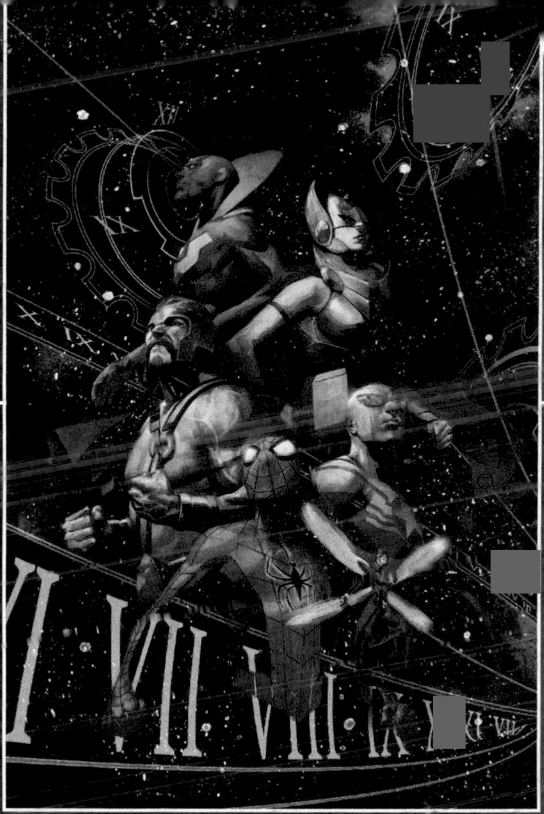

#3 VARIANT BY
JULIAN TOTINO TEDESCO

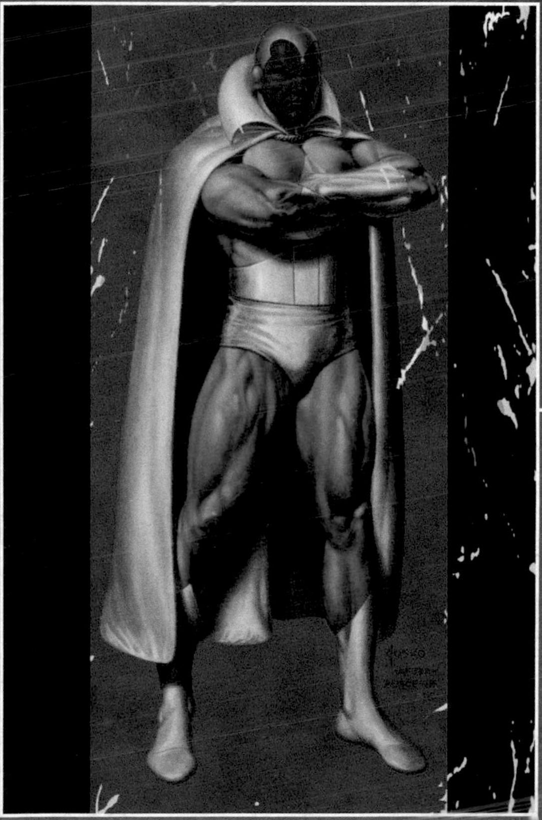

#4 CORNER BOX VARIANT BY
JOE JUSKO

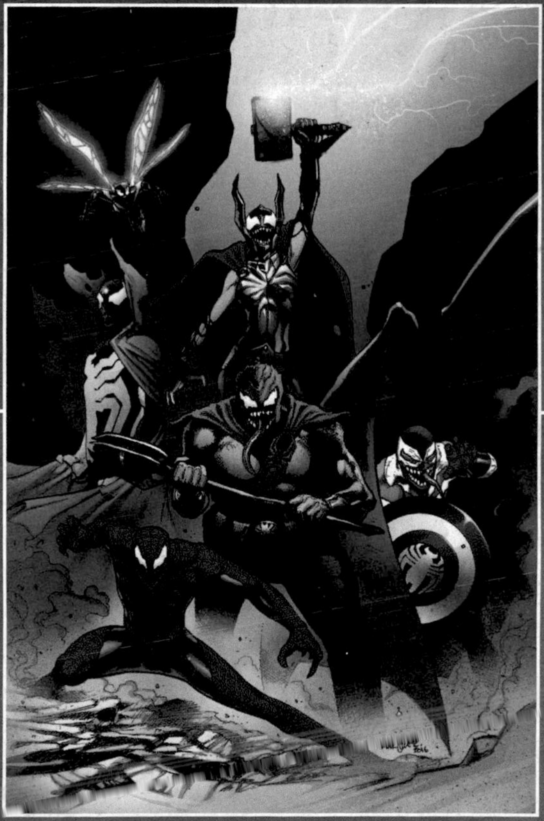

#5 VENOMIZED VARIANT BY
DAVID MARQUEZ & RICHARD ISANOVE

COMING THIS YEAR IN AVENGERS

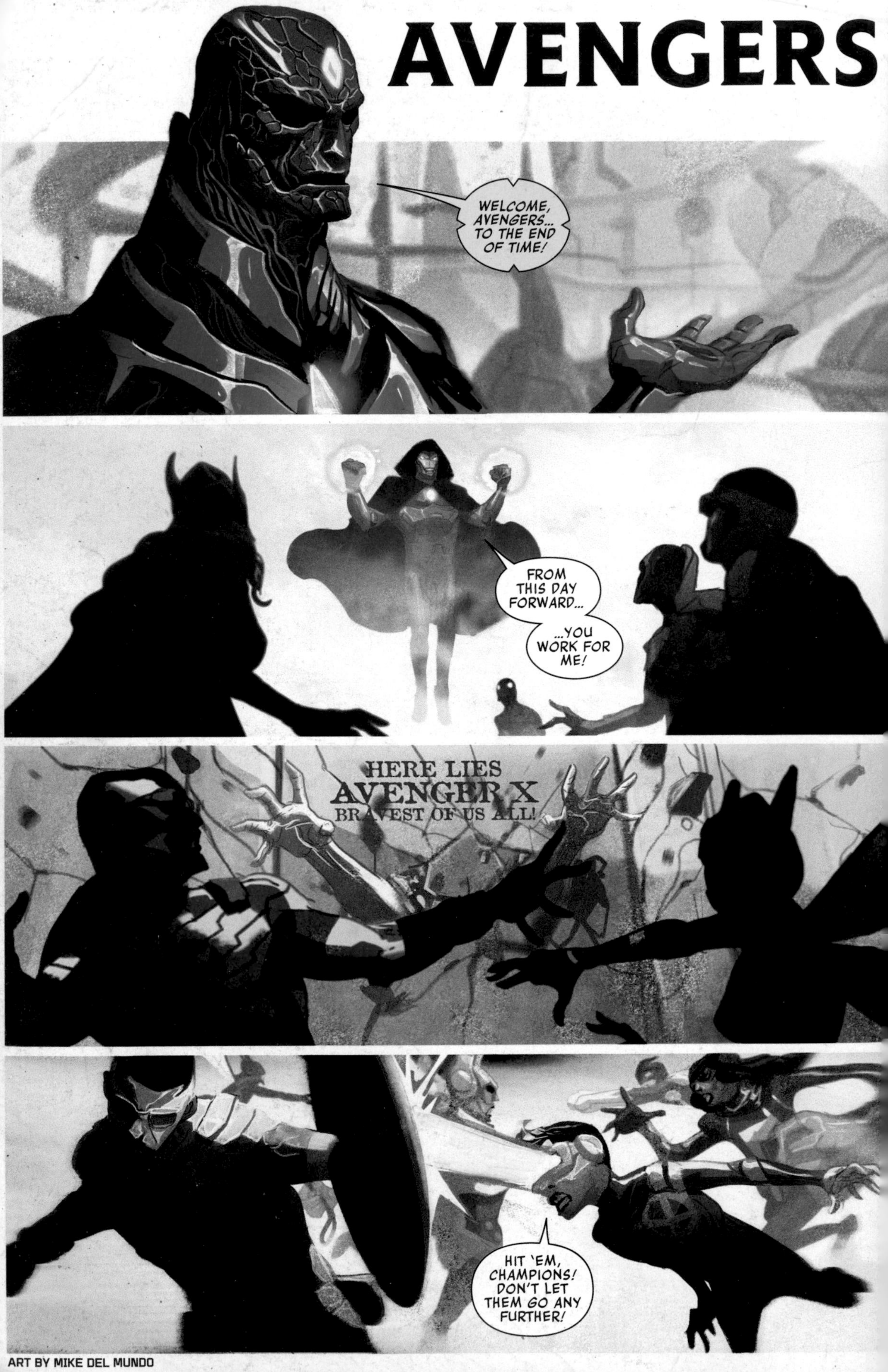

WELCOME, AVENGERS... TO THE END OF TIME!
FROM THIS DAY FORWARD...
...YOU WORK FOR ME!
HERE LIES AVENGER X BRAVEST OF US ALL!
HIT 'EM, CHAMPIONS! DON'T LET THEM GO ANY FURTHER!

ART BY MIKE DEL MUNDO